T0340832

# ADAPT
## AND BE
# ADEPT

ADVANCE PRAISE FOR
*Adapt and Be Adept*

"In the flood of books and articles about what people should do, or how guilty people should feel, about global warming, this book stands out: it is all about what people will do as climate change, or even the threat of climate change, alters the incentives, challenges, and opportunities that people face. It is thus far more realistic, honest, and helpful than much of the discussion about climate change policy."
—**Matt Ridley**, author of *How Innovation Works*
and *The Rational Optimist*

"With headlines of gloom and doom, it's no surprise that a large portion of the developed world population sees climate change as an imminent and existential threat to humanity. This book provides the missing, grounded hope, based upon our species' remarkable ability to adapt and flourish, driven in part by market forces, pricing, and reallocating risk. We do this every day, continually adjusting to supply and demand, risk and reward, in our normal behaviors, so why is it so novel to contemplate climate change with the same lens? This book tells us how we can adapt, are adapting, and will continue to adapt to the effects of climate change."
—**Lance Gilliland**, managing director,
Tudor, Pickering, Holt & Co.

"You don't have to agree with Anderson et al.'s faith in the markets—and I often don't—to know this book is important. Whatever we do politically, the planet will keep on warming and the money will keep on moving to higher ground, and these are the two inescapable truths of humankind's next centuries on Earth. Anyone who cares about the future should pay attention."
—**McKenzie Funk**, author of *Windfall* and writer for
*Harper's*, *National Geographic*, and *Rolling Stone*

"*Adapt and Be Adept* brings solid economic thinking to the challenge of harnessing market forces in the service of adaptation to a changing and variable climate, a topic too long neglected by policy makers."

—**G. Tracy Mehan III**, executive director for government affairs,
American Water Works Association, and
former assistant administrator for water,
US Environmental Protection Agency

# ADAPT
## AND BE
# ADEPT

## MARKET RESPONSES TO CLIMATE CHANGE

EDITED BY

### TERRY L. ANDERSON

WITH AN EPILOGUE BY

Bjorn Lomborg

CONTRIBUTORS

Ronald Bailey
Gregory W. Characklis
Kenneth W. Costello
Timothy Fitzgerald

Benjamin T. Foster
Matthew E. Kahn
Mark P. Mills
E. Barrett Ristroph

HOOVER INSTITUTION PRESS
STANFORD UNIVERSITY | STANFORD, CALIFORNIA

*With its eminent scholars and world-renowned library and archives, the Hoover Institution seeks to improve the human condition by advancing ideas that promote economic opportunity and prosperity, while securing and safeguarding peace for America and all mankind. The views expressed in its publications are entirely those of the authors and do not necessarily reflect the views of the staff, officers, or Board of Overseers of the Hoover Institution.*

*hoover.org*

**Hoover Institution Press Publication No. 719**

Hoover Institution at Leland Stanford Junior University,
Stanford, California 94305-6003

First printing 2021
27  26  25  24  23  22  21     7  6  5  4  3  2  1

Manufactured in the United States of America
Printed on acid-free, archival-quality paper

**Library of Congress Cataloging-in-Publication Data**
Names: Anderson, Terry L. (Terry Lee), 1946- editor.
Title: Adapt and be adept : market responses to climate change / edited by
    Terry L. Anderson.
Other titles: Hoover Institution Press publication ; 719.
Description: Stanford, California : Hoover Institution Press, Stanford University 2021. |
    Series: Hoover Institution Press publication ; no. 719 | Includes bibliographical
    references and index. | Summary: "This volume features seven essays exploring
    different ways market forces can help governments and populations adapt to the
    environmental and economic effects of climate change"—Provided by publisher.
Identifiers: LCCN 2020051684 (print) | LCCN 2020051685 (ebook) |
    ISBN 9780817924553 (paperback) | ISBN 9780817924560 (epub) |
    ISBN 9780817924577 (mobi) | ISBN 9780817924584 (pdf)
Subjects: LCSH: Climatic changes—Government policy. | Climatic changes—Economic
    aspects.
Classification: LCC QC903 .A2428 2021 (print) | LCC QC903 (ebook) |
    DDC 363.738/74561—dc23
LC record available at https://lccn.loc.gov/2020051684
LC ebook record available at https://lccn.loc.gov/2020051685

# Contents

# Acknowledgments

The Hoover Institution is indebted to the Koret Foundation for its generous support of the Adaptation to Climate Change project over the past four years. Prior to developing this volume, the project convened several research workshops and generated numerous scholarly and popular press articles. These products have highlighted the importance of emphasizing science in climate change policy debates as well as the demonstrated human ability to adapt to environmental changes. In short, this project gives us all reasons to be optimistic, rather than apocalyptic, about our future.

Many scholars, too numerous to name, have contributed to this project and laid the foundation for the ideas in this volume. In particular, I must acknowledge the input from Gary Libecap and Alice Hill for their past leadership on the project. Both have honed my thinking about the prospect of adapting to climate change.

There are many at the Hoover Institution who deserve acknowledgment. I thank former Hoover directors John Raisian and Tom Gilligan for having confidence in me to direct the project, and Chris Dauer always gives me confidence and guidance. Other staff at Hoover have contributed untold hours behind the scenes, especially Denise Elson. At the Hoover Institution Press, Danica Michels Hodge and Alison Law have led their team in editing and producing this volume and especially help we "airhead" academics clarify our writing. The De Nault family has supported my Hoover senior fellowship, giving me time to think and write about the "ideas defining a free society."

Finally, thanks to my wife, Monica, for proofreading "evry sentance I writ" (obviously not this one) and for putting up with my policy rants. She always hones my thinking, writing, and personality.

Terry L. Anderson
*John and Jean De Nault Senior Fellow*

# 1

# Introduction

Terry L. Anderson

The globe is warming, ice caps are melting, and sea levels are creeping up. The most convincing evidence to an economist, however, is not measurement with thermometers or yardsticks but the fact that people are reacting to price changes, whether the result of government policies or the result of asset markets. *Market forces are causing human beings to adapt to climate change, and that adaptation is the theme of this volume.*

Adaptation is occurring in part because other policies aimed at slowing global warming show little prospect of being implemented or, if implemented, of having much effect. First, the most common policy proposed for reducing global warming is regulation to reduce greenhouse gas (GHG) emissions. These are the basis for most international agreements, such as the Paris Accord. Not surprisingly, not all countries sign on to such agreements, and not all that do abide by them, especially those wanting more development, such as China and India. Moreover, because so much carbon is already stored in the atmosphere, these agreements are unlikely to have much effect on global temperatures. In the case of the Paris Accord, even if all countries met the targets, projected temperatures by 2100 would only be reduced by 0.05°C.[1]

Second, the alternative energy forms necessary to drive the global economy have inherent limits that, for the foreseeable future, will make a transition that eliminates hydrocarbons unlikely. Chapter 2 by Mark Mills explains why hydrocarbons are here to stay as a major share of the global energy supply, and therefore, why far more severe GHG regulations are unlikely to gain traction.

Third, and perhaps most important, politics, more than efficiency, drive climate policy. As Jeffrey Immelt said in answer to a question I posed at the 2008 ECO:nomics Conference sponsored by the *Wall Street Journal*, "If you're not at the table, you're on the menu." Being at the table means having lobbyists who influence policy. This is why climate change policies promoted by economists as efficient are seldom adopted. Such policy makes good "blackboard economics," as described in chapter 3 by Kenneth Costello. Behind the blackboard are special interest groups seeking subsidies, taxes, or regulations that make their products or services more profitable when they otherwise would not be. Economists refer to this as rent seeking, meaning that political outcomes have little resemblance to theoretical efficiency depicted in economic models. Timothy Fitzgerald, formerly an economist at the President's Council of Economic Advisers, explains in chapter 4 how rent seeking is playing out as climate change policy morphs into trade policy. These historically distinct areas are blending together as a result of "bootlegger and Baptist" coalitions that seek to limit trade. Yet trade offers economic gains that can allow humans to adapt more easily.

## Accepted but Ineffective Climate Policies

Most current policies proposed for reducing global warming or mitigating its effects require collective action. International agreements to reduce GHG emissions require global agreements that are difficult to enforce, even if agreed to. National and regional

GHG reduction is easier to enforce but has little hope of reducing global warming because the GHG emissions immediately mix in the global atmosphere so any effect they have cannot be separated from other GHG emissions. Hence, local economies bear costs with few identifiable benefits locally or globally. Moreover, GHG limits placed on a local economy most often result in "leakage" (see chapters 3 and 4), meaning emissions are shifted to economies without GHG regulations.

The policy that receives the most support from economists involves market-like mechanisms that incentivize individuals and corporations to reduce emissions. The two best known are carbon taxes and cap and trade. Even conservative economists, such as George Shultz, former secretary of treasury and state, and the late Gary Becker, Nobel laureate, call for carbon taxes on the grounds that they will promote an efficient solution to climate change. They argue that energy producers and consumers create "externalities," meaning they impose costs on others for which they are not liable. Shultz and Becker conclude that those who generate GHG "should bear the full costs of the use of the energy they provide," including the costs "imposed on society by the pollution they emit."[2] Such a tax "would encourage producers and consumers to shift toward energy sources that emit less carbon." Indeed, price changes resulting from a carbon tax will influence producer and consumer behavior, but they are not the result of a market. Again, as explained in chapter 3, it is easy to draw "blackboard" graphs making the case for carbon taxes but much harder to implement them as they are drawn.

Cap-and-trade policies are another example of the efficient blackboard economics favored by economists. Under cap and trade, the government places a cap on carbon emissions, allocates shares in the cap to carbon emitters, and allows the shares to be traded. This creates a market in the cap, the price of which is determined by willing buyers and willing sellers. As with a carbon tax, the price of the cap will affect producer and consumer behavior, but the quantity and its allocation are set through a political process, not through market forces.

Public investment in infrastructure is an effective way of mitigating, accommodating, or recovering from the effects of climate change. For example, seawalls can protect the coastline, flood control systems can reduce the effects of storm surge, and carbon capture or sequestration can lower atmospheric GHG.

Unfortunately, these public expenditures face the ever-present collective action problem: costs are generally spread among the many and benefits accrue to the few. This creates two problems. First, with benefits concentrated and costs diffuse, political rent seeking can promote investments that do not pass cost-benefit muster. Second, if the costs are not borne directly by asset owners who benefit, public investment in mitigation creates the potential for a moral hazard response, meaning people will take greater risks than they might otherwise because they are protected from the consequences. If seawalls reduce the risk of building in coastal areas and the increased risk is not priced—perhaps due to tax subsidies in construction of the seawalls or subsidized insurance—developers will have an incentive to build in places where climate change exacerbates risks. Or if dredging makes barge transportation more certain when water flows are low, movers of goods will continue using water transportation rather than considering forms of ground transportation or seasonal shipping accompanied by storage or both.

## Market Adaptation to Climate Change

Because the typical policy proposals for addressing climate change are costly and have been slow to materialize, they have inherent collective action problems, and they often have adverse consequences. This volume makes the case for more reliance on private action using asset, finance, and risk markets to incentivize individuals and groups to adapt to the effects of climate change.

To understand how this form of adaptation works its way through markets—especially land, capital, and other fixed asset values—assume for a moment that climate changes are *not* caused by anthropogenic GHG emissions but rather are the result of some force of nature beyond the control of human beings. Hence, climate change is not a result of private costs being less than social costs, because it is not human action causing the changes. Under this assumption, assets whose values are affected by climate will adjust, and asset owners will adjust, or adapt, how those assets are used. Beachfront properties subject to rising sea levels would be less valuable, inducing people to build differently or move to other locations. Agricultural land with more precipitation would be more valuable, inducing producers to use different crops or move production to different locations.

Relaxing the assumption that almost none of climate change is due to natural causes and assuming instead that climate change is due to anthropogenic GHG emissions yields the same conclusion about asset values. This conclusion follows the reasoning of Ronald Coase in his seminal article, "The Problem of Social Cost." He explained that competition for resources—the use of the atmosphere as a disposal medium for GHG or a medium for stabilizing climate—generates costs that are reciprocal: GHG emitters impose costs on people whose asset values are affected by climate change, or those asset owners impose costs on GHG emitters by regulating GHG emissions.[3]

Who gets to impose costs on whom depends on who has the right to emit or the right to have stable property values. Coase explains that parties can bargain to account for the costs, provided the property rights are clear and the costs of bargaining are low. Of course, neither of these conditions holds for the global atmosphere, because there are millions of GHG emitters and millions of asset owners spread across multiple political jurisdictions.

Who adapts and how they adapt depend on how atmospheric rents are allocated and how they change—that is, who captures the value of using the atmosphere as a GHG dump and who adapts in what ways to the consequences. Do owners of fossil fuel or generation facilities capture rents from using the atmosphere as a medium for the disposal of carbon, or do beachfront property owners capture the value of stable sea levels? It is not surprising that owners of beachfront property would rather continue receiving their rents from the beach, with waves lapping at their feet, and that coal-burning power plant owners would rather continue receiving rents from disposing of GHG in the atmosphere. To date, however, neither party has attained a political resolution to the question of who gets the rents, and without that resolution, the status quo seems to prevail, with the GHG emitters capturing benefits of atmospheric carbon disposal and the owners of land and capital adversely affected by climate change suffering reductions in asset values.

By focusing on market prices of land and capital that reflect the status quo, we begin to see how these prices induce market adaptation to climate change. Human beings are continually responding to changing environmental conditions (for example, rising sea levels or storm surges) and resource prices that reflect those conditions (such as falling recreational property values in the face of wildfires). As a result, the prospects of catastrophic climate change are reduced by human adaptation through market processes, entrepreneurial activities, and institutional evolution.

## Filling Missing Market Niches

The extent to which human beings react to climate change depends critically on the quantity and quality of information they have about the consequences. As Nobel laureate Friedrich Hayek noted in 1945, prices provide condensed information about the costs of production and the value of goods and services produced, appropriately discounted by uncertainty about technology and resource scarcity. How good that information is depends crucially on how complete markets are. If there are missing markets—meaning some inputs or outputs are not priced (see chapter 6)—the incentive to adapt is truncated. Tied to missing markets are the authority and the wherewithal (wealth) to take action. As E. Barrett Ristroph explains in chapter 5, Alaska Native Villages provide a case study of how a lack of authority or ability to act makes adaptation difficult, if not impossible.

Again using the example of a beachfront home, the price of that home will include the cost of the materials that went into construction, the quality of the construction, and the anticipated consequences of more frequent and intense hurricanes and storm surges, . to mention a few variables. Markets exist for construction materials and for real estate, but they will be missing for risks associated with climate change insofar as data on the climate effects are not robust, with uncertain consequences that vary considerably across time and space. Moreover, government insurance subsidies and disaster relief payments distort risk premiums and housing prices in ways that discourage adaptation.

Given the uncertainty of climate's effect on property values—including possibly warmer temperatures, lower temperatures, more precipitation, less precipitation, more humidity, or less humidity—it is difficult to measure the climate effects with much precision. Even having measures of the averages is of little help without knowing the variance, and the latter requires longer time trends. And knowing the means and variance of climate variables is only useful if those data can be translated into consequences. Will crop yields be lower or higher? Will new plant varieties mitigate the consequences? Will building techniques reduce the effects of climate change?

Information on risks and consequences is crucial if missing markets are to be filled, as explained in chapter 6 by Greg Characklis, Ben Foster, and Matthew Kahn. More and better information on how climate change affects assets will provide a foundation for the development of many products and services to facilitate adaptation. However, raw information related to climate change, including data related to natural phenomena, including sea level, precipitation, and temperature, is often not enough by itself to drive adaptation. Understanding the effects of climate change requires an understanding of how these natural systems interact with engineered and economic systems. Simply presenting hydropower producers, for example, with data on reduced stream flows will not inform them about the revenue losses they will experience from reduced electricity sales (the economic system) or how to optimize production (the engineered system). Only by accounting for all three systems—natural, engineered, and economic—will the information be available to allow asset owners, financial institutions, and risk arbitrageurs to price resources, products, and services that will incentivize people to adapt.

In short, climate change is about dealing with new averages and greater variation in climate measures and about providing the information and improved institutions that will incentivize adaptive measures. Doing so, however, also requires an understanding of the complex and interacting systems that determine climate change effects, all of which are time and place specific. With more and better information on what is happening to climate and what the consequences are, asset owners, financial institutions, and risk arbitrageurs can incorporate that information into prices— for example, housing prices, mortgages, and insurance rates—to incentivize people to adapt. However, subsidies for outputs and insurance can distort risk pricing (see chapter 6).

In addition to information on risks and consequences, as well as distortions caused by subsidies that encourage not adapting, other regulations interfere with adapting lifestyles to climate change. This is illustrated by E. Barrett Ristroph in chapter 5, where she discusses the importance of adaptation for Alaska Natives who already face the effects of global warming as sea ice melts, land erodes, permafrost thaws, and wildlife habitat changes. These changes leave Alaska Natives, like many minority populations in the United States, vulnerable because they depend on subsistence hunting and fishing to sustain their cultures and economies. Their ability to adapt is constrained by both the natural environment and the political environment, because Alaska Native Villages, the main units of local collective management, control whether, how, and when villages can move, as well as whether, how, and where Alaska Natives can hunt and fish. This case study could be replicated for other indigenous groups and small communities around the world.

Chapter 7 provides a timely example of how insurance regulations thwart information on wildfire risk from being produced by insurance markets and from being translated into prices that might induce people to adapt. Ronald Bailey makes the case that adaptation and the evolution of insurance and finance instruments require getting the government out of the way of that evolutionary process. In short, adaptation requires realistic insurance pricing without price controls and subsidies.

## To Adapt or Not to Adapt

When humans experience changes in their environment and are not prevented from adapting to the changes, they have shown a remarkable ability to do so. The following examples suggest the potential for adaptation (for more examples, see chapter 6).

Adaptation is McKenzie Funk's theme in his book *Windfall: The Booming Business of Global Warming*. Changes in the Arctic sea ice (the Melt) cause changes in water supplies (the Drought) and changes in coastal flooding (the Deluge), thus constituting three categories into which Funk pigeonholes entrepreneurial responses to climate opportunities. He asserts that his book is an answer to the increasingly urgent question "What *are* we doing about climate change?"[4] He provides many examples of climate entrepreneurs who aren't just talking about the weather; they are doing something about it.

Studies of real estate markets illustrate ongoing adaptation. A paper published in *Environmental Research Letters* by three Harvard University professors tested the hypothesis "that the rate of price appreciation of single-family properties in MDC [Miami-Dade County] is positively related to and correlated with incremental measures of higher elevation."[5] Using the value of 107,984 properties between 1971 and 2017, they found a positive relationship between price appreciation and elevation in 76 percent of the properties (82,068) in the sample. Again, it is important to emphasize that such changes in property values are more easily dealt with by people with the means to adapt.

A similar study by economists at the University of Colorado and Penn State found that beachfront homes in Miami exposed to rising sea levels sell at a 7 percent discount compared to properties with less exposure to coastal flooding, storm surge, and severe storms. Moreover, the discount has risen significantly over the past decade. Comparing rental rates to selling prices of coastal homes, they found that the discount in selling prices "does not exist in rental rates, indicating that this discount is due to expectations of future damage, not current property quality."[6]

Demographer Mathew Hauer reports in *Nature Climate Change* that sea level rise could displace 13 million people by the end of the century. This prediction is predicated on a six-foot sea level rise, an outer bound, but it does suggest that people will react to water lapping or surging at their doorstep. He also notes that "many communities will deploy a wide variety of adaptation measures, including sea walls, beach and marsh nourishment, pumps, or elevate homes and roads to protect both people and property. . . . However, the deployment of adaptation measures is driven by wealth for both cities and individuals."[7]

Though not armed with large data sets and sophisticated regressions, Massachusetts realtors are coming to the same conclusions. According to Jim McGue, a Quincy real estate agent, the northeaster that "happened here in March certainly underscores what a 100-year flood map is all about." Another broker, Maureen Celata from Revere, said a home that included a private beach sold for 9 percent less than its list price of nearly $799,000 and took fifty-five days to sell, which she called an "eternity."[8]

Wine producers in California, Bordeaux, and Tuscany beware. A study by Conservation International, published in the *Proceedings of the National Academy of Sciences*, forecasts that wine production in California may drop by 70 percent and regions along the Mediterranean by as much as 85 percent over the next fifty years.[9] The silver lining is that vintners will adapt by moving their grape production north, some predicting it will even move to places such as Montana, Wyoming, and Michigan, noted for their severe winters.[10]

In the future you may also see more signs on fruit saying, "Country of Origin—Canada," according to Canadian biologist John Pedlar, who sees more people in southern Ontario "trying their hand at things like peaches a little farther north from where they have been trying."[11] This is consistent with the US Department of Agriculture's Plant Hardiness Zone Map, which shows tolerant zones moving north.[12]

## Conclusion

There are many ways climate change can and will be incorporated into market prices and individual decisions, and there is some evidence that people are already adapting. How soon and how far adaptation progresses will depend importantly on implementing policies that produce clear price signals regarding the effect of climate change on asset prices. In his epilogue, Bjorn Lomborg concludes that "adaptive actions can typically deliver much more, faster and more cheaply than any realistic climate policy."

Even without complete property rights to the atmosphere and with the high cost of private negotiations to reduce GHGs, climate change connects in many ways through asset markets, which in turn encourage adaptation. Of course, adaptation is conditioned by information on risks and consequences as well as by policies that shift the risk through insurance programs and subsidies. Both available information (or lack thereof) and the structure of institutions are important factors in whether and how people adapt to climate change. Increased knowledge of the effects of climate change and improved institutional design will lead to prices and result in the development of the missing markets that will lead to more adaptation, unless the prices are distorted by political intervention.

## Notes

1. Bjorn Lomborg, "Impact of Current Climate Proposals," *Global Policy* 7, no. 1 (February 2016): 109–18.
2. George P. Shultz and Gary S. Becker, "Why We Support a Revenue-Neutral Carbon Tax," *Wall Street Journal*, April 7, 2013.
3. Ronald Coase, "The Problem of Social Cost," *Journal of Law and Economics* 3 (October 1960): 1–44.
4. McKenzie Funk, *Windfall: The Booming Business of Global Warming* (New York: Penguin, 2014), 11.
5. Jesse M. Keenan, Thomas Hill, and Anurag Gumber, "Climate Gentrification: From Theory to Empiricism in Miami-Dade County, Florida," *Environmental Research Letters* 13, no. 5 (May 2018): 1.
6. Asaf Bernstein, Matthew Gustafson, and Ryan Lewis, "Disaster on the Horizon: The Price Effect of Sea Level Rise," *Journal of Financial Economics* 134, no. 2 (2019): 254.
7. Mathew E. Hauer, "Migration Induced by Sea-Level Rise Could Reshape the US Population Landscape," *Nature Climate Change*, April 17, 2017.
8. Katheleen Conti, "Homes near Ocean Risk Losing Value, Even in a Hot Market," *Boston Globe*, April 23, 2018.

9. David Gelles, "Falcons, Drones, Data: A Winery Battles Climate Change," *New York Times*, January 5, 2017; Lee Hannah et al., "Climate Change, Wine, and Conservation," *Proceedings of the National Academy of Sciences* 110, no. 17 (2013): 6907–12.

10. Steven E. F. Brown, "Wine from Wyoming? How Yellowstone and Yukon Will Steal Napa's Crown," *San Francisco Business Times*, April 9, 2013.

11. Chelsey B. Coombs, "Climate Change Brings New Crops to Canadian Farms," *Climate Central*, July 16, 2015.

12. Dan Charles, "Gardening Map of Warming U.S. Has Plant Zones Moving North," *NPR*, January 26, 2012.

# 2

# Hydrocarbons Are Here to Stay

Mark P. Mills

The universe is awash in energy. For humanity, the challenge has always been to deliver energy in a useful way that is both tolerable and available when it is needed, not when nature or luck offers it. Whether it be wind or water on the surface, sunlight from above, or hydrocarbons buried deep in the earth, converting an energy source into useful power always requires capital-intensive hardware.

Given the world's population and the size of modern economies, scale matters. In physics, when attempting to change any system, one has to deal with inertia and various forces of resistance; it's far harder to turn or stop a Boeing than it is a bumblebee. Today's reality: hydrocarbons—oil, natural gas, and coal—supply 84 percent of global energy. That share has decreased only modestly from 87 percent two decades ago (figure 1).[1] Over those two decades, total world energy use rose by 50 percent, an amount equal to adding two entire United States' worth of demand.[2]

The small percentage-point decline in the hydrocarbon share of world energy use required over $2 trillion in cumulative global spending on alternatives over that period.[3] Popular visuals of fields festooned with windmills and rooftops laden with solar cells don't

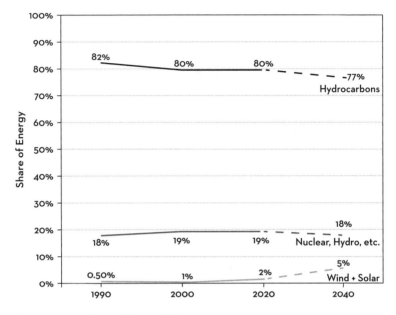

Figure 1.  How the World Is Fueled.

*Sources:* ExxonMobil, *Outlook for Energy: A View to 2040,* https://corporate.exxonmobil.com
/Energy-and-environment/Looking-forward/Outlook-for-Energy; Energy Information
Agency, "International Energy Statistics."

change the fact that these two energy sources today provide about
2 percent of the global energy supply and 3 percent of US energy
supply.

To completely replace hydrocarbons over the next twenty
years, global renewable energy production would have to
increase by at least ninetyfold.[4] For context, it took a half century
for global oil and gas production to expand by tenfold.[5] It is a
fantasy to think, costs aside, that any new form of energy infrastructure could now expand nine times more than that in under
half the time.

The daunting scale of meeting global energy needs often elicits
a common response: "If we can put a man on the moon, surely
we can [fill in the blank with any aspirational goal]." But trans-

forming the energy economy is not like putting a few people on the moon a few times. It is like putting all of humanity on the moon—permanently.

## Physics Realities of Wind and Solar

The technologies that frame the "new energy economy" vision distill to just three things: windmills, solar panels, and batteries.[6] While batteries don't produce energy, they are crucial for ensuring that episodic wind and solar power is available for use in homes, businesses, and transportation.

Over the decades, all three technologies have greatly improved and become roughly tenfold cheaper.[7] And while all three will continue to improve, the key to seeing the future is in recognizing underlying physics limits as well as the unsubsidized economic realities of each source today.

With today's technology, $1 million worth of utility-scale hardware will produce about 50 million kilowatt-hours (kWh) over a thirty-year operating period, using either wind or solar machines.[8] Meanwhile, $1 million worth of hardware for a shale rig will produce enough natural gas over thirty years to generate over 300 million kWh (figure 2).[9] The huge disparity in output arises from the inherent differences in energy densities that are features of nature.

This comparison illuminates the starting point in making a raw energy resource useful. For all forms of energy to become useful, additional technology is required. For gas, one necessarily spends money on a turbo generator to convert the fuel into grid electricity. For wind/solar, spending is required for some form of storage to convert episodic electricity into useful utility-grade, 24/7 power. In order to levelize this inherent cost disparity—that is, for wind + battery to match the stand-alone cost of electricity delivered by gas + turbine—the cost of grid-scale batteries would have to drop at least thirtyfold from today's level.[10]

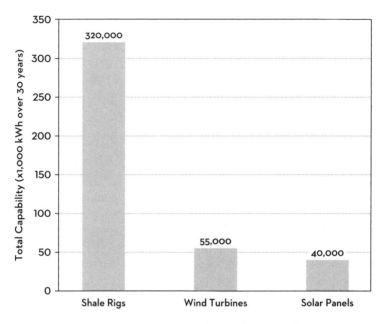

Figure 2. Total Thirty-Year Electricity Production from $1 Million in Hardware: Shale Rigs, Wind Turbines, and Solar Panels.

*Sources:* Lazard, *Lazard's Levelized Cost of Energy Analysis*, 2018, https://www.lazard.com /media/450784/lazards-levelized-cost-of-energy-version-120-vfinal.pdf; Gulfport Energy, Credit Suisse Energy Summit, 2019; Cabot Oil & Gas, "Where We Stand, Where We Are Going," Heikkinen Energy Conference, August 15, 2018, http://www.cabotog.com/wp -content/uploads/2018/08/Cabot-Oil-and-Gas-2018-Heikkinen-Energy-Conference -vFINAL.pdf.

## The High Cost of Ensuring Energy Availability

Availability is the single most critical feature of any energy infrastructure, followed by price. The eternal challenge has always been to produce lower costs without affecting availability, something even more critical in our data-centric, increasingly electrified society. Until the modern energy era, economic and social progress had been hobbled by the episodic nature of energy availability. That's why so far more than 90 percent of America's electricity and 99 percent of the power used in transportation come from sources that are easily stored and can easily supply energy any time on demand.[11]

Physics constrains the technologies and the costs for supplying availability.[12] For hydrocarbon-based systems, availability is dominated by the cost of equipment that can continuously convert fuel to power and do so for decades. Meanwhile, it's inherently easy to store the fuel needed to meet demand variability and weather supply chain failures. It costs less than one dollar a barrel to store oil or natural gas (in oil-energy equivalent terms).[13] Storing coal is even cheaper. Thus, unsurprisingly, the United States has on average about one to two *months'* worth of national demand in storage for each kind of hydrocarbon at any given time.[14]

For wind/solar, the features that dominate cost of availability are inverted. While solar arrays and wind turbines do wear out and also require maintenance, the physics and thus the additional costs of wear are less challenging than with combustion engines. But the complexity and challenges of battery electrochemistry make for an inherently more expensive and less efficient way to store energy and thus ensure availability.

With batteries, it costs roughly $200 to store the energy equivalent of one barrel of oil.[15] Thus, instead of months, barely two *hours* of national electricity demand can be stored by the combined total of all the utility-scale batteries currently on the grid plus all the batteries in the one million electric cars that exist today in America.[16]

Since hydrocarbons are so easily stored, idle conventional power plants can be dispatched—ramped up or down—to follow cyclical demand. There is, by definition, no means to "dispatch" the wind or sun. Wind-powered and sunlight-energized machines produce energy, averaged over a year, about 25–30 percent of the time, often less.[17] And this says nothing about seasonal variation for both average wind speeds and sunlight. Meteorological and operating data show that average output from wind and solar farms can drop as much as twofold during each source's respective low season.[18]

Meanwhile, the availability of conventional power plants is in the 80–95 percent range, day and night and year-round.[19]

A wind/solar grid would need to be sized to both meet peak demand *and* have enough extra capacity beyond peak needs to produce and store additional electricity when sun and wind are available. This means, on average, that a pure wind/solar system would have to be about threefold the capacity of a hydrocarbon grid— that is, one needs to build three kilowatts of wind/solar equipment for every kilowatt of combustion equipment eliminated. That cost disadvantage is real and generally ignored in claims of achieving so-called grid parity.[20]

## The Myth of Grid Parity

Nonetheless, the US Energy Information Agency (EIA) and other similar analysts report that wind and solar are getting close to grid parity with hydrocarbons in terms of calculating a theoretical levelized cost of energy (LCOE).[21] But in a critical and rarely noted caveat, the EIA states: "The LCOE values for dispatchable and nondispatchable technologies are listed separately in the tables because comparing them *must be done carefully*" (emphasis added).[22] Put differently, the LCOE calculations do not take into account the array of real, if ignored, costs needed to operate a reliable 24/7 and 365-day-per-year energy infrastructure—in particular, a grid that uses only wind/solar. Put simply, the real-world costs entail building extra operating capacity and storage.

The LCOE considers the hardware in isolation while ignoring system costs essential to supply 24/7 power. Equally misleading, an LCOE calculation, despite its illusion of precision, relies on a variety of assumptions and guesses subject to dispute, if not bias.

For example, an LCOE assumes that the future cost of competing fuels—notably, natural gas—will rise significantly. But that means the LCOE is more a forecast than a calculation. This is important because the levelized cost uses such a forecast to calculate a purported average cost over decades. The assumption that gas prices will go up is at variance with the fact that they have decreased over the past decade and the evidence that low prices are the new normal for the foreseeable future.[23] Adjusting the LCOE calculation to reflect a future where gas prices don't rise radically increases the LCOE cost advantage of natural gas over wind/solar.

An LCOE also incorporates the subjective feature of a discount rate, which is a way of comparing the value of money today versus the future. A low discount rate has the effect of tilting an outcome to make it more appealing to spend precious capital today to solve a future (theoretical) problem. Advocates of using low discount rates are essentially assuming slow economic growth, whereas a high discount rate effectively assumes that a future society will be far richer than today (not to mention have better technology).[24] Economist William Nordhaus's work in this field, in which he advocates using a high discount rate, earned him a 2018 Nobel Prize.

An LCOE also requires assumptions about capacity factors, the share of time the equipment actually operates when the sun shines and the wind blows. The EIA assumes, for example, 41 percent and 29 percent capacity factors, respectively, for wind and solar. But data from operating wind and solar farms reveal actual median capacity factors of 33 percent and 22 percent.[25] The difference between a 40 percent and 30 percent capacity factor translates into $3 million less in electricity produced over the twenty-year life of a two-megawatt wind turbine, a machine with an initial capital cost of about $3 million.

US wind farm capacity factors have been improving at a slow rate of about 0.7 percent per year over the past two decades.[26] That gain came mainly by reducing the number of turbines per acre to minimize wind interference, resulting in a 50 percent increase in land used per unit of wind energy produced.

LCOE calculations include costs for such things as taxes, loans, and maintenance. But here, too, mathematical outcomes give the appearance of precision while hiding assumptions. For example, assumptions about long-term maintenance and performance of wind turbines appear overly optimistic. Data from Britain, which is farther down the wind-favored path than the United States, point to far faster degradation in output than forecast.[27]

To address these issues, the International Energy Agency (IEA) recently proposed using a value-adjusted LCOE, or VALCOE, to incorporate the economics of flexibility and dispatchability. The VALCOE method found solar power in India, for example, to be far more expensive than coal, with the penalty widening the greater the share of solar on the grid.[28] And that reality is in fact reflected in the overall cost of electricity where the share of wind/solar has increased.

## More Hidden Costs

In Europe, the data show that the higher the share of wind/solar, the higher the average cost of grid electricity (figure 3).

Germany and Britain, well down the "new energy" path, have seen average electricity rates rise 60–110 percent over the past two decades.[29] The same pattern—more wind/solar and higher electricity bills—is visible in Australia and Canada.[30]

Since the share of wind power, on a per-capita basis, in the United States is still at only a small fraction of that in most of Europe, the cost impacts on American consumers are less dramatic and less visible. Nonetheless, average US residential electric costs have risen some 20 percent over the past fifteen years.[31] But that should not have been the case. Average electric rates should have gone down, not up.

Here's why: Coal and natural gas together supplied about 70 percent of electricity over that fifteen-year period.[32] The price of fuel accounts for about 60–70 percent of the cost to produce electricity when using hydrocarbons.[33] Thus, about half the average cost

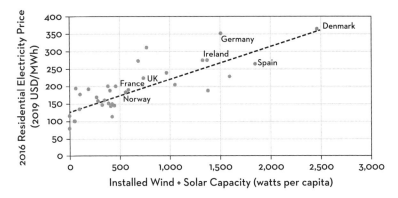

Figure 3. Correlation between Average Electricity Costs and More Wind/Solar Power in Europe.

*Source:* Eurostat, "Electricity Prices for Household Consumers—Bi-Annual Data (from 2007 Onwards)."

of America's electricity depends on coal and gas prices. Though the price of both those fuels has collapsed over that fifteen-year period, the savings have not translated into lower overall electric rates for consumers. That gap—the disappearance of lower costs—is largely attributable to higher costs coming from greater use of episodic wind and solar.

The increased use of wind/solar imposes a variety of hidden, physics-based costs that are rarely acknowledged in utility or government accounting. For example, when large quantities of power are rapidly, repeatedly, and unpredictably cycled up and down, the challenge and costs associated with balancing a grid (that is, keeping it from failing) are greatly increased. OECD analysts estimate that at least some of those "invisible" costs imposed on the grid add 20–50 percent to the cost of grid kilowatt-hours.[34]

Furthermore, maintaining existing power plants to be used as backup for wind/solar leads to other real but unallocated costs that emerge from physical realities. Increased cycling of conventional power plants increases wear-and-tear and maintenance costs. It also reduces utilization of those expensive assets, which means that capital costs are spread out over fewer kilowatt-hours produced—thereby arithmetically increasing the cost of each of those kilowatt-hours.[35]

If the share of episodic grid power becomes significant, the potential rises for complete system blackouts. That has happened twice after the wind died down unexpectedly (with some customers out for days in some areas) in the state of South Australia, which derives over 40 percent of its electricity from wind.[36]

After a total system outage in South Australia in 2018, Tesla, with much media fanfare, installed the (then) world's single largest lithium battery farm on that grid.[37] For context, to keep South Australia lit for one half day without wind would require eighty such "world's biggest" Tesla battery farms, and that's on a grid that serves just 2.5 million people.

The other way to achieve reliability is to use giant diesel-engine generators as backup (engines essentially the same as those that propel cruise ships or that back up data centers). Without fanfare, because of the rising use of wind, US utilities have been installing grid-scale engines at an unprecedented pace. Most burn natural gas, though a lot of them are oil-fired. Three times as many such big reciprocating engines have been added to America's grid over the past two decades as over the half century prior to that.[38] The grid now has over $4 billion in utility-scale, engine-driven generators; many more will be needed.

All these costs are real and are not allocated to wind or solar generators. But electricity consumers pay them. The way electric grids are being managed now is the equivalent of levying fees on *car* drivers for the highway wear and tear caused by heavy trucks, while simultaneously subsidizing the cost of fueling those trucks. That is, of course, precisely the inverse of how highways are managed.

The issue with wind and solar power comes down to a simple point: their usefulness is impractical *on a national scale* as a primary source of electricity. As with any technology, pushing the boundaries of practical utilization is possible but usually not sensible or cost effective. But today, we hear a constant refrain that "clean-tech energy" will bring a "new energy economy." And batteries are a central feature of such aspirations.

## Batteries Cannot Save the Grid or the Planet

It would indeed revolutionize the world to find a technology that could store electricity as effectively and cheaply as, say, oil in a barrel or natural gas in an underground cavern.[39] Such technology would render it unnecessary even to build domestic power plants. One could imagine shipping barrels of electrons around the world from nations where the cost to fill those barrels is lowest: solar arrays in the Sahara, coal mines in Mongolia (out of reach of Western regulators), or the great rivers of Brazil.

But in the universe we live in, the cost of storing energy in grid-scale batteries is about two-hundred-fold more than the cost of storing natural gas to generate electricity when it's needed.[40] That's why we store, at any given time, months' worth of national energy supply in the form of natural gas or oil, but only minutes' worth of electricity.

Consider Tesla, the world's best-known battery maker: $200,000 worth of Tesla batteries, which collectively weigh over 20,000 pounds, are needed to store the energy equivalent of one barrel of oil.[41] A barrel of oil, meanwhile, weighs 300 pounds and can be stored in a $20 tank. Even a 200 percent improvement in underlying battery economics and technology won't close such a gap.

Policy makers enthusiastically embrace mandates and subsidies to vastly expand the use of batteries at grid scale, but astonishing quantities of batteries—and the underlying minerals—will be needed to keep country-level grids energized with batteries.[42]

A grid based on wind and solar necessitates going beyond managing daily variability of wind and sun. It also means preparation for longer periods when there will be far less wind and sunlight combined, even long periods when there will be none of either. While uncommon, such a combined event—daytime continental cloud cover with no significant wind anywhere, or nighttime with no wind—has occurred more than a dozen times over the past century—effectively, once every decade. Historical data show there have also been far more frequent one-hour periods when 90 percent of the nation's wind/solar electric supply would have disappeared.[43]

So how many batteries would be needed to store, say, two days' worth of the nation's electricity? (Note, again, that an average of two months of hydrocarbon demand is in storage.) The $5 billion Tesla Gigafactory in Nevada is one of the world's biggest battery manufacturing facilities.[44] The total annual production yields a quantity of batteries that could store three *minutes'* worth of US electricity demand. A quantity of batteries able to store two days' worth of US electricity demand would thus require one thousand years of Gigafactory production.

Wind/solar advocates propose to minimize battery usage with enormously long transmission lines on the observation that it is always windy or sunny somewhere. While theoretically feasible (but not always, given country-level total wind/solar outages), the length of transmission needed to reach somewhere "always" sunny/windy also entails substantial reliability and security challenges. (And, it bears noting, long-distance transport of energy by wire is twice as expensive as by pipeline.)[45]

## Building Massive Quantities of Batteries Would Have Epic Implications for Mining

Meanwhile, a battery-centric future means a world that will dramatically increase mining to access gigatons more materials.[46] And this says nothing about the fact that it takes, on average, ten times more materials (per unit of energy produced) to fabricate wind turbines and solar arrays compared to conventional generation.[47]

It starts with the fact that about sixty pounds of batteries are needed to store the energy equivalent of one pound of hydrocarbons. Meanwhile, about fifty pounds of various materials are mined, moved, and processed for each pound of battery produced.[48] Such underlying realities translate into enormous quantities of minerals—including lithium, copper, nickel, graphite, rare earths, and cobalt—that would need to be extracted from the earth to fabricate batteries for grids and cars.[49]

Even without grid demand, if electric cars alone replace 20 percent of all cars in two decades (which would require a nearly hundredfold growth in the number of electric vehicles), the mining required to make batteries will dominate the production of many minerals. Lithium battery production today already accounts for about 40 and 25 percent, respectively, of all lithium and cobalt mining.[50] In a battery-centric future, global mining for various minerals would have to expand by more than 200 percent for some minerals and as much as 2,000 percent, or more, for others. It will be a global "gold rush" for lithium, graphite, cobalt, copper, nickel, manganese, and rare earths.[51]

A battery-centric energy future guarantees more mining, elsewhere, and rising import dependencies for America. Most of the relevant mines in the world are in Chile, Argentina, Australia, Russia, the Congo, and China. Notably, the Democratic Republic of Congo (DRC) produces 70 percent of global cobalt, and China refines 40 percent of that output for the world.[52]

Essentially no attention has been afforded the radical increase in import dependencies—associated with energy minerals and "clean-tech" hardware—arising from replacing hydrocarbon liquids and gases. For a sense for what this implies, consider that wind and solar, which supply less than 4 percent of America's energy, will have to expand exponentially (as noted earlier) to replace the hydrocarbons that supply over 80 percent of our energy. And while net hydrocarbon consumption is met almost entirely from domestic sources, nearly all of the green energy materials (and hardware) are produced overseas.[53]

Concerns over mineral dependencies have been flagged in study after study for years, not least in one from the National Academy of Sciences in 1999. As it stands today, the United States is 100 percent dependent on imports for some seventeen key minerals and cannot supply even half its needs for another twenty-eight. As recently as 1990, the United States was the world's primary producer of minerals. Today, it is in seventh place. Opening new mines has been out of favor for decades.

In an acknowledgment of these dependency challenges, the Dodd-Frank Act of 2010 included a new Securities and Exchange Commission requirement that companies report use of "conflict minerals," not least because of direct linkages between, say, consumer-tech batteries and child labor for cobalt in the DRC.[54] While that provision was motivated by the mineral supply chain dependencies for tech products, we should now consider the fact that the quantity of minerals needed for the green energy vision would entail an entirely new scale of material demands.

The one million electric cars on America's roads already contain more cobalt than one billion smartphones. Note that today's electric vehicles account for only 0.5 percent of America's cars. And the materials required for grid-scale batteries will dwarf those used for electric vehicles. The accounting looks the same for the entire panoply of energy minerals—not least the rare earths often in the news—including those needed to build wind and solar hardware.

But most clean-tech hardware is built overseas (using minerals also sourced overseas). For wind turbines, the United States imports some 80 percent of the electrical components (all but fiberglass and steel).[55] About 90 percent of solar panels are imported.[56] Even if the panels were assembled here, the United States fabricates only 10 percent of the global supply of the critical underlying silicon material. China produces half.[57] And while Tesla (which accounted for nearly 80 percent of all domestic electric vehicle sales in the United States in 2019) manufactures domestically, essentially all the critical minerals originate overseas.[58]

In the clean-tech vision, global oil and gas supply chains will be replaced with equally critical but bigger mineral supply chains. An analysis from The Hague Centre for Strategic Studies summarized the "security dimension" of green energy by drily noting that "import dependent countries may use military capabilities to secure mineral resources."[59]

Nonetheless, lithium batteries have finally enabled electric vehicles to become viable, inspiring a rush of the world's manufacturers to produce appealing battery-powered vehicles. This has emboldened bureaucratic aspirations for outright bans on the sale of internal combustion engines, notably in Germany, France, England, and unsurprisingly, California.

Optimists forecast that the number of electric vehicles in the world will rise from today's nearly 10 million to some 500 million in two decades.[60] But because there will be some 2 billion cars in the world by 2040, and cars use only 30 percent of all petroleum, this hundredfold increase in electric vehicles will (arithmetically) yield less than a 10 percent decrease in global oil demand by 2040.[61] And it may even increase carbon dioxide emissions.

It requires the energy equivalent of about one hundred barrels of oil to fabricate the batteries to store a single barrel of oil-equivalent energy.[62] Since China dominates global battery manufacturing and is on track to supply nearly two-thirds of all production, it's relevant that 70 percent of China's grid is coal-fired (forecast to still be at 50 percent in 2040).[63] This means that over the life span of such batteries, the outcome could be an *increase* in net carbon dioxide emissions from replacing internal combustion engines in many regions of the world.[64]

In any event, batteries don't represent a revolution in personal mobility equivalent to, say, going from the horse and buggy to the car—an analogy often invoked.[65] Driving an electric vehicle is more analogous to changing what horses are fed and, for the United States, importing the new fodder.

## Moore's Law Misapplied

Faced with all the realities outlined above, new-energy-economy enthusiasts nevertheless believe that true breakthroughs are inevitable. That's because, it is claimed, energy tech will follow the trajectory seen in recent decades with computing and communications. The world will yet see the equivalent of an Amazon or "Apple of clean energy."[66]

This idea is seductive because of the astounding advances in silicon technologies that so few forecasters anticipated decades ago. Today's smartphones are not only far cheaper; they are far more powerful than a room-size IBM mainframe from thirty years ago. That transformation arose from engineers inexorably shrinking the size and energy appetite of transistors, and consequently increasing their number per chip roughly twofold every two years—the Moore's law trend, named for Intel cofounder Gordon Moore.

The compound effect of silicon progress has indeed caused an information revolution. Over the past sixty years, Moore's law has seen the efficiency of how logic engines *use* energy improve by over a billionfold.[67] But a similar transformation in how energy is *produced* or *stored* isn't just unlikely; it can't happen given the physics we know today.

In the world of people, cars, planes, and large-scale industrial systems, increasing speed or carrying capacity causes hardware to expand, not shrink. The energy needed to move a ton of people, heat a ton of steel or silicon, or grow a ton of food is determined by properties of nature whose boundaries are set by laws of gravity, inertia, friction, mass, and thermodynamics.

If combustion engines, for example, could achieve the kind of scaling efficiency that computers have since 1971—the year the first widely used integrated circuit was introduced by Intel—a car engine would generate a thousand times more horsepower and shrink to the size of an *ant*.[68]

If photovoltaics scaled by Moore's law, a single postage-stamp-size solar array would power the Empire State Building. And if batteries scaled by Moore's law, a battery the size of a book, costing three cents, could power an airliner to Asia. But only in the world of comic books does the physics of propulsion or energy production work like that. In our universe, power scales the other way.

An ant-size engine—which has been built—produces roughly one hundred thousand times *less* power than a Prius. An ant-size solar photovoltaic array (also feasible) produces a thousand times less energy than an ant's biological muscles. The energy equivalent of the aviation fuel actually used by an aircraft flying to Asia would require a pile of Tesla-type batteries weighing five times more than that aircraft.[69]

The challenge in storing and processing information using the smallest possible amount of energy is distinct from the challenge of producing energy or of moving or reshaping physical objects. The two domains entail different laws of physics.

The world of logic is rooted in simply knowing and storing the fact of the binary state of a switch—that is, whether it is on or off. Logic engines don't produce physical action but are designed to manipulate the *idea* of the numbers 0 and 1. Unlike engines that carry people, logic engines can use software to do "magic" things such as compress information through clever mathematics and thus reduce energy use. No comparable compression options exist in the world of humans and hardware.

Of course, wind turbines, solar cells, and batteries will continue to improve in cost and performance, as will drilling rigs and combustion turbines. And of course, digital technology will bring important, even dramatic, efficiency gains in the production and management of all energy and physical systems. But the outcomes won't be as miraculous as the invention of the integrated circuit or the discovery of petroleum or nuclear fission.

## The Physics Limits of Green Dreams and Energy Revolutions

Nonetheless, new-energy-economy advocates commonly claim that we should expect a rapid decline in future costs for wind/solar/ battery tech. It's true that the two decades of commercialization after the 1980s saw a greater than tenfold reduction in the cost of solar and wind hardware. But the future won't emulate the past. Instead gains in these technologies are now on a standard asymptote, a law of diminishing returns (figure 4).

This is a normal phenomenon in all physical systems. Throughout history, engineers have achieved big gains in the early years of a technology's development, whether wind or gas turbines, steam or sailing ships, internal combustion or photovoltaic cells. Over time, as engineering approaches nature's limits, gains in efficiency, speed, or other equivalent metrics, such as energy density, then shrink from double-digit percentages to fractional percentage changes. Such progress is economically meaningful but not revolutionary.

The physics-constrained limits of energy systems are unequivocal. Solar arrays *can't* convert more photons than those that arrive from the sun. Wind turbines *can't* extract more energy than exists in the kinetic flows of moving air. Batteries *are* bound by the physical chemistry of the molecules chosen, just as combustion engines are bound by the physics of the Carnot efficiency limit.

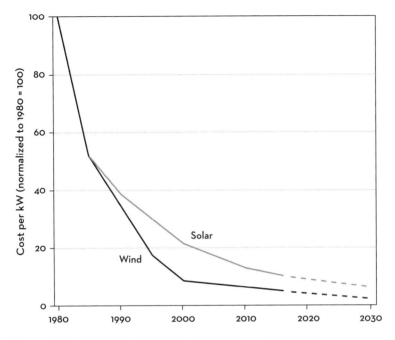

Figure 4. Cost Reductions for Wind and Solar Power, 1980–2030.

*Sources:* Data drawn from Massachusetts Institute of Technology, Energy Initiative, *The Future of Solar Energy: An Interdisciplinary MIT Study*, 2015; Johannes N. Mayer, *Current and Future Cost of Photovoltaics*, Agora Energiewende, February 2015; David Feldman, Galen Barbose, Robert Margolis, Mark Bolinger, Donald Chung, Ran Fu, Joachim Seel, Carolyn Davidson, Naïm Darghouth, and Ryan Wiser, *NREL Photovoltaic Pricing Trends: Historical, Recent, and Near-Term Projections*, National Renewable Energy Laboratory (NREL), August 25, 2015; Ryan Wiser, Karen Jenni, Joachim Seel, Erin Baker, Maureen Hand, Eric Lantz, and Aaron Smith, *Forecasting Wind Energy Costs and Cost Drivers*, Lawrence Berkeley National Laboratory, June 2016; Ran Fu, David Feldman, and Robert Margolis, *U.S. Solar Photovoltaic System Cost Benchmark: Q1 2018*, NREL, November 2018.

At high temperatures, for example, 80 percent of the chemical energy that exists in fuel can be turned into power. Early engines operated at 10 percent efficiency, while today's best achieve 50–60 percent efficiency. While there's still room for gains, none can broach the physics limit. Wind/solar technologies are now on the same spectrum of limits after seeing enormous gains in the first decades after their invention.

For wind, the boundary is called the Betz limit, which dictates how much of the kinetic energy in air a blade can capture; that limit is about 60 percent.[70] Capturing all the kinetic energy would mean, by definition, no air movement and thus nothing to capture. There needs to be wind for the turbine to turn. Modern turbines already exceed 45 percent conversion.[71] That leaves some useful gains to be made but, as with combustion engines, nothing revolutionary.

For silicon photovoltaic (PV) cells, the physics boundary is called the Shockley-Queisser limit: a maximum of about 33 percent of incoming photons are converted into electrons. State-of-the-art commercial PVs achieve just over 26 percent conversion efficiency. While researchers keep unearthing new nonsilicon options that offer tantalizing performance improvements, all have similar physics boundaries, and none is remotely close to manufacturability.

Future advances in wind turbine and solar economics are now centered on incremental engineering improvements. For both technologies, all the underlying components—concrete, steel, and fiberglass for wind; silicon, copper, and glass for solar—are already in mass production and well down asymptotic cost curves in their own domains.

While there are no surprising gains in economies of scale available in the green supply chains, that doesn't mean costs are immune to improvement. In fact, all manufacturing processes experience continual improvements in production efficiency as volumes rise. This experience curve is called Wright's law, first documented in 1936. Experience leading to lower incremental costs is to be expected, but again, it's not a revolutionary improvement.

As for batteries, there are promising options for improvements in the underlying physical chemistry. New nonlithium materials in research labs offer as much as a 200 percent or even 300 percent gain in inherent performance.[72] But again, such gains don't constitute the tenfold or even hundredfold advances already seen since

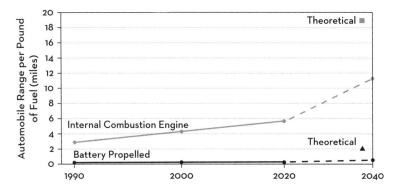

Figure 5. Battery vs. Hydrocarbon Energy Density for Propulsion.
*Sources:* Author calculations; Michael M. Thackeray, Christopher Wolverton, and Eric D. Isaacs, "Electrical Energy Storage for Transportation—Approaching the Limits of, and Going Beyond, Lithium-Ion Batteries," *Energy & Environmental Science* 5 (May 2012): 7854–63; Richard Van Noorden, "The Rechargeable Revolution: A Better Battery," *Nature* 507, no. 7490 (March 2014): 26–28; Anton Wahlman, "The New 39 MPG Toyota SUV vs. Tesla Model 3: Same Fuel Cost Per Mile," *Seeking Alpha*, November 20, 2018; Kevin Bullis, "70 mpg, without a Hybrid," *MIT Technology Review*, October 25, 2010; Justin Hughes, "Toyota Develops World's Most Thermally Efficient 2.0-Liter Engine," *The Drive*, March 1, 2018, https://www.thedrive.com/tech/18919/toyota-develops-worlds-most-thermally-efficient-2-0-liter-engine.

the early days of combustion chemistry. And even such prospective improvements will still leave batteries miles away from the real competition: petroleum.

There are no subsidies and no engineering from Silicon Valley or elsewhere that can close the physics-centric gap between the energy densities of batteries and oil (figure 5). The energy stored per pound is the critical metric for vehicles and, especially, aircraft. The maximum potential energy contained in oil molecules is about 1,500 percent greater, pound for pound, than the maximum in lithium chemistry.[73] That's why aircraft and rockets are powered by hydrocarbons. And that's why a 20 percent improvement in oil propulsion (eminently feasible) is more valuable than a 200 percent improvement in batteries (still difficult).

Finally, when it comes to limits, it is relevant to note that the technologies unlocking shale oil and gas are still in the early days of engineering development, unlike the older technologies of wind, solar, and batteries. Tenfold gains are still theoretically possible in terms of how much energy can be extracted by a rig from shale rock before approaching physics limits. That fact helps explain why shale oil and gas added 2,000 percent more to US energy production over the past decade than wind and solar combined.[74]

## Digitalization Won't Uberize the Energy Sector

A lot of hope and hype has been afforded to what analytics and artificial intelligence could do to optimize energy technologies. Digital tools are already improving and can further improve all manner of efficiencies across entire swaths of the economy, and it is reasonable to expect that software will yet bring significant improvements in both the underlying efficiency in fabricating and using wind/solar/battery machines and the efficiency of how such machines are integrated into infrastructures. Silicon logic has improved, for example, the control and thus the fuel efficiency of combustion engines, and it is doing the same for wind turbines. Similarly, software epitomized by Uber has shown that optimizing the efficiency of *using* expensive physical assets lowers costs. "Uberizing" all manner of capital assets is inevitable.

Uberizing the electric grid without hydrocarbons is another matter entirely.

### The Peak Demand Problem That Software Can't Fix

In the energy world, one of the most vexing problems involves optimally matching electricity supply and demand (figure 6). Here the data show that society and the electricity-consuming services used by people are generating a growing gap between peaks and valleys of demand. The net effect for a hydrocarbon-free grid will be to increase the need for batteries to meet those peaks.

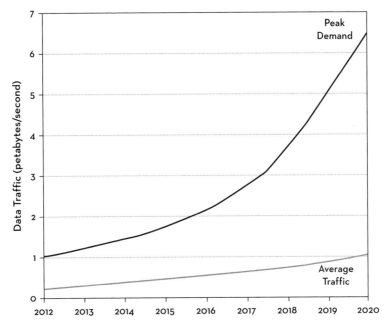

Figure 6. Peak vs. Average Demand for Data.
*Source:* Cisco, *Visual Networking Index: Forecast and Trends, 2017–2022 White Paper,*
February 27, 2019, https://www.cisco.com/c/en/us/solutions/collateral/executive-perspectives
/annual-internet-report/white-paper-c11-741490.html.

All this has relevance for encouraging electric vehicles. In terms of managing the inconvenient cyclical nature of demand, shifting transportation fuel use from oil to the grid will make peak management far more challenging. People tend to refuel when it's convenient; that's easy to accommodate with oil, given the ease of storage. Electric vehicle refueling will exacerbate the already episodic nature of grid demand.

To ameliorate this problem, one proposal is to encourage or even require off-peak electric vehicle fueling. The jury is out on just how popular that will be or whether it will even be tolerated.

Although kilowatt-hours and cars—key targets in the new-energy-economy prescriptions—constitute only 60 percent of the energy economy, global demand for both is centuries away from saturation. Green enthusiasts make extravagant claims about the effect of Uber-like options and self-driving cars. However, the data show that the economic efficiencies from Uberizing have so far increased the use of cars and urban congestion. Similarly, many analysts now see autonomous vehicles amplifying, not dampening, that effect.

That's because people, and thus markets, are primarily focused on economic efficiency and not on energy efficiency. Economic efficiency can be associated with reducing energy use, but it is also, and more often, associated with increased energy demand. Cars use more energy per mile than a horse, but they offer enormous gains in economic efficiency. Computers similarly use far more energy than pencil and paper.

## Uberizing Improves Energy Efficiencies but Increases Demand

Every energy conversion in our universe entails built-in inefficiencies: converting heat to propulsion, carbohydrates to motion, photons to electrons, electrons to data, and so forth. All entail a certain energy cost, or waste, that can be reduced but never eliminated. But, in no small irony, history shows—as economists have often noted—that improvements in efficiency lead to increased, not decreased, energy consumption.

If, at the dawn of the modern era, affordable steam engines had remained as inefficient as those first invented, they would never have proliferated, nor would the attendant economic gains and the associated rise in coal demand have happened. We see the same thing with modern combustion engines. Today's aircraft, for example, are three times as energy efficient as the first commercial passenger jets in the 1950s. That didn't reduce fuel use but rather propelled air traffic to soar and led to a fourfold rise in jet fuel burned.

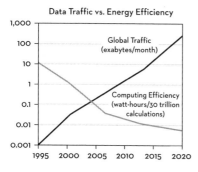
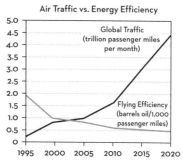

Figure 7. Increasing Energy Efficiency Increases Demand.

*Sources:* Cisco, *Visual Networking Index: Forecast and Trends, 2017–2022 White Paper*, February 27, 2019, https://www.cisco.com/c/en/us/solutions/collateral/executive-perspectives/annual-internet-report/white-paper-c11-741490.html; Jonathan Koomey, Stephen Berard, Maria Sanchez, and Henry Wong, "Implications of Historical Trends in the Electrical Efficiency of Computing," *IEEE Annals of the History of Computing* 33, no. 3 (March 2011): 46–54; Timothy Prickett Morgan, "Alchemy Can't Save Moore's Law," *Next Platform*, June 24, 2016, https://www.nextplatform.com/2016/06/24/alchemy-cant-save-moores-law/; Joosung Lee and Jeonhgoon Mo, "Analysis of Technological Innovation and Environmental Performance Improvement in Aviation Sector," *International Journal of Environmental Research and Public Health* 8, no. 9 (July–September 2011): 3777–95; International Air Transport Association, *Air Passenger Market Analysis*, December 2018, https://www.iata.org/en/publications/economics/.

Similarly, it was the astounding gains in computing's energy efficiency that drove the meteoric rise in data traffic on the internet—which resulted in far more energy being used by computing. Global computing and communications now consume the energy equivalent of three billion barrels of oil per year—*more* energy than global aviation.[75]

The purpose of improving efficiency in the real world, as opposed to the policy world, is to reduce the cost of enjoying the benefits from an energy-consuming engine or machine. So long as people and businesses want more of the benefits, declining cost leads to increased demand, which, on average, outstrips any savings from the efficiency gains. Figure 7 shows how this efficiency effect has played out for computing and air travel.

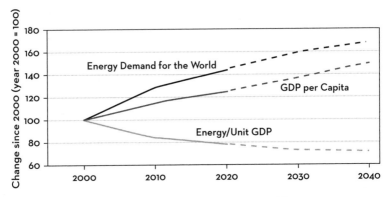

Figure 8. As Global Efficiency Improves, Energy Demand Rises.

*Sources:* ExxonMobil, *2018 Outlook for Energy: A View to 2040*, https://corporate.exxonmobil
.com/Energy-and-environment/Looking-forward/Outlook-for-Energy; PWC Global,
*The World in 2050*, 2019, https://www.pwc.com/gx/en/issues/economy/the-world-in-2050
.html#keyprojections.

Of course, the growth in demand for a specific product or service can subside in a (wealthy) society when limits are hit: the amount of food a person can eat, the miles per day an individual is willing to drive, the number of refrigerators or light bulbs per household, and so on. But a world of eight billion people is a long way from reaching any such limits.

The macro picture of the relationship between efficiency and world energy demand is clear (figure 8). Technology has continually improved society's energy efficiency. But far from ending global energy growth, efficiency has enabled it. The improvements in cost and efficiency brought about through digital technologies will accelerate, not end, that trend.

## Energy Revolutions Are Still beyond the Horizon

When the world's poorest four billion people increase their energy use to just 15 percent of the per-capita level of developed economies, global energy consumption will rise by the equivalent of adding an entire United States' worth of demand. In the face of such projections, there are proposals that governments should constrain demand, or even ban certain energy-consuming behaviors. One academic article proposed that the "sale of energy-hungry versions of a device or an application could be forbidden on the market, and the limitations could become gradually stricter from year to year, to stimulate energy-saving product lines."[76] Others have offered proposals to reduce dependency on energy by restricting the size of various infrastructure or requiring the use of mass transit or carpools.

The issue here is not only that poorer people will inevitably want to—and will be able to—live more like wealthier people but that new inventions continually create new demands for energy. The invention of the aircraft means that every $1 billion in new jets produced leads to some $5 billion in aviation fuel consumed over two decades to operate them. Similarly, every $1 billion in data centers built will consume $7 billion in electricity over the same period.[77] The world is buying both at the rate of about $100 billion a year.

The inexorable march of technology progress for things that *use* energy creates the seductive idea that something radically new is also inevitable in ways to *produce* energy. But sometimes the old or established technology is the optimal solution and nearly immune to disruption. We still use stone, bricks, and concrete, all of which date to antiquity. We do so because they're optimal, not old. So are the wheel, water pipes, electric wires—the list is long. Hydrocarbons are, so far, optimal ways to power most of what society needs and wants.

And insofar as petroleum itself is concerned, the popularized idea that oil is an "old fuel," about to enter the buggy-whip dustbin of history, isn't supported by either the trends of the past two decades or the physics of transporting peoples and goods. With some 98 percent of all transportation powered by oil-burning machines, even the earlier noted optimistic case for electric vehicles in the coming decades would leave the world with greater than 80 percent of transportation fueled by petroleum. And that would still require roughly the same total annual production as today, since overall transportation demands will increase.

The 2019–20 oil price wars initiated by Saudi Arabia and Russia (prior to the coronavirus crisis and its associated epic demand and price collapse) were widely seen as an attempt to push from the market America's productive shale fields—which had, by January 2020, led to the United States becoming the world's largest producer. While that strategy was indisputable, some also claimed the market grab was a sign of desperation on the part of OPEC and Russia, which were seeking to sell as much as possible before clean-tech progress obviated the need for oil. As we've outlined earlier, without regard to which countries supply petroleum, there is no usefully foreseeable time frame without oil demand remaining comparable to today's levels.

Even the use of coal, the oldest of the three hydrocarbons, is unlikely to decrease in the coming decades. More than a decade ago, Google focused its vaunted engineering talent on a project called "RE<C," seeking to develop renewable energy cheaper than coal. After the project was canceled in 2014, Google's lead engineers wrote, "Incremental improvements to existing [energy] technologies aren't enough; we need something truly disruptive. . . . We don't have the answers."[78] Those engineers rediscovered the physics and scale realities of energy systems. Those realities explain why China, despite its aggressive wind/solar construction and rhetorical compliance with green-energy climate goals, is still planning to build hundreds of gigawatts of new coal-fired power plants within its borders and for dozens of other nations.[79]

An energy revolution will come only from the pursuit of basic sciences. As Bill Gates has phrased it, the challenge calls for scientific "miracles." These will emerge from basic research, not from subsidies for yesterday's technologies. The internet didn't emerge from subsidizing the dial-up phone, nor the transistor from subsidizing vacuum tubes, nor the automobile from subsidizing railroads.

However, 95 percent of private-sector R&D spending and the majority of government R&D is directed at "development" and not basic research.[80] If policy makers want a revolution in energy, the single most important action would be to radically refocus and expand support for *basic* scientific research.

Hydrocarbons—oil, natural gas, and coal—are the world's principal energy resource today and will continue to be so in the foreseeable future. We will use more wind turbines, solar arrays, and batteries in the future. But the physics of energy dictates that this won't constitute a revolution or elimination of hydrocarbons. There is simply no possibility that the world is undergoing—or can undergo—a near-term transition to an entirely new energy economy.

## Energy Productivity and Wealth: Keys for Adaptation to Everything

Over the past two centuries—the rise of the hydrocarbon era— society has seen a radical collapse in the share of an economy's GDP devoted to acquiring fuel and food. This has been one of the single most significant structural changes in civilization over the long march of human progress (see figure 9). Put in classical economic terms, energy supply has become far more productive. And as all economists (and some policy makers) know, gains in productivity create greater wealth for society—wealth that can be put to work for other social and environmental purposes.

More wealth is always required to build resilience and adaptation into society's infrastructures and thus protect civilization from any and all of nature's attacks—including, but far from limited to, future climate changes regardless of the proximate cause. Since, as we've summarized above, clean-tech energy technologies are far less productive than hydrocarbon tech in most applications, if

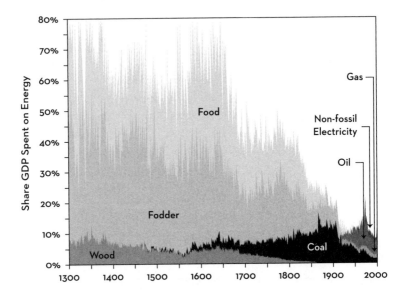

Figure 9. Acquiring Fuel and Food as a Share of GDP.

*Source:* Florian Fizaine and Victor Court, "Energy Expenditure, Economic Growth, and the Minimum EROI of Society," *Energy Policy* 95 (August 2016): 172–186, https://doi.org /10.1016/j.enpol.2016.04.039.

policy makers impose greater use of green machines, society will see a reversal of history's long-term trend of increasing energy productivity. The consequences of such a path are severe enough that it's extremely unlikely that it will be long tolerated.

## Notes

Figures 1–8 in this chapter are based on data analysis conducted by Mark Mills, senior fellow at the Manhattan Institute for Policy Research, for *The "New Energy Economy": An Exercise in Magical Thinking*, March 26, 2019, https://www.manhattan -institute.org/green-energy-revolution-near-impossible.

1. British Petroleum, *BP Energy Outlook: 2018 Edition*, https://www.bp.com /content/dam/bp/business-sites/en/global/corporate/pdfs/energy-economics /energy-outlook/bp-energy-outlook-2018.pdf.

2. British Petroleum, *BP Energy Outlook: 2018*.

3. International Energy Agency, *World Energy Investment 2018: Investing in Our Energy Future*, July 2018, https://www.iea.org/reports/world-energy -investment-2018; REN21, "Renewables 2018 Global Status Report."

4. John W. Day, Christopher F. D'Elia, Adrian R. H. Wiegman, Jeffrey S. Rutherford, Charles A. S. Hall, Robert R. Lane, and David E. Dismukes, "The Energy Pillars of Society: Perverse Interactions of Human Resource Use, the Economy, and Environmental Degradation," *BioPhysical Economics and Resource Quality* 3, no. 2 (2018), https://doi.org/10.1007/s41247-018-0035-6.

5. Day et al., "The Energy Pillars of Society."

6. Biofuels and nuclear energy are also, obviously, nonhydrocarbons, but neither is a central feature for new-energy-economy visionaries. Biofuel, in any case, has clear limits, since it regresses to farming to fuel society. Nearly 40 percent of US corn production is used to produce ethanol that supplies less than 5 percent of America's transportation fuel. And after a half century of government support, nuclear power supplies 5 percent of global energy.

7. Historical trends from Massachusetts Institute of Technology, Energy Initiative, *The Future of Solar Energy: An Interdisciplinary MIT Study*, 2015, https://energy.mit.edu/wp-content/uploads/2015/05/MITEI-The -Future-of-Solar-Energy.pdf; Johannes N. Mayer, *Current and Future Cost of Photovoltaics*, Agora Energiewende, Feb. 2015, https://www.ise .fraunhofer.de/content/dam/ise/de/documents/publications/studies /AgoraEnergiewende_Current_and_Future_Cost_of_PV_Feb2015_web .pdf; David Feldman, Galen Barbose, Robert Margolis, Mark Bolinger, Donald Chung, Ran Fu, Joachim Seel, Carolyn Davidson, Naïm Darghouth, and Ryan Wiser, "NREL Photovoltaic Pricing Trends: Historical, Recent, and Near-Term Projections," National Renewable Energy Laboratory, August 25, 2015; Ryan Wiser, Karen Jenni, Joachim Seel, Erin Baker, Maureen Hand, Eric Lantz, and Aaron Smith, *Forecasting Wind Energy Costs and Cost Drivers*, Lawrence Berkeley National Laboratory, June 2016, https:// emp.lbl.gov/sites/all/files/lbnl-1005717.pdf.

8. Capital costs and capacity factors from Lazard, *Lazard's Levelized Cost of Energy Analysis*, 2018, https://www.lazard.com/media/450784/lazards -levelized-cost-of-energy-version-120-vfinal.pdf. Our calculations here (a) overstate wind and solar output since both degrade in operational efficiency over time, and (b) optimistically assume equal cost for the technologies needed to convert wind/solar and natural gas into grid-useful power, whereas battery $/kW is actually over twice the cost of a natural gas generator.

9. This calculation includes a production decline curve. Capital cost and total recovery/production data are from Gulfport Energy, Credit Suisse Energy Summit, 2019; and Cabot Oil & Gas, Heikkinen Energy Conference, 2018. Additional data for the calculations drawn from Vello Kuuskraa, Advanced Resources International, "Perspectives on Domestic Natural Gas Supplies and Productive Capacity" workshop, Growing the North American Natural Gas Production Platform, Energy Policy Research Foundation, April 19, 2018; gas turbine kWh/Btu from General Electric, "Breaking the Power Plant Efficiency Record," GE Power, https://www.ge.com/power/about/insights/articles/2016/04/power-plant-efficiency-record; US Energy Information Agency (EIA), *Capital Cost Estimates for Utility Scale Electricity Generating Plants* (Washington, DC: US Department of Energy, 2016), https://www.eia.gov/analysis/studies/powerplants/capitalcost/pdf/capcost_assumption.pdf; solar and wind capacity factors from EIA, "Electric Power Monthly," May 2018, https://www.eia.gov/electricity/monthly/epm_table_grapher.php?t=epmt_6_07_b. Calculations do not include the ~$1,000/kW capital cost of a turbine generator for natural gas or the cost of battery storage for wind/solar of ~$1,500–$4,000/kW. EIA, "U.S. Battery Storage Market Trends," May 2020; the latter cost is as critical as the former for utility-scale grid operation.

10. Prachi Patel, "How Inexpensive Must Energy Storage Be for Utilities to Switch to 100 Percent Renewables?" *IEEE Spectrum*, September 16, 2019.

11. EIA, "What Is U.S. Electricity Generation by Energy Source?," https://www.eia.gov/tools/faqs/faq.php?id=427&t=3.

12. Mark P. Mills, "The Clean Power Plan Will Collide with the Incredibly Weird Physics of the Electric Grid," *Forbes*, August 7, 2015.

13. "Why Too Much Oil in Storage Is Weighing on Prices," *The Economist*, March 16, 2017; Nathalie Hinchey, "Estimating Natural Gas Salt Cavern Storage Costs," Center for Energy Studies, Rice University, 2018, http://www.usaee.org/usaee2017/submissions/OnlineProceedings/Nathalie_Hinchey_Gas_Storage_Model_USAEE_Houston_Student_Paper.pdf.

14. EIA, "Natural Gas Storage Dashboard," https://www.eia.gov/naturalgas/storage/dashboard/; EIA, "Petroleum and Other Liquids," https://www.eia.gov/petroleum/; EIA, "Coal Stockpiles at U.S. Coal Power Plants Have Fallen Since Last Year," November 9, 2017, https://www.eia.gov/todayinenergy/detail.php?id=33692.

15. Lazard, *Levelized Cost of Energy Analysis*. Utility-scale lithium battery LCOE @ $108–$140/MWh converts to $180–$230/BOE (barrel of oil energy equivalent).

16. EIA, "U.S. Battery Storage Market Trends," May 2018; Office of Energy Efficiency and Renewable Energy, "One Million Plug-in Vehicles Have Been Sold in the United States," November 26, 2018, https://www.energy.gov/eere /vehicles/articles/fotw-1057-november-26-2018-one-million-plug-vehicles -have-been-sold-united.

17. Landon Stevens, "The Footprint of Energy: Land Use of U.S. Electricity Production," *Strata*, June 2017.

18. EIA, "Wind Generation Seasonal Patterns Vary across the United States," February 25, 2015, https://www.eia.gov/todayinenergy/detail.php?id=20112; *EnergySkeptic*, "Wind and Solar Diurnal and Seasonal Variations Require Energy Storage," June 4, 2015, http://energyskeptic.com/2015/wind-and-solar -diurnal-and-seasonal-variations-require-energy-storage.

19. Lazard, *Levelized Cost of Energy Analysis*.

20. Stephen Brick and Samuel Thernstrom, "Renewables and Decarbonization: Studies of California, Wisconsin, and Germany," *Electricity Journal* 29, no. 3 (April 2016): 6–12.

21. EIA, *Levelized Cost and Levelized Avoided Cost of New Generation Resources in the* Annual Energy Outlook 2020, February 2020, https://www.eia.gov /outlooks/aeo/pdf/electricity_generation.pdf. Gas @ $41/MWh, wind $56, solar $60.

22. EIA, *Levelized Cost and Levelized Avoided Cost*, 2.

23. EIA, *Annual Energy Outlook 2019*, January 2019, https://www.eia.gov /outlooks/aeo/data/browser/#/?id=3-AEO2019&cases=ref2019&sourcekey =0; Mark P. Mills, "The Real Fuel of the Future: Natural Gas," Manhattan Institute, Sept. 24, 2018, https://media4.manhattan-institute.org/sites/default /files/R-MM-0918.pdf.

24. Jason Hickel, "The Nobel Prize for Climate Catastrophe," *Foreign Policy*, December 6, 2018; Thomas Tanton, *Levelized Cost of Energy: Expanding the Menu to Include Direct Use of Natural Gas*, T2 and Associates, August 2017.

25. Stevens, "The Footprint of Energy."

26. Lee M. Miller and David W. Keith, "Observation-Based Solar and Wind Power Capacity Factors and Power Densities," *Environmental Research Letters* 13, no. 10 (October 2018).

27. Gordon Hughes, *The Performance of Wind Farms in the United Kingdom and Denmark*, Renewable Energy Future Foundation, 2012.

28. Brent Wanner, "Commentary: Is Exponential Growth of Solar PV the Obvious Conclusion?," IEA, February 6, 2019, https://www.iea.org/commentaries/is -exponential-growth-of-solar-pv-the-obvious-conclusion.

29.  Frédéric Simon, "Germany Pours Cold Water on EU's Clean Energy Ambitions," EURACTIV, June 12, 2018; Strom-Report, "Electricity Price Development," 2018, https://strom-report.de/#strompreisentwicklung-2018.

30.  Joanne Nova, "Electricity Prices Fell for Forty Years in Australia, Then Renewables Came," JoNova (blog), February 2018, http://joannenova.com.au /2018/02/electricity-prices-fell-for-forty-years-in-australia-then-renewables -came/.

31.  EIA, "U.S. Natural Gas Electric Power Price," February 2019, https://www.eia .gov/dnav/ng/hist/n3045us3a.htm.

32.  EIA data show that the combined contribution from coal and natural gas slightly declined, from 70 percent in 2008 to 63 percent today; shifting 7 percent of US supply from low-cost to high-cost generation also increases average rates. "Electric Power Monthly," April 2020, https://www.eia.gov /electricity/monthly/epm_table_grapher.php?t=epmt_1_01.

33.  IEA, "Projected Costs of Generating Electricity," February 27, 2019.

34.  OECD, *Nuclear Energy and Renewables: System Effects in Low-Carbon Electricity Systems*, 2012, https://www.oecd-nea.org/ndd/pubs/2012/7056 -system-effects.pdf; Barry Brook, "Renewable Energy's Hidden Costs?" Energy Central, Mar. 23, 2013, https://energycentral.com/c/ec/renewable -energys-hidden-costs.

35.  George Taylor and Thomas Tanton, *The Hidden Costs of Wind Electricity*, American Tradition Institute, December 2012, https://eelegal.org/wp-content /uploads/2013/09/Hidden-Cost.pdf.

36.  Australian Energy Market Operator, *South Australian Renewable Energy Report*, November 2017, https://www.aemo.com.au/-/media/Files/Electri city/NEM/Planning_and_Forecasting/SA_Advisory/2017/South-Australian -Renewable-Energy-Report-2017.pdf; Daniel Wills and Sheradyn Holderhead, "AEMO Report on Heatwave Rolling Blackouts Reveals Low Wind Power, Inability to Turn on Gas-Fired Pelican Point Led to Power Cuts," *Advertiser* (Adelaide, Australia), February 15, 2017; Charis Chang, "Why South Australia's Blackouts Are a Problem for Us All," News.com.au, February 10, 2017.

37.  James Thornhill, "Musk's Outback Success Points to Bright Future for Battery Storage," *Bloomberg*, December 4, 2018.

38.  EIA, "Natural Gas-Fired Reciprocating Engines Are Being Deployed More to Balance Renewables," February 19, 2019, https://www.eia.gov/todayinenergy /detail.php?id=37972&src=email; Kurt Koenig and Grant Ericson, "Reciprocating Engine or Combustion Turbine?," Burns McDonnell, https://

www.districtenergy.org/HigherLogic/System/DownloadDocumentFile.ashx
?DocumentFileKey=9b1819fc-c305-f909-4004-5de98aa3eac0.

39. Tantalizing scientific discoveries are possible but still largely dreams. See, e.g., R. Colin Johnson, "Superconducting Graphene Beckons," *EE Times*, September 16, 2015.

40. Even this likely understates battery costs. The 200:1 ratio emerges from *Lazard's Levelized Cost of Storage: 2018*. Lazard's assumption of 84–90 percent battery efficiency (electricity in vs. output) may be optimistic, since data from operating grid storage systems reveals efficiencies of 41–69 percent. See John Baker, James Cross, and Ian Lloyd, *Lessons Learned Report: Electrical Energy Storage, Northern Power Grid*, December 8, 2014, http://www.networkrevolution.co.uk/wp-content/uploads/2014/12/CLNR_L163-EES-Lessons-Learned-Report-v1.0.pdf.

41. Manufacturing cost from "Tesla Is Approaching the Anticipated Magic Battery Cost Number," *Inside EVs*, June 28, 2018, https://insideevs.com/news/338670/tesla-is-approaching-the-anticipated-magic-battery-cost-number.

42. EIA, "U.S. Battery Storage Market Trends," 2018; Jason Deign, "European Utilities Muscle into Energy Storage," *Green Tech Media*, November 26, 2018, https://www.greentechmedia.com/articles/read/european-utilities-muscle-in-on-energy-storage#gs.2qDRDWae.

43. Matthew R. Shaner, Steven J. Davis, Nathan R. Lewis, and Ken Caldeira, "Geophysical Constraints on the Reliability of Solar and Wind Power in the United States," *Energy & Environmental Science* 11, no. 4 (February 2018): 914–25.

44. Trefis Team, "Gigafactory Will Cost Tesla $5 Billion but Offers Significant Cost Reductions," *Forbes*, March 11, 2014.

45. Bonneville Power Administration and Northwest Gas Association, *Comparing Pipes & Wires*, http://www.northwestchptap.org/nwchpdocs/transmission_and_n_gas_comparing_pipes_and_wires_032304.pdf.

46. Pieter van Exter, Sybren Bosch, Branco Schipper, Benjamin Sprecher, and René Kleijn, *Metal Demand for Renewable Electricity Generation in the Netherlands*, Dutch Ministry of Infrastructure and Water Management, 2018, https://www.metabolic.nl/publication/metal-demand-for-renewable-electricity-generation-in-the-netherlands.

47. US Department of Energy (DOE), *Quadrennial Technology Review: An Assessment of Energy Technologies and Research Opportunities*, September 2015, 390.

48. Ore grades: lithium (Nicholas LePan, "Not All Lithium Mining Is Equal: Hard Rock (Pegmatites) vs. Lithium Brine," *TSX Media*, July 17, 2018,

https://tsxmedia.com/2018/07/17/not-all-lithium-mining-is-equal-hard-rock-pegmatites-vs-lithium-brine/); nickel (Greg Ashcroft, "Nickel Laterites: The World's Largest Source of Nickel," *Geology for Investors*, https://www.geologyforinvestors.com/nickel-laterites/); copper (Vladimir Basov, "The World's Top 10 Highest-Grade Copper Mines," Mining.com, February 19, 2017, http://www.mining.com/the-worlds-top-10-highest-grade-copper-mines/); graphite (Fred Lambert, "Breakdown of Raw Materials in Tesla's Batteries and Possible Bottlenecks," *electrek*, November 1, 2016, https://electrek.co/2016/11/01/breakdown-raw-materials-tesla-batteries-possible-bottleneck).

49. Elena Timofeeva, "Raw Materials Supply for Growing Battery Production," Influit Energy, June 11, 2018, http://www.influitenergy.com/supply-chain-and-raw-materials-for-growing-battery-production.

50. Marcelo Azevedo, Nicolò Campagnol, Toralf Hagenbruch, Ken Hoffman, Ajay Lala, and Oliver Ramsbottom, *Lithium and Cobalt: A Tale of Two Commodities*, McKinsey & Company, June 2018, https://www.mckinsey.com/~/media/mckinsey/industries/metals%20and%20mining/our%20insights/lithium%20and%20cobalt%20a%20tale%20of%20two%20commodities/lithium-and-cobalt-a-tale-of-two-commodities.ashx.

51. Henry Sanderson, Tom Hancock, and Leo Lewis, "Electric Cars: China's Battle for the Battery Market," *Financial Times*, March 5, 2017; Jamie Smyth, "BHP Positions Itself at Centre of Electric-Car Battery Market," *Financial Times*, August 9, 2017.

52. Terence Bell, "World's Biggest Cobalt Producers," *The Balance*, October 23, 2018, https://www.thebalance.com/the-biggest-cobalt-producers-2339726.

53. Klaus J. Schulz, John H. DeYoung Jr., Robert R. Seal II, and Dwight C. Bradley, "Critical Mineral Resources of the United States—Economic and Environmental Geology and Prospects for Future Supply," USGS Professional Paper 1802, 2017, https://pubs.er.usgs.gov/publication/pp1802.

54. US Government Accountability Office, *Conflict Minerals: 2018 Company Reports on Mineral Sources Were Similar in Number and Content to Those Files in the Prior Two Years*, September 2019, https://www.gao.gov/assets/710/701232.pdf.

55. Ryan Wiser and Mark Bolinger, *2018 Wind Technologies Market Report*, Department of Energy, Office of Energy Efficiency and Renewable Energy, August 2019, https://www.energy.gov/sites/prod/files/2019/08/f65/2018%20Wind%20Technologies%20Market%20Report%20FINAL.pdf#page=32&zoom=100,93,712.

56. EIA, "2018 Annual Solar Photovoltaic Module Shipments Report," July 2019.

57. Debra Sandor, Sadie Fulton, Jill Engel-Cox, Corey Peck, and Steve Peterson, "System Dynamics of Polysilicon for Solar Photovoltaics," *Sustainability* 10, no. 1 (January 2018): 160–87.

58. Zachary Shahan, "Tesla Gobbled Up 78% of U.S. Electric Vehicle Sales in 2019," *CleanTechnica*, January 16, 2020, https://cleantechnica.com/2020 /01/16/tesla-gobbled-up-81-of-us-electric-vehicle-sales-in-2019/#:~:text =Tesla%20Gobbled%20Up%2078%25%20Of%20US%20Electric%20 Vehicle%20Sales%20In%202019*,-January%2016th%2C%202020.

59. Marjolein de Ridder, *The Geopolitics of Mineral Resources for Renewable Energy Technologies*, The Hague Centre for Strategic Studies, August 2013.

60. IEA, "Global EV Outlook 2017"; British Petroleum, *BP Energy Outlook: 2019 Edition*, https://www.bp.com/content/dam/bp/business-sites/en/global /corporate/pdfs/energy-economics/energy-outlook/bp-energy-outlook-2019 .pdf.

61. EIA, *Global Transportation Energy Consumption: Examination of Scenarios to 2040 using ITEDD*, September 2017, https://www.eia.gov/analysis/studies /transportation/scenarios/pdf/globaltransportation.pdf.

62. Jens F. Peters, Manuel Baumann, Benedikt Zimmermann, Jessica Braun, and Marcel Weil, "The Environmental Impact of Li-Ion Batteries and the Role of Key Parameters: A Review," *Renewable and Sustainable Energy Reviews* 67 (January 2017): 491–506; Qinyu Qiao, Fuquan Zhao, Zongwei Liu, Shuhua Jiang, and Han Hao, "Cradle-to-Gate Greenhouse Gas Emissions of Battery Electric and Internal Combustion Engine Vehicles in China," *Journal of Applied Energy* 204 (October 2017): 1399–1411.

63. Sanderson, Hancock, and Lewis, "Electric Cars"; Jeff Desjardins, "China Leading the Charge for Lithium-Ion Megafactories," *Visual Capitalist*, February 17, 2017, https://www.visualcapitalist.com/china-leading-charge -lithium-ion-megafactories/; EIA, "Chinese Coal-Fired Electricity Generation Expected to Flatten as Mix Shifts to Renewables," September 27, 2017, https:// www.eia.gov/todayinenergy/detail.php?id=33092.

64. Qiao et al., "Cradle-to-Gate Greenhouse Gas Emissions."

65. Tony Seba, "Clean Disruption," YouTube, June 9, 2017, https://www.youtube .com/watch?v=2b3ttqYDwF0&t=6s.

66. Diane Cardwell, "Testing the Clean-Energy Logic of a Tesla–Solar City Merger," *New York Times*, June 23, 2016.

67. Max Roser and Hannah Ritchie, "Technological Progress," *Our World in Data*, 2019, https://ourworldindata.org/technological-progress#citation; Timothy

Morgan, "Alchemy Can't Save Moore's Law," *Next Platform*, June 24, 2016, https://www.nextplatform.com/2016/06/24/alchemy-cant-save-moores-law.

68. S. Brown, S. Menon, and C. Hagen, "Investigation of Scaling Laws for Combustion Engine Performance," Oregon State University, 2016, https://sites01.lsu.edu/faculty/smenon/wp-content/uploads/sites/133/2017/02/WSSCI_Provo_v5.pdf.

69. Author's calculations. For useful perspectives, see Toyohashi University of Technology, "Unveiling of the World's Smallest and Most Powerful Micro Motors," Physics.org, May 1, 2015, https://phys.org/news/2015-05-unveiling-world-smallest-powerful-micro.html; Ella Davies, "The World's Strongest Animal Can Lift Staggering Weights," BBC Earth, November 21, 2016; Leeham News and Analysis, "Updating the A380: The Prospect of a Neo Version and What's Involved," March 2014, https://leehamnews.com/2014/02/03/updating-the-a380-the-prospect-of-a-neo-version-and-whats-involved.

70. Marisa Blackwood, "Maximum Efficiency of a Wind Turbine," *Undergraduate Journal of Mathematical Modeling: One + Two* 6, no. 2 (Spring 2016): 1–10.

71. Lee Teschler, "Wind Turbines for Low Wind Speeds Defy Betz Limit Efficiency," *Machine Design*, May 29, 2014. Note, clever, not commercial and actual, efficiency appears closer to 40 percent, and even this claim is no 10x improvement.

72. Azevedo et al., *Lithium and Cobalt.*

73. Michael M. Thackeray, Christopher Wolverton, and Eric D. Isaacs, "Electrical Energy Storage for Transportation—Approaching the Limits of, and Going Beyond, Lithium-Ion Batteries," *Energy & Environmental Science*, no. 7 (May 2012): 7854–63.

74. EIA, "Monthly Energy Review," Table 1.2: "Primary Energy Production by Source," February 2019.

75. Mark P. Mills, "Energy and the Information Infrastructure Part 1: Bitcoins & Behemoth Datacenters," Real Clear Energy, Sept. 19, 2018.

76. Sofie Lambert and Mario Pickavet, "Can the Internet Be Greener?," *Proceedings of the IEEE* 105, no. 2 (February 2017): 179–82.

77. Lambert and Pickavet, "Can the Internet Be Greener?"

78. Ross Koningstein and David Fork, "What It Would Really Take to Reverse Climate Change," *IEEE Spectrum*, November 18, 2014.

79. Darrell Proctor, "China Ramping Renewables, and Building More Coal Plants," *Power*, November 28, 2019, https://www.powermag.com/china-ramping-renewables-and-building-more-coal-plants.

80. Mark P. Mills, "Basic Research and the Innovation Frontier," Manhattan Institute, February 2015.

# 3

# The Political Realities of Climate Policy

## Kenneth W. Costello

Climate change poses a daunting challenge for economists, political scientists, and policy makers: it features a global shared resource magnified by massive uncertainty over both physical and economic processes, we all contribute to its cause, and we all potentially bear the costs of its consequences.[1] Three policy challenges result: (1) taking collective action, where cooperation of countries is essential to achieve targeted reductions in greenhouse gas (GHG) emissions, (2) incentivizing individuals to reduce their GHG emissions, and (3) identifying the preferred institutional arrangement—namely, markets versus government—to alleviate the damages from climate change.

Policy makers face the task of trading off the risk of doing too little to combat climate change with excessive spending or regulating. The ideal policy position on climate change depends critically on the size and likelihood of negative outcomes, in view of the best available scientific and other fact-based evidence. Reasonable people can disagree over the opportunity cost of an overly active climate strategy versus the cost of a passive one. Thus, they can agree on the scientific evidence but differ over the preferred strategy, which becomes more of a value judgment.

For example, the preferred strategy depends critically on people's risk aversion to negative outcomes, given the available scientific evidence and other relevant information. Some people may worry more about an incorrect scientific conclusion that climate change has a high risk when in fact it has a low risk; the opportunity cost comes in the form of excessive resources allocated to slowing climate change, which could result in less economic growth. Other people may have more concern about an incorrect conclusion that climate change has a low catastrophic risk when in fact it has a high risk; to them, the opportunity cost is the excessive damage from climate change resulting from an overly passive policy.

Nobel laureate Ronald Coase coined the term *blackboard economics* to describe the difference between what economists consider an ideal state, usually in terms of economic efficiency or social welfare, and what government officials do in advancing their objectives. He once remarked in an interview that blackboard economics is "economics which you can put on the blackboard, in which you study an imaginary system. It's not empirically based at all. It's not concerned with what really happens. It's what you imagine could happen and what you imagined didn't happen. . . . That's called blackboard economics. It's something you can put on the blackboard but that doesn't exist."[2]

What blackboard economics tells us is especially germane for various climate actions, including a carbon tax, which may appear to be the preferred policy but in reality is less attractive. Blackboard economics abstract from the prevailing politics, the acquisition of tolerably accurate information on the social cost of carbon, the institutional setting, and the likelihood that the tax will achieve its objective. Because of politics, for example, a carbon tax is less likely to balance social and private benefits than to appease those in charge politically.

Numerous examples exist where actual public policies in all areas of society deviate far from what blackboard economics would say is ideal. The public choice literature confirms this divergence between ideal and actual outcomes. Such divergence typically results from information deficiencies, institutional realities, and the government's incentive to serve its self-interest and appease special interests rather than the public good. Climate policy certainly falls into a space where government action would likely have adverse consequences.

Friedrich Hayek's "pretense of knowledge" prevails where policy makers are under the illusion that they can predict the distant future with reasonable accuracy and that they alone can solve problems without the aid of markets. This presumptuousness has triggered much harm from ill-conceived government actions, notably large-scale centralized planning, in a wide range of areas across the economy. Supporters of a carbon tax fall into this trap, falsely believing that there are reasonably accurate calculations for the damages from carbon emissions and the cost of abatement.

This paper suggests that, given the obstacles and other problems faced by conventional climate policy, such as carbon-emission caps, carbon taxes, and targeted subsidies for alternative energy, more attention should focus on measures that strengthen market signals for individuals to adapt to climate change. These measures may include adaptation based on the pricing mechanism, companies satisfying consumers and investors with clean products, and governmental assistance for basic research in clean-energy technologies (for instance, nuclear power, renewable energy, and hydropower) and climate engineering. Each of these has taken a back seat to GHG-emissions mitigation policies.

## The Political Economy of Top-Down Climate Policy

Climate change actions involve managing a global shared resource (i.e., the atmosphere). From a public policy perspective, a global shared resource differs from a national or local shared resource because there exist no mechanisms—either market- or government-driven—to deal with it effectively or without high transaction costs. International law requires countries to consent to joining international agreements, which makes such agreements in effect voluntary. The fact that one country benefits from them does not detract from the benefits enjoyed by other countries. The reality that controlling climate change in one country cannot deprive others of the benefits motivates individual countries to not pay for mitigation. William Nordhaus, for example, considers free riding as the main culprit for the lack of progress in climate policy. While free riding is not uncommon, it is especially prevalent for global public goods.[3] Aggravating this problem are the differences in the marginal valuation of climate control across countries, making international cooperation difficult.

The issues raised by climate change are numerous, including (1) data- and computer-based forecasting models, like integrated assessment models (IAMs);[4] (2) uncertainty over the physical and economic effects of climate change;[5] (3) lack of property rights to the atmospheric commons; (4) the proportion of the observed climate change over hundreds of years that is man-made and natural;[6] (5) the cost of reaching and enforcing international cooperation; (6) the time gap between the incurred costs and the realization of benefits; and (7) the preferred institutional design, which determines the role of government relative to markets.

Some analysts label catastrophic climate change as a high-impact, low-probability (HILP) event, known as a "black swan" event. These events are generally unpredictable with potentially severe consequences. They pose special challenges because of a far-reaching effect, poorly understood risks, costly actions to mitigate the damage, and the unclear role for individuals and groups, including governments, in sharing the responsibilities for mitigating the damage from a catastrophe. HILP events can have economy-wide effects. The benefits of any actions toward GHG-emissions reduction consequently become harder to measure. In dealing with black swan events, policy makers should heed the advice sometimes attributed to Mark Twain: "It ain't what you don't know that gets you into trouble. It's what you know for sure that just ain't so."[7]

Evidence in different contexts has shown that probability neglect, meaning the sole focus on outcome and disregard for its probability, helps explain excessive reactions to low-probability, catastrophic events. Responses to tragedies and other highly damaging events often occur right after incidents with high public exposure.[8] This results in political responses that have little to do with blackboard economics and everything to do with the politics of who bears the cost and reaps the benefits. Climate change would seem susceptible to this conundrum.

Climate models produce probabilistic predictions about the effect of GHG emissions. Scientists still debate over the threshold GHG emissions and temperature change ("tipping point") before a catastrophe would strike. Especially troublesome are the worst-case scenarios. While the uncertainty is great, to most analysts the risk is too great to ignore. How do individuals and politicians react to low-probability, high-cost events (e.g., catastrophic outcomes)? Hedging (i.e., acting to avoid a serious consequence) is a rational individual response, but questions remain as to when, how, and how realistic the information is to which individuals and politicians respond.

Hedging allows individuals and organizations to protect themselves against a major disaster that could cause serious damage. Discussion has centered on four major actions or a combination of them to mitigate the chances of climate catastrophe: (1) reduce new GHG emissions (e.g., via a carbon tax), (2) extract some of the GHG emissions presently in the atmosphere (e.g., via reforestation, direct air carbon capture), (3) lower the climate sensitivity for a given stock of GHG emissions in the atmosphere (e.g., via geoengineering), and (4) mitigate the damage from a given level of climate change (e.g., adaptation).

## Economic Obstacles

Climate change poses a daunting economic challenge, partially because it involves a global shared resource, and the damage it can cause is highly uncertain. GHG emissions disperse throughout the world, no matter where the emissions originate.[9] Curtailing GHG emissions requires countries to inconvenience their citizens while largely benefiting people elsewhere or not yet born. That partially explains why many countries are reluctant to execute aggressive action like a carbon tax or a cap-and-trade mechanism.

The distant benefits that would come from climate action diminish the urgency, from both a political and economic perspective, to act today. Added to this are uncertainties over the nature and magnitude of those benefits, as well as the fact that abatement costs incur much sooner. The question of the right discount rate (which measures the rate at which future benefits diminish in today's dollars) becomes decisive in policy making but invites contention over how to define and measure it.[10] One risk in assigning a low discount rate to future benefits is that it could justify spending today on climate change that would deprive the present generation of resources allocated to other priorities with more immediate benefits.

Uncertainty can affect behavior in different directions: people, government, and organizations sometimes act overconfidently by overstating the sureness of their decision. They believe something like the following: "We just know that spending more money on climate change is cost-beneficial. We observe how damaging climate change can be, so we can never throw too much money at mitigating its effects." Others may rationalize doing nothing presently because of the high degree of uncertainty: "Since we have highly imprecise estimates of what the benefits will be, we shouldn't throw any money at climate change until we get better estimates." Doing nothing today, however, does not preclude waiting for new information to act or to adapt to climate change if its effects become serious in the future.[11]

Controls on GHG emissions would directly affect goods and services, such as electricity and transportation, whose costs would likely escalate. If controls include banning fossil fuels, the costs could be substantial. We have an abundance of fossil fuels at affordable prices, which explains why over 80 percent of the world's energy still comes from fossil fuels. This raises the question of whether we want to or can wean ourselves from fossil fuels over the next two or three decades, given the possible serious economic consequences.

Another economic obstacle to climate policy is the requirement that virtually all countries cooperate; otherwise, "leakage" will occur, where emissions "migrate" to noncooperative countries. One prime example is industries locating in jurisdictions with a lenient climate policy. A subtler example is the United States undertaking aggressive action that increases the price of gasoline, thereby causing its citizens to drive less; this may lower global oil prices, driving up the demand for oil in other countries. Such aggressive policies would be an inconvenience to US citizens while doing little to slow climate change. It is reasonable to believe that an aggressive US-only climate policy would be more nominal than substantive.

## Political Obstacles

The target of controlling temperatures at 1.5–2.0°C above pre-industrial levels—sometimes referred to as a deep-decarbonization scenario—is the focal point for climate debate but not for political action, which is not surprising.[12] If the target is unattainable, should the dialogue then shift to how the world could adapt to higher temperatures using market price signals and incentives?

To judge from his writings, Ronald Coase would have predicted the difficulty of countries reaching agreement on climate policy. He would attribute this condition to high transaction costs and a lack of property rights to the atmosphere. We have seen the futility of collective action since the 1990s, the latest example being the UN Climate Change Conference in Madrid (COP25). As one commentator remarked, the meeting ended with "an ideological divide around carbon credits that is fundamentally motivated by economic self-interest."[13] One perception is that because the atmosphere is a global shared resource, any policy should require government-driven, worldwide collective action. Since changes in GHG emissions would affect the entire world, any successful coordination would require virtual unanimity rather than just coalition building. But as past experience has shown, reaching mutual consent among multiple heterogenous countries is a Herculean task.

Some may interpret the absence of international coordination signals as a market or collective-action failure. Desirable coordination for society at large requires that the benefits exceed the costs, which may not be possible when property rights are not well defined (which is true for use of the atmosphere) and the transaction costs are high. As an illustration, the need to compensate poor countries affected by climate change may impose a high cost on other countries, making reaching an agreement and enforcing it difficult. Failure to reach coordination could then make economic sense from a global perspective.

Aggravating this problem is the fact that those countries with the most to gain from controlling climate change have the least financial capability. Wealthy countries have more resources and site-specific technology to adjust to changing climate than developing countries have. Developing countries are most vulnerable to climate change because they have fewer resources to adapt to it. Besides, there is no easy way to induce cooperation from developing countries as long as they view emissions reduction as disrupting their economic growth. As a rule, growth-oriented economies will relegate climate change to the back burner.

Politicians would generally prefer to hide or diffuse the costs of climate mitigation and concentrate on the benefits. This explains the appeal of subsidies over taxes. Subsidies encourage rent seeking by special interests and allow policy makers to determine which technologies to champion. Subsidies for renewable energy have been especially attractive because of the claim that they would improve air quality and create new jobs, while their costs are concealed in the larger government budget. It is harder to sell the public on a carbon tax whose costs are more visible and concentrated on consumers.

Another problem is that a victory under one regime in aggressively attacking climate change is vulnerable to reversal under a future one. The highly politically charged views on climate change mean that when a different administration takes power, it will likely rescind the policies of the previous administration. The odds that an adequate number of countries will sustain their commitment to an international agreement over several decades are long.

William Nordhaus proposes the formation of a climate club to redress the problem of free ridership, which would make international cooperation more likely. Club members would pay dues in the form of GHG-emissions mitigation while penalizing nonmembers through tariffs, such as for exports to club-member countries. Nordhaus concedes that a climate club is presently only a theoretical concept. But, he contends, the alternatives offer little hope: weak national plans that achieve minimal reductions, geoengineering that has unknown risks of dangerous side effects, or doing nothing and risking a catastrophic outcome.[14] Nordhaus concludes that a climate club and carbon prices around the world are prerequisites for slowing climate change.[15] If that is true, then we cannot expect this outcome to happen. A market approach such as price-driven adaptation and other nongovernmental actions will therefore have to play a prominent role to avoid the serious consequences of climate change.

## A Cautionary Tale about a Carbon Tax

A carbon tax has special appeal to mainstream economists of various stripes, who support it largely on theoretical grounds. For example, more than 3,500 economists from both sides of the political spectrum, including twenty-seven Nobel laureates, four former chairs of the Federal Reserve, and almost all former chairs of the Council of Economic Advisers, signed the "Economists' Statement on Carbon Dividends Organized by the Climate Leadership Council" advocating a carbon tax.[16]

Advocates claim that as a Pigouvian-type tax on carbon dioxide emissions, such a tax sends price signals to consumers and producers that align with the social cost of production inclusive of the damage from carbon emissions, stimulate R&D on clean technologies, and avoid command and control, subsidies, or other inherently inefficient measures. To say it differently, the Pigouvian rationale for a tax is that treating the atmosphere as a commons results in decentralized market prices failing to reflect all the costs of using the global atmosphere as a carbon sink.

Further, high transaction costs and the absence of property rights make it infeasible for countries to reach agreement on the use of the global atmosphere. Overall, then, the decentralized market is unable to produce an optimal amount of carbon emissions.

## Real-World Obstacles

An idealized Pigouvian tax—which advocates argue is efficient and economically benign—must satisfy, however, a set of conditions that policy makers cannot presume to exist: (1) it must replace regulations rather than adding to them in controlling GHG emissions;

(2) the additional revenues for government should lower distortionary taxes such as the personal income tax or corporate income taxes; (3) the revenues should steer away from uneconomical projects or funding of energy sources favored by certain interest groups; and (4) it requires a tolerably accurate estimate of the social cost of GHG emissions and abatement rather than estimates based on political and other empirically invalid factors. Especially when none of these conditions hold, the efficacy of a carbon tax to improve the state of affairs becomes highly suspect.

## Blackboard Economics and Public Choice

What Coase said about blackboard economics is instructive for a carbon tax as well as other public policies that appear attractive on the "blackboard": policy analysts should account for world realities rather than merely resorting to a theory with simplified assumptions detached from reality. Even Pigou himself recognized the difficulties of establishing the right level for a tax, given the politics: "It is not sufficient to contrast the imperfect adjustments of unfettered private enterprise with the best adjustment that economists in their studies can imagine. For we cannot expect that any State authority will attain, or will even whole-heartedly seek, that ideal. Such authorities are liable alike to ignorance, to sectional pressure and to personal corruption by private interest. Every public official is a potential opportunity for some form of self-interest arrayed against the common interest."[17]

For a carbon tax, policy makers should consider the politics, the profound problems with measuring the social cost of carbon, and other real-world challenges (e.g., administrative difficulties). Analysts refer to the damage from carbon emissions as the social cost of carbon (SCC), which many argue is the appropriate metric for setting a carbon tax. Our knowledge of the SCC, however, is so speculative as to make estimates highly suspect. The SCC is dependent on parameters that are subjective ("garbage in, garbage out"): interest groups, politicians, and bureaucrats can come up with an SCC that best advances their agenda, and they have. For example, the SCC is highly sensitive to both the discount rate, since alleged major damages would begin only after several decades have passed, and the temperature change and welfare losses (which are region and country specific) from a ton of carbon emissions.

It is highly doubtful that a US-only carbon tax would have a detectable effect on climate change. Even supporters of a carbon tax do not claim that it would.[18] If the demand for carbon-based energy is highly inelastic, for example, people may be willing to pay the tax and continue emitting carbon. This weakens the argument of those who believe that even if a carbon tax fails the cost-benefit test, it can still act as a form of insurance by avoiding worst-case scenarios for climate change. The overall result would be that the government collects huge tax revenues with little effect on global temperatures.

On the blackboard, a carbon tax would offset implicit subsidies to nonclean-energy, carbon-based goods and services. But in the real world, the SCC is so conjectural that we have little idea of what tax would be necessary to make this offset. Moreover, if the subsidies are detrimental to policy goals, they should be directly eliminated by simply removing them.

Estimates of the SCC require forecasts that relate damages to carbon emissions and global temperature change. We know today that those forecasts are grossly uncertain, seriously diminishing their use in setting a carbon tax. A US carbon tax would actually do little to reduce carbon emissions outside the United States, where the climate change battle will be won or lost. The reason is that over 85 percent of carbon emissions originate in foreign countries.

Those countries that institute a carbon tax bear the emission-reduction costs while the benefits accrue globally. A widely accepted estimate of the global social cost of carbon (i.e., the social benefit of reducing carbon emissions) is around $50 per ton. But the benefit to the United States would be around just $7 per ton, according to 2017 estimates from the US Environmental Protection Agency.[19] If the United States or any country institutes a carbon tax alone, its citizens will likely realize negative benefits. This means that setting a carbon tax at the global social cost of carbon could burden US citizens more than what they receive in climate-related benefits. For policy makers to justify it, they would have to convince the citizenry that the tax will trigger other countries to institute a carbon tax. It would also be terribly difficult to get global agreement on a carbon tax, as experience has shown. One reason is that there exists no single social cost of carbon: the cost differs across countries. Mitigating climate change therefore does not benefit everyone equally. Some countries would balk at establishing a carbon tax, inevitably feeling that the tax is both excessive and unfair.

Even with a carbon tax, climate activists would likely continue to push for more stringent, inefficient regulations and subsidies for clean technologies. They would never agree to a carbon tax unless it were extremely high, but even then, it would likely fail to achieve the 1.5–2.0°C target that many activists advocate.

A high tax rate would also surely face strong opposition from politicians and those who would be adversely affected. We know from the past that governmental action leading to higher energy prices evokes a public outcry.

We also know that environmentalists are generally skeptical of "pollution" taxes; they prefer subsidies for clean-energy technologies and caps on emissions. Subsidies reflect heavy-handed regulation and require policy makers with imperfect information to choose specific technologies for preferential treatment.

Some advocates of a carbon tax argue that, when found to be appropriate, it would be easier to undo a tax compared to alternative approaches. But based on experiences with other taxes, beneficiaries (e.g., clean-energy producers, government) will likely exert strong political opposition to the abolition of a tax.

A carbon tax also faces the problem of leakage. A fundamental flaw in state carbon taxes is that states are unable to do a border adjustment. If the governor of Oregon tries to solve her budget problems by imposing a carbon tax, the tax could cause massive leakage to neighboring states. This explains why a carbon tax would work only as a federal policy. But even then, economic activity could move to other countries.

What, then, would be the purpose of a carbon tax, or any climate policy, if it fails to reduce the welfare losses from the external effects of carbon emissions? We will surely see fewer carbon emissions, but if no discernible change in global temperature occurs, then why go through the trouble of creating the tax in the first place?

## The Complications of a Dynamic World

Even if one can reasonably calculate the starting point for a carbon tax, projecting how it should change over time would be highly susceptible to error. The optimal carbon tax derives from the condition that the marginal abatement cost equals the marginal damage from carbon. Assume that over time new low-cost, clean-energy technologies emerge on the market. The carbon tax should decline, just as a technological improvement for the production of a good would have the same effect on its market price. Over time, the marginal-damage schedule for carbon should also shift. Better ways to adapt to climate change might become available (i.e., actions that reduce the damage for every level of carbon emissions in the atmosphere), or new information might lower or increase the damage from each unit of carbon—for example, adaptation might become more economically attractive than carbon mitigation. Again, these dynamics would affect the optimal tax, where the marginal abatement cost equals the marginal damage. It would be far-fetched to think that the government would adjust a carbon tax in a timely fashion in response to such changes.

Abstracting from these dynamics would enlarge the margin of error, where the carbon tax would allow emission of either an excessive or deficient amount of carbon into the atmosphere. Especially given the likelihood that any changes in the carbon tax over time are politically driven, a distortive tax could conceivably cause more harm than good. But even if government tries to base the tax on objective, best-available information (which is unlikely), it would fall short of making accurate calculations. Notwithstanding a consensus among experts on the damage from carbon, the bureaucrats and politicians would likely choose a metric aligned with their self-interest or with the interests of those who hold current power. The implication is that an action intended to do good can easily turn into a suboptimal tax with a large welfare loss.

The blackboard economics version of a carbon tax relies on both deductive reasoning and static analysis (e.g., no change in technologies, a constant ratio of damage to carbon emissions) to demonstrate on the blackboard how a carbon tax would produce an optimal outcome. This approach fails to acknowledge the complexities involved by making simplistic, blackboard assumptions in establishing the tax at which the marginal abatement cost equals the marginal damage from carbon. It mistakenly glosses over real-world constraints while still rationalizing a carbon tax that is unequivocally superior to the status quo.

Given unrealistic assumptions, highly imperfect information, and a dynamic world, the blackboard criticism of public policy seems well placed for a carbon tax. Public choice economics would also predict the improbability of an actual carbon tax achieving a blackboard outcome: the combination of distorted incentives to appease special interests and the self-interest of government officials, along with the lack of knowledge about how a complex world works, would avert a blackboard outcome. As in other matters, bureaucrats and politicians would identify more with their self-interest and willingly pursue it, even if it makes matters worse in the aggregate.

## Polarized Views Make Reconciliation Difficult

Divergent views on climate change start with the credibility of the scientific evidence. People may question the certainty underlying the scientific evidence. They may also have trouble distinguishing scientifically sound evidence from advocacy evidence. Disagreement may then shift to the relevance of this evidence for public policy. Here, self-interest motives and ideology play key roles. People tend to adhere to their prior beliefs irrespective of the scientific evidence. These beliefs carry over to the relative costs they place on an overly aggressive climate policy relative to an overly passive policy. All of these factors contribute to the difficulty of reaching political consensus. They bolster the argument for a bottom-up approach where individuals and others transmit their differing preferences in market transactions.

A statistical concept called Bayes's theorem relates people's prior beliefs to their later beliefs based on new evidence. It also identifies people's biases.[20] Assume that two groups of people presently have disparate views on the risks of climate change; the first group believes the risks are low, while the second group believes the risks are high. If new scientific evidence shows potentially high risk, one would expect the first group to change its beliefs by assigning a higher risk to climate change than it did previously. But if this group finds changing its public position on climate change clashes with its economic interests or ideology, it might instead hire experts to rebut the new findings. The second group would tend to respond similarly if the new evidence showed little risk—for example, by harshly criticizing the new evidence—from climate change.

Bad decisions can result when people disregard new evidence, unless they can demonstrate that this evidence is not credible, or when they overreact to new evidence by ignoring their prior beliefs, which presumably had some rationale. People generally accord more plausibility to the evidence on climate change—or other things, for that matter—when it coincides with their prior beliefs. On a broad range of issues, a recent tendency in our country is that when new evidence contradicts those beliefs, people tend to attack both the evidence and those producing it.

Another explanation for divergent views on climate change involves differences over the interpretation of the scientific evidence for public policy. One group may interpret evidence of even a low probability of climate risk to justify a precautionary approach. Another group may interpret the same evidence to justify doing nothing or very little.

People also assign differences to the trade-offs between the risks of climate change and the economic losses from phasing out fossil fuels over the next few decades—that is, they differ in the weight assigned to various objectives, like cheap energy or innocuous climate change. Some people may contend that experience and existing knowledge have demonstrated trivial and manageable risks from climate change. They may then argue that because the benefits from fossil fuels are huge, phasing them out over the next several years would inevitably stifle economic growth, especially in less-developed countries, where oil, coal, and natural gas are critical factors in breaking out of their poverty cycle.

A concept in philosophy, Pascal's wager, helps explain people's different risk tolerance for climate change relative to other risks. Pascal's wager posits that humans bet with their lives that God either exists or does not. One argument is that a rational person should live as though God exists. If God does not actually exist, such a person will have a finite loss, like giving up some pleasures in this life, whereas if God does exist, one stands to receive eternal benefits in heaven and avoid eternal damnation in hell.[21]

The analogy to climate change is that some people are willing to spend a substantial amount of money to avoid a radical change in global temperature that is catastrophic. They are willing to pay a high premium to avoid a highly harmful event, even if the odds are overwhelmingly against it happening. Other people prefer taking a chance by spending little on climate change today and instead allocating resources to other activities that would have more immediate benefits to society. They are in effect betting that climate apocalypse is a myth.

Differences in trade-offs might derive more from the self-interest of the groups than from what they feel is in the collective interest. One observation is that people on both sides of the climate change debate so far seem to exhibit non-Bayesian behavior: they are non-receptive to new factual evidence that could change their prior positions on climate change.[22] The result is that people's beliefs diverge. Inertia seems to prevail in people updating their prior beliefs by sifting the latest scientific evidence; open minds would consider new evidence to reevaluate positions. This state of affairs exemplifies the difficulty of shifting the present highly polarized debate on climate change. One implication is policy instability: the party in power will likely reverse the climate actions of the previous party in power if it held a disparate view on climate change. In the United States, for example, the positions of the two major political parties are too far apart presently for anyone to believe that they will form a consensus position in the foreseeable future.

## Turning to Markets

How can markets address climate change? What are their advantages over top-down government actions? The presumption is that because producers and consumers fail to account for the social cost of GHG emissions in their decisions, a market failure exists that is correctable only by nonmarket intervention—namely, the government. This thinking invites valid criticism, but it regrettably has dominated the narrative on how to address the climate problem.

Another misperception is that any global problem requires global action. A counter view is that the odds for global action—

where countries reach agreement on climate policy—are long. Even within a country, consensus for specific action may be hard to achieve. One does not have to look farther than the United States. One glaring observation is that much of the motivation for aggressive action—for example, deep decarbonization with hurried phaseout of fossil fuels—derives from rent seeking, where special interest groups are the true drivers of proposed change. Rent seeking could involve environmentalists expending resources to persuade the government to enact a stringent climate change law. Opponents of such a law would counter by also expending resources to prevent passage of the law. The total costs incurred by both groups constitute real economic costs from the politicization of climate change.

Rent seeking tends to concentrate the benefits to these groups while spreading the costs to the general population. A good example is interest groups pressuring state utility regulators and legislatures to use subsidies to promote energy efficiency, distributed generation, electric vehicles, and other clean-energy technologies. Each of these actions has the primary objective of reducing GHG emissions. The result has been cost subsidization, which is unfair to both utility customers who do not benefit and competing third-party providers. Unfortunately, the evidence confirms that an increasing number of states have been at the forefront of bad policies that have inflicted a regressive-tax-type wound on lower-income people. The reason is that lower-income households spend a larger percentage of their incomes on electricity, and these policies tend to increase electricity prices.

Either for ideological or monetary reasons, special interests want to shape future climate policy, and the sooner the better. Their self-interest motive is limited to benefiting themselves, not the broader public interest. Their vision of the future entails filling up their pockets (e.g., clean-energy vendors) or satisfying their followed doctrine (e.g., environmentalists). They have relentlessly lobbied politicians and bureaucrats at all levels of government for special favors funded by taxpayers and energy consumers. This reality by itself warrants consideration of nongovernmental options to address climate change.

Markets can be especially effective in mitigating the climate problem when prices reflect demand and supply conditions. Consumers and investors can reveal their preference for financial assets or products and services that explicitly account for climate change. They have done so already, and we should expect this development to proliferate in the future.

Markets are also more flexible than government in adapting to changing and unexpected developments. Governmental actions often reflect decisions based on static information. These actions tend to remain immutable even as the government accumulates new information, while market and other conditions vary. In contrast, markets have an incentive to accommodate their actions to changed conditions. This lowers the chances for costly mistakes that government often makes in its central planning endeavors. Especially for climate change, where massive uncertainties prevail, flexibility and adaptability are key factors in sound decision making.

## Less Regulation of the Energy Industries

One example of a market-driven approach is the restructuring of the electric industry, allowing markets to develop and resulting in the sharp decline of coal usage as an energy source for a generation. Under typical economic regulation, a utility fails to recover the full cost for a physical asset, like a generating facility, when technological or other changes prematurely shorten the economic life of the asset. This encourages utilities to stay with the old technology even when it would be economical, and perhaps more environmentally benign, to adopt a new technology.

Market-based pricing would make energy storage and other environmentally friendly technologies more economical. Retail competition has been shown to bolster green pricing, where utility customers pay extra for electricity produced from clean energy.[23]

Another example is the transformation of the natural gas industry, which has played a large role in the displacement of coal for electricity generation; for example, shale gas has made natural gas more abundant and economical for various end uses. This has accelerated the retirement of coal plants. The shift from coal to natural gas was a major factor in lowering US carbon emissions from electricity production by 28 percent over the period 2005–17. Even after accounting for methane emissions, the most credible studies conclude that switching from coal to natural gas has mitigated GHG emissions. As an additional benefit, natural gas emits less air pollutants, such as sulfur dioxide, mercury, and nitrogen oxide, than coal.

## Satisfying the Preferences of Market Participants

Under a market-based approach, the decision to spend money on reducing climate change hinges on the preferences of consumers, investors, and even employees. Climate action would ultimately depend more on the value the market places on climate change. A bottom-up approach places the top priority on pricing and market incentives. Its flexible rules accommodate the demands of individual market players. For example, markets allow companies to charge a higher price for carbon-free or low-carbon products as consumers reveal their demands for a cleaner environment.

It seems no different for consumers to pay more for a food product that looks more appealing or is healthier than for consumers to pay more because the company lowers its carbon footprint. Such consumers may believe that they have a moral obligation to future generations, or they may have a self-interest reason. It really does not matter what the reason is for consumers to pay a premium for low-carbon products. A caveat is that market participants may act on the basis of erroneous information from sensational reporting by the press on the severity and immediacy of damages from climate change—for example, probability inflation because of distorted media coverage of the scientific evidence, which places an excessively high focus on catastrophic events and assumes that the science is settled. The media seems to assign more precision to climate models and more accuracy to their predictions than warranted by the evidence; they omit the fact that the worst-case scenarios or catastrophic outcomes are not expectations in the statistical sense. The media and others fall into the trap of focusing on the possibility of major catastrophe without reporting the probability of occurrence.

Under the auspices of the recently popular concept of corporate social responsibility (CSR), various sources are pressuring companies to become more conscious of climate change and act to reduce their carbon footprint.[24] When propelled by government mandates or by CEOs advancing a personal agenda, CSR diverts companies' attention away from their core objective to profit from the goods and services they produce. Milton Friedman was emphatic and correct in criticizing this perverted form of capitalism.[25]

But when companies are pursuing so-called social-oriented activities because that is what their investors, consumers, and employees want, that is another matter: they are simply responding to the preferences of market participants.[26] If market participants want companies to reduce their carbon footprint, then as profit maximizers companies should respond accordingly: more investors would be willing to provide capital funds, consumers to pay a higher price, and employees to work with lower compensation.

Contrary to the predictions of some CSR skeptics, satisfying their stakeholders would not make these companies go out of business. It would, in fact, help companies prosper by accommodating those who directly affect their profits. Free-market advocates should have no qualms with this market-based approach: it would certainly be superior to government mandates driven by bureaucrats, special interests, or the whims of CEOs, as it reflects the preferences of the marketplace, which Friedman would be unlikely to find offensive. Voluntary market transactions really epitomize Coasian bargaining: with low transaction costs and well-defined property rights, sellers and buyers cooperate in consummating a mutually beneficial deal.

## Adaptation with Market-Based Pricing

The best scientific evidence shows that warming of Earth's atmosphere will grow gradually, allowing ample time for adaptive measures to mitigate the effects of climate change. As learned from basic economics in other contexts, people adapt when change implies a need to reoptimize.

Adaptation strategies have the feature of evolving over time in response to new information. Adaptation demands the latest information on when, where, and how much the effects of climate change will occur. It can raise the tipping point at which GHG concentrations become catastrophic. Rather than controlling GHG emissions, it limits the damage that emissions can cause. Adaptation can act as a safety net or hedge in the event that the reduction in GHG emissions falls short of preventing a climate catastrophe.

Adaptation does not require international cooperation—which, as shown earlier, is highly unlikely. Arguably, it is a more effective, less costly, and more practical solution than trying to achieve a stringent temperature-change target that may be unreachable.

Both the benefits and costs from adaptive actions would be local.[27] Taking unreciprocated actions in reducing GHG emissions, in contrast, would inevitably fail a cost-benefit test viewed from the locale, as benefits would inevitably fall short of local abatement costs.

Actions can start with individuals, markets, or local governments and community groups. Adaptation therefore lends itself to a wide range of rational private and local collective actions. The pricing mechanism is critical for adaptation to efficiently adjust to climate change.[28] A simple example relates to water. If climate change decreases water supply and increases the demand for water, the price level will rise, which induces innovation, substitution away from water, and more efficient use of water.[29] In recent years, emphasis has shifted to reducing water usage, as water supplies have become more limited and expensive. Some government measures include arbitrarily imposing a price ceiling, rationalizing that it would ease the pain on users. But this approach is wrongheaded: constraining prices aggravates scarcity in the long run and harms water users. As scarcity intensifies, the opportunity cost of increasing water supplies rises—resulting, for example, in more money taken from alternative activities. One efficient action is to allocate scarce water to the most valuable uses through market-based pricing, which conflicts with the prevailing political view. In sum, efficient pricing could alleviate the societal damage from water scarcity triggered by climate change.

As previously discussed, there are high transaction costs of negotiating, monitoring, and enforcing a global agreement. (Most cooperative multilateral bodies lack real power to enforce compliance with collective decisions.) This condition makes producing a public good—namely, a lower-carbon atmosphere—through the consent of heterogeneous countries highly unlikely. In markets, when long-term contracts have high transaction costs, entities often turn to self-supply in the form of vertical integration.[30] For climate change, this means not relying on others by taking adaptive actions on a local level. With adaptation, the locale would have greater control over the risk of climate change, compared with relying primarily on carbon mitigation, which requires cooperation from other jurisdictions.

The message here is that countries and regions with activist climate policies, such as California, should consider shifting their focus to adaptive measures, whose benefits and costs are local, rather than trying to lead the efforts in reducing GHG emissions, hoping that other jurisdictions will follow. It is illusory to believe that other jurisdictions will do likewise unless it is in their self-interest.

## Conclusion

Climate actions should rely more on market forces. The emphasis has been on a government-driven approach dominated by carbon mitigation measures. As a cardinal rule, any public policy dialogue should steer away from "rhetorical heat" (hype and spin) and toward "analytical light." This is especially true for climate change. Basing climate action on the evidence and rational decision making, however, is easier said than done, and it has especially been absent in the ongoing dialogue on climate change.

The pursuit of a government-driven approach with international participation seems unrealistic. It is likely that this logjam will continue indefinitely, unless countries begin to perceive climate change as a short-term threat that demands aggressive action. Market approaches seem more feasible and effective. Market forces have produced impressive reductions in carbon emissions through competition in the electric and natural gas sectors.

Climate policy must compete with other potentially catastrophic threats and alternative uses for scarce resources—for example, from an asteroid impact, nuclear or biological terrorism, or a highly deadly virus. Devoting excessive resources to climate change can prevent the reduction of other threats, which would have a greater benefit.

For the electric industry, a fixation on climate change threatens other policy objectives, like reasonable and stable rates, affordable energy bills, economic growth, and reliable utility service. The opportunity cost is the welfare loss from forgoing alternative actions to attack climate change. These actions could help those in need of immediate assistance, especially low-income households, or foster economic growth, which could improve the well-being of the general population. There is the intergenerational issue of whether people today should sacrifice under an aggressive climate policy to benefit people in the far-out future, who are likely to have a much higher standard of living. Some climate activists view anything less than a maximum effort to address climate change as a social injustice. But one can legitimately rejoin by arguing that an obsession with climate change can deprive impoverished people of the resources required for survival or progress.

A drastic abatement policy—something much more stringent than, say, the emission reductions specified in proposed international agreements—is difficult to justify based on best-guess scenarios for GHG emissions, temperature change, economic impacts, and abatement costs. As Martin Weitzman argues, the case for a stringent policy might, however, be justified as protection against a catastrophic outcome.[31] But whether such protection is worth the cost, which would be extremely high, is an open question.

Public choice theory predicts that government, composed of bureaucrats and politicians, lacks the necessary information and the right incentives to pursue efficient policies that are in the public good. We cannot expect any climate policy dominated by interest-group politics to be immune from this problem. We have seen this in the form of subsidies for renewable energy. Economists consider most subsidies to be inefficient, often politically motivated, and enduring too long. Their preference is to have the government reallocate funds for basic research. But political forces have given higher priority to existing clean technologies with their strong lobbyists than to potential future ones.

Reshaping the energy sector for the main purpose of aggressively combating climate change poses both economic and political risks. Many climate activists want to wean us off fossil fuels as soon as possible. We have seen a two-prong attack on natural gas. The first is opposition to natural gas as a bridge fuel to clean energy in electricity generation. The second is what industry observers call "electrification," where consumers switch from natural gas and other fossil fuels to electricity for direct use like transportation, or water and space heating.

Two justifications for state and local action, although unlikely to pass a cost-benefit test for the respective jurisdiction, originate from moral or social justice grounds and the reasoning that other jurisdictions will follow. Then the question is who should decide to act: Does this view coincide with the consensus in the particular jurisdiction? In line with the common problem of special interests dominating government action, some local actions may stem more from lobbying and other activities of powerful political groups that advance their agenda at the expense of the majority. Public choice theory predicts this outcome: the efforts of vocal minorities who stand to gain economically or ideologically drive government action over the majority, who individually lose little but collectively lose a lot.

One cannot ignore the importance of new technologies to soften the clash between the goals of climate stabilization and economic growth. Some observers support countries suppressing economic growth to reduce GHG emissions, while other observers believe that economic growth, especially in poor countries, can reduce vulnerability to climate change by infrastructure and industrial development.[32] It is a common perception that developed countries would be more adaptable to extreme climate change than poor countries. Suppressing economic growth aligns with the Club of Rome's prediction over forty-five years ago that greater economic growth spelled catastrophe for the world. The prediction turned out to be grossly wrong, but accompanying it was the fixation that economic growth was bad, which has led to public policies that have done great damage to the world.

New technologies could make it cheaper for countries to meet climate targets—for example, by making it economical to use renewable energy for electricity generation in the absence of subsidies. Countries would then more likely sustain their commitment to an international agreement on carbon reductions. Unbearable future costs to abate GHG emissions would instead increase the chances of countries reneging on those commitments. Technological advances would make the politics easier.

Finally, one hypothesis is that aggressive climate change policy will only happen when some highly tragic and publicized event has direct links to climate change that are believed by the general population. Why, for example, do we spend much more on terrorism and other threats than on climate change? Some possible reasons are that (1) most of the benefits from domestic actions go to other countries, (2) the benefits are abstract to many people, and (3) the United States has not yet faced a serious threat of climate change because of its wealth. Until the time when everyone is stuck in the same lifeboat, we should expect to continue seeing much political posturing in containing climate change.

The reader should take these conjectural comments as positive (how the world works) rather than normative (how the world should work). The main message of this chapter is that any climate action should proceed cautiously and shift its emphasis from politically driven strategies rationalized by blackboard economics to a market path based on property rights or lack thereof. Politicians and bureaucrats seem more interested in how their actions affect their notion of equity, their own self-interest, influential interest groups, and their ideologies. These actions tend to clash with the well-being of the general citizenry.

# Notes

1. Some analysts label the climate problem a tragedy of the commons, which Garrett Hardin, the creator of the term, describes as involving a shared resource that society overuses with no incentive for mitigation. "The Tragedy of the Commons," *Science* 162, no. 3859 (December 1968): 1243–48.

2. Transcript of the *EconTalk* podcast with Russ Roberts (host), May 21, 2012, at https://www.econtalk.org/coase-on-externalities-the-firm-and-the-state-of-economics/-audio-highlights.

3. William D. Nordhaus, "Climate Clubs: Overcoming Free-Riding in International Climate Policy," *American Economic Review* 105, no. 4 (April 2015): 1339–70.

4. Robert Pindyck, who has done widely cited work on the economics and modeling of climate change, once commented,

   > What have these IAMs (and related models) told us? I will argue that the answer is very little. . . . The models are so deeply flawed as to be close to useless as tools for policy analysis. Worse yet, their use suggests a level of knowledge and precision that is simply illusory, and can be highly misleading. . . . An IAM-based analysis suggests a level of knowledge and precision that is nonexistent, and allows the modeler to obtain almost any desired result because key inputs can be chosen arbitrarily ("Climate Change Policy: What Do the Models Tell Us?" *Journal of Economic Literature* 51, no. 3 [September 2013]: 861–62, 870).

   A 2015 analysis by the European Commission statistician Andrea Saltelli and her colleagues states, "The uncertainties associated with mathematical models that assess the costs and benefits of climate change policy options are unknowable. Such models can be valuable guides to scientific inquiry, but they should not be used to guide climate policy decisions." Andrea Saltelli et al., "Climate Models as Economic Guides: Scientific Challenge or Quixotic Quest?," *Issues in Science and Technology* 31, no. 3 (Spring 2015): 79–84. Perhaps the best we can hope for is to have models estimating boundary points with the high likelihood of outputs falling between low and high levels.

5. According to Frank Knight, risk applies to situations where we do not know the outcome of a given situation but can, with reasonable accuracy, measure the odds. Frank H. Knight, *Risk, Uncertainty, and Profit* (Boston: Riverside Press, 1921). Uncertainty, on the other hand, applies to situations where we lack the information needed to set accurate odds in the first place. In the

jargon of statistics, risky outcomes have known probability distributions, while uncertain outcomes have unknown ones. Uncertainty inevitably forces decision makers to rely heavily on value judgment. This is especially true in evaluating the benefits of "climate change" investments.

6. Strong scientific evidence points to human activity as the major source of climate change. NASA, "The Causes of Climate Change," NASA, https://climate.nasa.gov/causes. Human activity has produced increased GHG concentrations, which result from the combination of carbon dioxide, methane, nitrous oxide, and other gases. How much of climate change results from human activity, compared to natural causes, remains an issue. A bigger area of dispute is the size of the effects of GHG concentrations on temperature and the world economy.

7. For a discussion of black swan events, see Nassim Nicholas Taleb, *The Black Swan: The Impact of the Highly Improbable* (New York: Random House, 2010). Some climate activists would argue that catastrophic climate change is not so improbable if it lies within the "fat tail" portion of a probability distribution. Fat tails convey the likelihood of catastrophic damage being greater than expected under the statistical assumption of a normal distribution—that is, severe climate change will occur more frequently than predicted by a normal distribution. It implies that when evaluating or designing a climate policy, we need to pay greater attention to the likelihood and possible consequences of extreme outcomes, especially when warning signs become visible. See William D. Nordhaus, "The Economics of Tail Events with an Application to Climate Change," *Review of Environmental Economics and Policy* 5, no. 2 (Summer 2011): 240–57.

8. Cass R. Sunstein, "Probability Neglect: Emotions, Worst Cases, and the Law," *Yale Law Journal* 112, no. 1 (January 2002): 61–107.

9. One distinctive feature of carbon emissions relative to conventional air pollutants is that once entering the atmosphere, much of the emissions remain for over a hundred years. Thus the only way to lower the emissions is by dramatically reducing the inflow. As noted in one article, "Holding global warming steady at its current rate would require a worldwide 60–80 percent cut in emissions, and it would still take decades for the atmospheric concentration of carbon dioxide to stabilize." David G. Victor et al., "The Geoengineering Option: A Last Resort against Global Warming," *Foreign Affairs* 80, no. 2 (March/April 2009): 64–76.

10. Lawrence H. Goulder and Roberton C. Williams III, "The Choice of Discount Rate for Climate Change Policy Evaluation," National Bureau of Economic Research, NBER Working Paper 18301, August 2012.

11. One paradigm for a wait-and-see strategy toward climate change is real options theory. It suggests that action should procced incrementally until we know more. Waiting may be a rational response to a slow-moving uncertain peril in an environment of fast-changing technology. On the downside, there exists the risk of a potentially high cost from irreversibility in waiting too long to avoid a "tipping point," which is the threshold at which the societal damage from GHG emissions becomes extremely severe. That means that preventive action failed to occur when it could have avoided a catastrophic situation. It also may be unrealistic that we will have available more precise information on the timing of the tipping point or the benefits from reducing global temperature change, say, to 2°C in the foreseeable future.

12. See William D. Nordhaus, "Projections and Uncertainties about Climate Change in an Era of Minimal Climate Polices," Cowles Foundation Discussion Paper No. 2057, December 2016, 1.

13. Andy Stone, "Madrid Climate Conference Failed, but Silver Lining Exists," *Forbes*, December 20, 2019.

14. Geoengineering is a large-scale effort directed at altering the earth's climate, usually to reverse or offset the effects of GHG emissions. It involves limiting the amount of sunlight reaching the earth's surface via solar radiation management. It reflects some of the sun's energy back into space, counteracting temperature rise (or having a cooling effect) caused by increased levels of GHG emissions in the atmosphere—for example, by seeding the atmosphere with sulfur particles. See Oxford Geoengineering Programme, "What Is Geoengineering?" (2018), http://www.geoengineering.ox.ac.uk/www .geoengineering.ox.ac.uk/what-is-geoengineering/what-is-geoengineering.

15. William D. Nordhaus, "Climate Change: The Ultimate Challenge for Economics," Nobel Lecture in Economic Sciences, Stockholm University, December 8, 2018; William D. Nordhaus, "Climate Clubs," 1339–70.

16. See "Economists' Statement on Carbon Dividends Organized by the Climate Leadership Council," https://www.econstatement.org.

17. Arthur C. Pigou, *The Economics of Welfare* (London: Macmillan, 1920), 196–97.

18. See the commentary of David Bailey and David Bookbinder: "Carbon tax proponents (such as ourselves) take as a given that adding or subtracting the U.S. emissions avoided through a carbon tax will have no discernible impact on global temperatures." David Bailey and David Bookbinder, "The Conservative Case against Market-Oriented Climate Policy," Niskanen Center, July 5, 2015, https://www.niskanencenter.org/the-conservative-case -against-market-oriented-climate-policy.

19. See also Michael Greenstone, Statement to the US House Committee on Oversight and Reform, Hearing on Economics of Climate Change, December 19, 2019, https://epic.uchicago.edu/wp-content/uploads/2019/12/Greenstone-Testimony-12192019-FINAL.pdf.

20. See Sharon Bertsch McGrayne, *The Theory That Would Not Die: Bayes' Rule Cracked the Enigma Code, Hunted Down Russian Submarines and Emerged Triumphant from Two Centuries of Controversy* (New Haven, CT: Yale University Press, 2011).

21. See Alan Hájek, "Pascal's Wager," in *Stanford Encyclopedia of Philosophy* (Summer 2018 Edition), ed. Edward N. Zalta, https://plato.stanford.edu/entries/pascal-wager.

22. It could be true, as speculated by some observers, that so-called climate deniers do not ignore the scientific evidence. They may actually believe in climate change and think it is partially caused by human activity but prefer not to reveal it because it would bolster the case for costly climate action, which they oppose.

23. See Devin Hartman, "Environmental Benefits of Electricity Policy Reform," R Street Policy Study No. 82 (January 2017), 2, 10.

24. Over the past several months, the idea that corporations have a responsibility to the broader society beyond their responsibility to their shareholders has accelerated. The Business Roundtable shifted its views from companies existing to serve stockholders to endorsing "stakeholder capitalism." Several companies have announced their plans to spend stockholder money to attack climate change and to engage in investment and production activities that are climate sensitive. Lucian A. Bebchuk and Roberto Tallarita, "The Illusory Promise of Stakeholder Governance," working draft, Harvard Law School, March 2020.

25. Milton Friedman, "The Social Responsibility of Business Is to Increase Its Profits," *New York Times Magazine*, September 13, 1970.

26. In reviewing the *Wall Street Journal* and other publications over the past several months, one readily sees how investors and consumers in particular are pressuring companies to lower their carbon footprint. Some companies have committed to spending hundreds of millions and even billions of dollars to attack climate change. Amazon, for example, expects to spend $10 billion to address climate change in an initiative called the Bezos Earth Fund.

27. Ostrom supports local or bottom-up action as being more diverse, less vulnerable to politics, and more sensitive and accommodating to local conditions. She contends that local activity could expand and ultimately become

a global effort. While emphasizing the need for individuals and communities to reduce GHG emissions, Ostrom recognizes the necessity for international cooperation to have a major effect on climate change. Elinor Ostrom, "Collective Action and the Evolution of Social Norms," *Journal of Economic Perspectives* 14, no. 3 (Summer 2000): 137–58; Ostrom, "Beyond Markets and States: Polycentric Governance of Complex Economic Systems." Nobel Prize lecture, December 8, 2009.

28. A top-down approach to adaptation would include such measures as stricter building codes, federal subsidization of community-scale relocation, and new regulations on the siting of new buildings. Each of these measures would be susceptible to rent seeking and the other adverse outcomes of politicized adaptation.

29. Studies have shown that water is far too cheap in many if not most parts of the country and senior water rights are allocated excessively to farmers; for example, farmers in the west use 80 percent of the water and usually at a below-market price. Because of its politically motivated pricing, government is the culprit for these inefficient outcomes.

30. Paul L. Joskow, "Vertical Integration," in *Handbook of New Institutional Economics*, ed. C. Menard and M. Shirley (Dordrecht, Netherlands: Springer, 2005), 319–48; Oliver E. Williamson, "Transaction-Cost Economics: The Governance of Contractual Relations," *Journal of Law and Economics* 22, no. 2 (October 1979): 233–61.

31. Martin L. Weitzman, "Fat-Tailed Uncertainty in the Economics of Catastrophic Climate Change," *Review of Environmental Economics and Policy* 5, no. 2 (Summer 2011): 275–92.

32. See John Cassidy, "Steady State: Can We Have Prosperity without Economic Growth?," *New Yorker*, February 10, 2020, 24–27.

# 4

# Merging Trade and Climate Policy

Timothy Fitzgerald

The international political case for climate change action has reached a fevered pitch. Two factors contribute to the crescendo: on one hand scientists report a pattern of data whose modeling results suggest the current trajectory will soon lead humanity into a historically unprecedented period of climatic change, while on the other hand the failure of climate diplomacy to deliver a concrete policy road map has increased frustration in countries around the world. The 2015 Paris Agreement was hailed as a breakthrough international agreement, but subsequent events have revealed that it lacked key details about how the objectives would be achieved by each participant, and those details have not all been forthcoming. Economists can contribute to the policy debate in at least two important ways.[1] One is by helping develop politically viable policy options in an area that has suffered from a chronic failure of international coordination. A second is by increasing research efforts on existing policy options, including adaptation strategies.

Escalating demands for climate action have expanded in scope to embrace trade policy. Proposals appear forthcoming for an explicit merger of climate and trade policy in the near future. It seems that historically bright lines between trade and climate policy are fading as merged policies that address climate and trade objectives become more likely. A variety of justifications have been provided for why trade must be included to ensure climate policy success, ranging from complaints that emissions targets might be undermined by imports to strategic considerations and attempts to convince trading partners to adopt similar climate objectives. Since 2018 the international trading order has been disrupted by a sharp reversion to unilateral tariff policies, especially by the United States. New unilateral tariffs triggered retaliatory tariffs and other restrictions, all of which reversed a decades-long trend toward greater globalization and trade policy harmonization. The effects of this recent disruption deepen the threat from an indelicate merger. Climate protectionism or trade retaliation under the auspices of climate policy could choke trade and undermine the economic well-being of citizens around the world.

Broadly speaking, three strategies might be used to achieve climate policy goals.[2] The first is mitigation, which has featured most prominently in policy debates, focusing on emissions reductions and complementary sequestration actions to help stabilize atmospheric concentrations of key substances that contribute to climate change.[3] Such emissions reductions come with explicit and opportunity costs. A second strategy is to embrace adaptation, as humans might find ways to acclimate to future climatic conditions. It is important to recognize that such adaptation is also costly, though some adaptations are clearly cost effective. Importantly, some adaptations are more cost effective than some amount of mitigation would be. Third, in an effort to reduce the climatic effects of an increased global stock of greenhouse gases in the atmosphere, amelioration interventions such as geoengineering might be tried. Aldy and Zeckhauser argue for each of these three strategies to be deployed in concert. Intuitively, a cost-effective climate strategy would equate net benefits from action in each of the three strategies. Importantly, trade policy interacts in different ways with the three approaches.[4]

Emissions contributing to global climate change pose a number of challenges, particularly with regard to trade. First, the total stock of emissions in the atmosphere affects the pace at which climate change proceeds. Other pollution problems may depend on the rate of emissions or the spatial distribution of emissions, both of which can result in "hot spots" that suffer higher damages. Second, these emissions are particularly long lived in the global atmosphere, persisting for decades after they are released. Third, the atmosphere does a very effective job of mixing emitted substances, making it prohibitively difficult to assign liability for stocks of emissions to particular parties. Taken together, these conditions make emissions from any one location a perfect substitute for emissions from anywhere else.

Trade includes embodied emissions in products and also requires energy for transport. Alternative transport modes have different emissions profiles. Ships are less energy intensive than airplanes. In the absence of a coordinated universal mitigation program, trade may lead to "leakage" of emissions by substituting emissions from less-restricted sources for those that are more restricted. A simple example illustrates leakage. Suppose a country produces steel in a process that involves some emissions. Then the country imposes a tax to reduce emissions, which operates as intended and raises costs for steel producers, ultimately driving up the market price of steel. Consumers of steel observe that they could now import steel more cheaply even after paying transportation charges, in part because of the higher cost of embodied emissions. The imported steel would likely come from a producer that does not incur higher costs for emissions and may even use a more emissions-intensive production process.

Domestic consumers still consume the domestically produced steel and thus contribute to the overall reduction domestically. But they also consume steel that required emissions somewhere else in the world—and for a uniformly mixed global stock pollutant the source of the emissions does not matter, in contrast to a local pollutant. The domestic consumer is therefore responsible for more emissions than the domestic production, and some emissions have *leaked* out of the country to other sources. Global emissions have not decreased by as much as the domestic target thanks to the desire and ability of domestic consumers to continue to use steel.

This leakage has been widely studied, with varying estimates of the extent of the problem. As a general matter, econometric analyses of policy history in Europe find little evidence of leakage, whereas computable general equilibrium (CGE) models project higher leakage rates based on theoretical linkages.[5] Because CGE models simulate alternative states of the world, they rely on theoretical predictions to make forecasts, which may miss the reality. In contrast, adaptation strategies rely in part on providing humans with more resources, both physical and intellectual, to make adaptive investments. Trade has a long and distinguished history of making humans better off. Thus the projection of trade differs under these two prongs of climate policy—mitigation and adaptation. While amelioration strategies are not yet well developed, it is possible that trade in ameliorative technologies could play a role in that prong as well. Trade-offs between climate and trade policy would optimally keep the best attributes to help adaptation without undermining contemporaneous mitigation efforts. As trade and climate policy overlap more and the relationships become more detailed and intricate, avoiding tossing the baby out with the bathwater is a pertinent concern.

The promise of international cooperation for climate policy is enabled in part by a more globalized world. In 2002–17, the nominal value of international merchandise trade increased by 170 percent according to World Trade Organization (WTO) data. Concern about the success of globalization has contributed to recent policy efforts to revise the trajectory of the postwar international trading order. While the United States has taken a leading role in disrupting the trade order, nativist politicians are ascendant in many countries around the world. Importantly, those countries have very different strategic incentives regarding climate. While some (e.g., Britain and the United States) have a long history of relatively high emissions, they have reduced the emissions intensity of their economies.[6] In contrast, developing countries with nativist political leaders (e.g., India and Brazil) have a very different strategic outlook on climate issues. Any merger between climate and trade will force policy makers to balance concerns over climate and trade because of the direct linkages between the two. Because integrating trade and climate policy provides political and economic cover for unilateral actors, it is important to consider alternatives to a scenario in which countries independently impose, in the name of climate action, intentionally high tariffs that serve domestic protectionist objectives. Avoiding such climate protectionism is an important policy goal.

There are hopes for achieving trade and climate mitigation objectives through a unified policy. A central proposal has been to impose an emissions-based border tax, sometimes called a border carbon adjustment (BCA). Aaron Cosbey and his colleagues provide a detailed review of the mechanism.[7] BCAs are not yet imposed between countries, but current proposals anticipate a world in which they are used to achieve climate objectives. The European Union has entertained introducing a BCA scheme since 2019. Imposing these new tariffs leads to two distinct concerns. First, border adjustments are a second-best policy (next to a globally uniform emissions charge) that will impose an efficiency cost in an attempt to prevent emissions leakage. Second, in today's international trade environment, new tariffs imposed by any party will likely be met by a retaliatory response. This has been the case with a variety of tariffs imposed since 2018.[8] BCAs are intended to adjust relative prices between a collection of linked and unlinked economies.[9] In the current state of the world, the scope of potentially linked economies is small, meaning that a BCA would be applied to many trading partners. The need for BCAs is small in a linked world, where all firms face similar climate policies, but international climate policy efforts have not yet delivered on that score. These facts lead to a concern that unilateral climate action in response to domestic political pressure would also include a BCA, and that initial tariff action might spur a noncooperative, protectionist response. This could lead to protectionism masked as climate action. Relatively new climate and entrenched industrial concerns may share an interest in new trade barriers, leading to what Bruce Yandle termed a "Baptist and bootlegger" dynamic advocating for additional regulation.[10] In this case, the climate interests and environmentalists are the Baptists. Just as Baptists were interested in restricting alcohol consumption on its own merits, many groups see emissions mitigation and reduction of emissions leakage as a virtuous undertaking. The bootleggers in this case are domestic producers who see economic gain in restricting competition. Bootleggers have a smaller market when alcohol is legal and so have a vested interest in prohibition. By the same token, domestic producers of emissions-intensive goods like steel or cement often complain about import competition and see tariffs as a way to protect their domestic market. Nativist political leadership may also support protectionist impulses, adding more bootleggers to the bandwagon.

Michael Mehling and his coauthors advocate for imposing BCAs *rather* than unilateral protectionist tariffs.[11] While such a strategy recognizes that climate and trade policy can be accomplished in a single instrument, it fails to embrace the complementary political economy factors that could contribute to application of BCAs in an uncoordinated way and resulting climate protectionism. It seems to be a pure Baptist exhortation to link climate and trade, with an implicit admission that bootlegging protectionists will be happy with the end result.

Aaron Cosbey and his colleagues frame BCAs in a useful way; coupled with a domestic emissions charge, a BCA effectively shifts the tax system away from production-based taxes and toward consumption-based taxes.[12] Such a shift is conceptually simple: a production-based tax is assessed based on productive activities, while a consumption-based tax is levied on consumption. The economic incidence of both types of taxes will be shared between producers and consumers, though potentially not at equal rates. From a climate policy perspective, either basis could work. The reorientation connects to a broader literature considering the design of emissions taxes. McAusland and Najjar model a purely consumption-based tax and conclude that the transaction costs inherent in verifying embodied emissions might make it prohibitively costly.[13] Nonetheless, a BCA is an attempt to correct the shortcomings of a policy that addresses emissions in one place but not another by accounting for flows of embodied emissions between the two places. Other coincident distortions in the tax system are also relevant. The trade treatment of different classes of goods differs *ex ante*, with generally lower barriers on carbon-intensive goods.[14] Thus a BCA advocate could argue that the intervention simply levels the field with respect to emissions.

Levying a BCA effectively doubles down on the mitigation prong to address climate. The value of abated emissions is modest at relatively low levels of emissions mitigation, but as mitigation aspirations increase, the incentive to avoid higher costs via trade leads to leakage. As the marginal value of abated emissions climbs, so too does the opportunity cost of leakage. Despite its costs, the BCA becomes more attractive if the only feasible strategy is mitigation. Adaptation and amelioration alternatives can help deflate the urgency of BCAs.

While the idea of BCAs has been discussed by academics and policy makers for some time, putting them to work in a viable system is a larger challenge.[15] Some of the same implementation issues arise as in the carbon-pricing and climate-trade approaches. These detailed issues have helped confound international climate negotiations. Given that monitoring and enforcement issues are prominent in the international trade community, expanding domestic climate implementation across international borders will raise a number of difficult issues that require coordination to solve. If these issues are not addressed, a climate-trade merger could result in imposing expansive nontariff atop tariff barriers, increasing the odds of an outcome that curtails trade even more than intended.

A uniform upstream tax would obviate many of these remedies by changing the relative price of inputs and letting producers and consumers react to the altered prices. That would imply that fossil fuels giving rise to emissions face the same charge everywhere in the world. International climate negotiations have recognized this as the preferable solution for decades but have failed to implement such a policy because of political realities that prevent implementation. Support for a globally uniform policy breaks down in part because of differences in consumption and income across countries. The relative costs of implementing a consumption-based tax are distinct from the costs of implementing a BCA, though both mechanisms require similar types of verification and monitoring. Shifting to a consumption-based tax will likely increase the share of costs borne by consumers, while a BCA requires additional layers of trade monitoring and enforcement. Even without those costs to consider, the differences in income, emissions trajectories, and negotiating power dim the prospects for uniform multilateral solutions, further motivating study of second-best remedies like BCAs. Using a BCA to prevent leakage and achieve climate goals is an admission that a universal carbon price is an unlikely political and policy outcome.

## Climate Policy Options and Trade

Political urgency for climate action can be satisfied in a number of ways. The strategic incentives for countries and individuals present a significant impediment to achieving climate goals. The different strategic incentives across heterogeneous countries have been a major sticking point in international negotiations for decades, with little prospect of relief. The correlation of contemporaneous and historical emissions with affluence and economic power underscores the difficulty. The remaining options for climate action raise the specter of including trade in the policy response.

Climate adaptation also has implications for trade in goods and people. Any adaptation strategy—unilateral or multilateral—will require additional resources that might be obtained via trade, both to generate the needed surplus for investments and to obtain adaptive goods directly. For example, technology imports might allow for greater adaptive resilience in the face of severe weather. Some investments might achieve both mitigation and adaptation goals: investment in electric microgrids with resilient renewable generation could reduce emissions and increase resilience.

## Unilateral

Unilateral action to achieve climate goals is one possible solution to the current international deadlock, but it is not incentive compatible: a country acting unilaterally would bear the full costs of reducing emissions but would share the benefits with all other countries in the world. Uncoordinated action is likely to result in negligible gains toward climate goals, while potentially imposing large explicit and opportunity costs on a first mover. The effect of unilateral climate policy on trade can compound the costs. The global atmosphere has public-good attributes that discourage individual contributions without cooperation. Several distinct costs are incurred by a unilateralist.

One area of primary concern is that unilateral emissions mitigation is likely to raise costs for domestic producers. These costs are passed along to consumers, at least for goods that are domestically produced and consumed. Some energy-intensive goods, such as electricity, are largely untraded in certain parts of the world. In that case, the cost pass-through can be offset by recycling revenues back to consumers. The provincial carbon tax in British Columbia is revenue neutral to offset income effects.[16] The ability to return revenues to citizens helps avoid the need to impose strong border measures. The British Columbia program works by adding taxes to fossil fuels and thereby limits the number of monitored products. Unilateral standards or targets that do not generate revenue do not have the opportunity for recycling, even as cost increases may still be passed through to consumers.

Not all goods can be provided domestically, leading to concern about competitiveness effects for domestic firms through two pathways. First, domestic firms may be subject to greater import competition. Second, domestic exporters with higher costs may find it harder to compete in foreign markets. The effect of either of these indirect mechanisms is distinct from the primary intention of unilateral action in reducing emissions. Joseph Aldy articulates several pathways through which policies might affect competitiveness.[17] An empirical estimate pins the competitiveness effects at maximum one-sixth of the overall effect on manufacturing of introducing carbon pricing.[18] That means that if introducing carbon pricing costs manufacturing firms six dollars, only one dollar is attributable to competitiveness effects. Brendan Casey and his colleagues exploit differential regional and state-level pricing of carbon emissions in the United States to isolate the effects on manufacturing employment and output, and find substantial effects that indicate leakage out of the regulated states.[19] In states where it is imposed, a carbon price equivalent to ten dollars per ton reduces employment, output, and profits by 3–4 percent, most of which is recouped in other states without carbon prices, reducing concern about international leakage from subnational policies. Jared Carbone and Nicholas Rivers use CGE modeling to conclude that only small changes (< 2 percent) in social welfare result even from ambitious emissions reduction goals, in part because of presumptive gains from emissions abatement.[20]

Not all unilateral mitigation strategies persist. Kate Crowley identifies a viable political movement founded in economic self-interest as the proximate cause of the repeal of Australia's carbon price in 2016.[21] That episode underscores the fragile position that unilateralists may find themselves in, without foreign collaborators and with domestic political enemies keen to capitalize on any misstep. It is notable that the policy reversal in Australia was motivated more by narrow economic interest than advocacy for an alternative economic approach to climate issues. While the Australian experience is somewhat extreme, insofar as an implemented policy was reversed, similar domestic political forces may also help explain the failure to act unilaterally or to participate in multilateral or plurilateral efforts.

### Multilateral and Plurilateral Options

Coordinating emissions reductions through a mitigation strategy poses a classic public-good provision problem. Proposals for how to solve this problem have attracted environmental economists since at least Thomas Crocker and David Montgomery.[22] Approaches aimed at affecting prices and those aimed at quantities, such as emissions fees and tradable emissions permits or allowances, have guided successful policies reducing greenhouse gas (GHG) emissions. Some of these approaches involve several or many partners. Plurilateral examples include the Emissions Trading System (ETS) in the European Union as well as smaller regional efforts like the Regional Greenhouse Gas Initiative (RGGI) in the United States. However, the imposition of any of these schemes effectively raises the cost of activities with embodied carbon emissions. Given the demand for those services across countries and income levels, raising costs for end users has proved to be politically unpopular.

One reason why such policies have not taken off is the political opposition they engender.

Nordhaus articulated the notion of "carbon clubs," or voluntary plurilateral groups working together to reduce emissions. The same idea is familiar in international trade as preferential trade agreements.[23] Rather than engaging on equal terms with all countries, many of whom may not be trading partners, many countries have opted into regional preferential trading arrangements (e.g., Mercosur, NAFTA). These agreements have delivered important increases in trade, even considering that they are more likely to form among partners that are more likely to trade with one another than among countries that do not trade.[24] Carbon clubs may form along similar lines, with like-minded countries banding together while holdouts remain outside clubs. While club formation results in progress toward climate goals, incentives for individual countries to free ride are strong. Punishing free riders is one motivation behind a BCA, but the broader problem of linkage remains under a club approach.

Clubs do not eliminate the public-good issue but may form if the share of benefits is high enough relative to costs. If a pollutant is a uniformly mixed global stock pollutant, like many GHGs, the source of emissions does not matter; the marginal cost of an additional unit of emissions is the same. This creates the same problem for small clubs as for individual countries: the costs of emissions are higher than the share of global benefits. As a carbon club increases in size, this disparity narrows. In a fully linked climate policy world, all producers would face the same emissions cost. Even after adjusting for local purchasing power, this economic solution is not politically palatable. The variation across countries has proven to be too large. In addition, the cost of reaching a comprehensive multilateral agreement is high, as decades of failure of international climate talks can attest.

One reality of environmental policy in general is the heterogeneity of performance across firms.[25] In the international policy context, that same heterogeneity has been a stumbling block; a more uniform set of perspectives would make a solution easier to craft. Differences in mitigation efforts and potential are clearly an issue in crafting a voluntary multilateral solution.[26] The reality of differences between countries makes the ability of any carbon club to stick together a primary concern.[27]

## The Threat of Trade Linkage

### Border Carbon Adjustment

The possibility that a unilateral BCA could lead to veiled protectionism has been recognized for some time.[28] Some observers consider that to be a potential benefit; Dieter Helm and his coauthors argue that the threat of a unilateral BCA should enhance the viability of international climate negotiations.[29] By threatening to upset the trade equilibrium, unilateral actors might convince partners to join it in pursuing more serious climate action. The same philosophy is shared by architects of the disruptive Trump trade policy, though not in pursuit of climate objectives. Initial assessment of that policy suggests that the United States has borne a greater share of the costs of increasing tariffs, without clearly moving toward a desired objective.[30]

While a BCA can mitigate leakage, it cannot eliminate it, because of the terms of trade effects of the tariff.[31] That is, when a tariff is imposed, the relative buying power of currencies may also change in a way to undercut the tariff. Böhringer, Balistreri, and Rutherford find that a BCA can reduce leakage by a substantial one-third, though a nontrivial 8 percent leakage persists.[32] Fell and Maniloff document evidence of similar leakage rates econometrically, studying a regional initiative in the United States where a BCA was not possible between participating and nonparticipating states.[33]

Climate policy is motivated by achieving 100 percent of theoretically possible gains, rather than conceding that some leakage is unavoidable. BCAs may well reduce leakage, but they also stand to substantially reduce economic well-being.[34] Welfare implications depend critically on the costs of increasing concentrations of GHGs. There is a substantial debate about the appropriate level for the social cost of carbon, the calculation of which depends in large measure on avoided costs. If costs of climate change are larger, then the welfare cost of a BCA is somewhat smaller, and vice versa. Successful adaptation strategies lower avoided costs and therefore increase the welfare cost of a BCA. Put another way, mixing policy approaches increases the cost of a BCA. Böhringer, Carbone, and Rutherford consider the value of BCAs from a negotiation standpoint: they may provide a valuable threat point to achieve cooperative climate policy.[35] This is a similar argument to that advanced by Helm, Hepburn, and Rutha.[36] Since those studies, however, changes in the international trade policy arena would seem to weaken this argument. In particular, they do not consider the case in which BCAs are met with retaliation.

BCAs are not the only policy option for policy makers seeking to link climate goals across countries. There has been substantial work on a variety of other linkages between trading partners as an approximation to coordination.[37] Some researchers have concluded that BCAs do not pass a welfare test.[38] Output quotas are another alternative, though Fischer and Fox find that they lead to greater efficiency loss than a price-based instrument.[39] Output quotas could be enforced on a national level, requiring little if any coordination. There could be strategic incentives eroding enforcement for some countries. For example, a country that relies heavily on a particular emissions-intensive industry might be less rigorous in setting or enforcing quotas or favor particular politically connected firms within an industry even if those firms are relatively emissions intensive.

Use of BCAs raises a number of new and difficult enforcement questions and promises a series of novel implementation costs.

Previous work indicates that implementation costs are likely to be substantial, compounded by the heterogeneity in trade.[40] While a substantial apparatus exists to monitor trade flows and typify them by product and value, there is little infrastructure in place to identify and verify embodied emissions along supply chains and assess the appropriate measure at the time of border crossing. Fowlie and Reguant present a conceptual framework for targeting monitoring efforts to minimize emissions leakage.[41] While some sectors are indeed better candidates for deploying monitoring, a linked trade-climate regime must ultimately solve this problem for all trading partners and products. The variance in embodied emissions within relatively uniform classes of products, such as iron and steel, cement, and electric power, underscores the magnitude of the challenge for customs authorities.[42]

While many industries are moving toward product verification throughout the supply chain (e.g., organic and GMO-free agricultural commodities, fish caught with eco-friendly technology), others have a long way to go to provide the kind of granular information that would be needed to implement a universal BCA (e.g., renewable electric power, which is subject to verification that it reduces emissions relative to a baseline). To ensure compliance with BCAs or similar information-hungry trade barriers, it may be necessary to offer discounts for providing information or impose penalties for failing to provide verifiable information. For a given climate policy objective, such mechanisms will raise the overall trade barrier that is needed.

The problem of double-counting compounds as emissions from traded fossil fuels becomes embedded in other products, which are themselves traded. To maintain the integrity of the emissions accounting system, the same ton of carbon cannot be counted twice. Care must be taken to avoid unintentionally counting emissions twice. Consider a hypothetical example. A ton of Australian coal is exported to China, where it is burned to create steel. That steel is then exported to South Korea, where it is transformed to a machined part. That part is in turn exported to Mexico, where it is assembled into an automotive part, which is finally exported to the United States for final assembly. The emissions of the original ton of coal are embodied in every link of the value chain, perhaps with additional emissions inputs added at every step. Only the added emissions need to be tracked so as to avoid counting the emissions from coal at every step. If care is not taken to properly avoid double-counting, or if it proves too costly to identify and verify the marginal emissions added in each link of the value chain, then a tariff will apply to all embodied carbon. That is the penalty for not providing verified emissions. Tariffs on embodied emissions (rather than just marginal emissions) would steeply increase trade barriers and could potentially increase the cost of achieving mitigation targets.[43]

Imposing tariffs raises an important diplomatic issue: trade is not randomly distributed, but rather occurs most often with allies and other friendly nations. The imposition of tariffs therefore primarily affects those allied nations, along with domestic purchasers and consumers. This creates an additional nexus of opposition to any tariff policy and may favor the formation of club approaches. The expansion of preferential trade agreements into the environmental realm—such as the addition of a climateless environment chapter to the US-Mexico-Canada Agreement—is a small step in this direction.

In the worst case, imposing a BCA may trigger a response from trading partners. To the extent that partners respond in kind by raising protective barriers, or even imposing BCAs of their own, the impasse in international climate diplomacy is simply extended into trade policy. Retaliation increases welfare costs, in large part because it is not symmetric. Tariffs on steel are not met with tariffs on steel; tariffs on embodied emissions will not necessarily be met with tariffs on embodied emissions. So carbon tariffs will most likely be met by retaliation on products with comparative advantage, which are unlikely to be equally emissions intensive.

The mechanism of BCAs has been the subject of considerable discussion about legal challenges that might be made in the event that they are implemented in the international setting.[44] BCAs are a specific application of border adjustment taxes, which are subject to special consideration under General Agreement on Tariffs and Trade (GATT) rules. Differential tariffs across countries violate the principle of most-favored-nation status, and rebates for exporters may constitute export subsidies in violation of WTO standards. Michael Mehling and his colleagues address these issues straight on, arguing that specific design features are needed to maintain legal viability and effectiveness.[45] These recommendations form the current best design practices for BCAs, and they reflect the difficult implementation choices policy makers must make: BCAs should serve as temporary instruments organized through a hypothesized new international body, apply only to imports so as to avoid export subsidy prohibitions, be applied only to energy-intensive trade-exposed (EITE) sectors, offer no country exemptions, be subject to stringent reporting and monitoring standards, prohibit revenue recycling, and be subject to a handful of other provisions to ensure uniformity and transparency. Collectively, these recommendations underscore the substantial new implementation apparatus that will be required to comply with current international law.

## Climate Protectionism

Cosbey and his coauthors provide guidance for implementation of BCAs, emphasizing that the welfare implications of any BCA are likely to depend on implementation details.[46] There are many such details, because a BCA is not necessarily an extension of a domestic emissions price. Balistreri, Kaffine, and Yonezawa demonstrate that an optimal BCA may be set above or below a domestic emissions price, implying some discretion.[47] This in turn invites protectionist bootleggers to join climate Baptists in setting BCAs as a regulation with multiple beneficiaries.[48] In cases where a BCA is imposed along with a new emissions price, a restrictive import barrier (or a generous export rebate) might be used to compensate domestic interests. Given the strong political economy linkages of energy-intensive trade-exposed industries, this is more likely than if the most-affected industries were less important.

Energy-intensive industries that are responsible for a large proportion of industrial emissions also tend to be exposed to trade. Some of these industries, such as steel and iron, have advocated for greater trade protection. The domestic political economy of taking aggressive climate action has been unfavorable due to the influence of particular energy- and emissions-intensive industries. While not all of these industries could be persuaded to accept climate policy in exchange for trade protection (e.g., steel versus electricity generation), combining climate and trade policy offers an opportunity to broaden the domestic coalition in support.

## A Snapshot of World Carbon Trade

Proposals to implement BCAs must contend with existing trade flows. Understanding the current state of affairs is fundamental to considering policy design. Most human-caused emissions come from fossil fuels, which themselves are widely traded. Those products are not primarily the target of BCAs, largely because the emissions expended to mine and ship the fuels are counted rather than the future emissions from the fuels themselves. Instead, a BCA requires monitoring a larger and more diverse collection of products, even if the approach focuses on particular energy-intensive sectors. The differences in production and consumption patterns around the world put countries in a variety of positions on the introduction of climate-linked trade measures. Those differing vantages may affect policy implementation in substantive ways as strategic advantages are pressed.

A first step is understanding the current intersection between emissions and trade. Fortunately, detailed data about world trade flows are readily available. Davis and Caldeira present an innovative measure of the carbon intensity of trade flows around the world.[49] Sato documents alternative approaches to the measurement of embodied emissions in trade and highlights the lack of standardized methodology.[50] One motivation for merging trade and climate policy is the indication that traded products account for an increasing share of global emissions over time. This should not be a cause for alarm, and trying to limit trade because of embodied emissions is likely to toss the baby out with the bathwater.

Erecting barriers to manufactured products with substantial embodied emissions, such as automobiles, may give incentives to domestic producers to produce inferior alternatives (including from an embodied emissions perspective). Domestic politicians are excited by the prospect of promoting manufacturing, and erecting trade barriers is one way to increase potential gains for new entrants.

By some measures, crude oil is the most widely traded product in the world.[51] In 2018, at least 45 percent of global crude oil production crossed an international border; trade in refined products adds an additional 26 percent of final production.[52] If all refined barrels were not also traded as crude, then well over two-thirds of global consumption would have been traded at some point. The trade in both crude oil, which is almost strictly an intermediate good, and refined products, which are both intermediate and final consumption goods, underscores both the complexity of tracking trade flows for emissions purposes and the possibility of serious double-counting of emissions. Table 1 reports the share of product that is traded and the share of emissions. Petroleum accounts for 34 percent of global emissions, according to 2015 figures published by the IEA. Concentrating on crude oil only, nearly a fifth of global emissions are traded internationally.

Table 1. Global Trade in Fossil Fuels, 2018

| Product | Pct. Traded Internationally BP Statistical Review | Pct. Global Emissions (2015) |
|---|---|---|
| Crude Oil | 54.7 | 34.3 |
| Refined Products | 25.9 | |
| Coal | 22.7 | 45.1 |
| Natural Gas | 32.1 | 19.9 |

Note: BP Statistical Review of World Energy 2019 mixes international and interregional trade movements, including some, but not all, international movements, with the balance covered under the umbrella of interregional movements. Hence the proportion of traded product is conservative. For natural gas, the above reflects international shipments by pipeline and interregional shipments of LNG—therefore the total exceeds the "total trade" on an interregional basis.

Sources: British Petroleum, BP Statistical Review of World Energy; World Trade Organization; International Energy Agency; author calculations.

Coal and natural gas are not subject to the same sort of double-counting as crude and refined petroleum because a large portion of those fuels is used directly rather than refined. Adding a similar calculation for coal and natural gas suggests that another sixth of global emissions is traded internationally. Combined with crude oil, a conservative 35 percent (because refined products are excluded) of global emissions cross borders just as fossil fuels. Yet the future emissions of these fuels are not counted in the embodied emissions; only the emissions incurred in mining and delivering them are counted. Given that the vast bulk of human-caused emissions come from these three categories of products, if the objective is to account for emissions without exploding monitoring and verification costs, the prevalent trade in fossil fuels that lead to the most emissions is an opportunity.

Recall the hypothetical ton of Australian coal that winds up embodied in part of an American automobile, as described above. If the emissions of the ton of coal are accounted for initially, then all subsequent links of the value chain carry that adjustment forward. All other components of the automobile could have a similar accounting. In the absence of a multilateral uniform policy to reduce emissions, a patchwork merger of trade and climate will

Table 2.  Leading Countries in Embodied $CO_2$ Trade, 2015

| Top Embodied $CO_2$ Importers, 2015 | | | Top Embodied $CO_2$ Exporters, 2015 | | |
|---|---|---|---|---|---|
| Rank | Country | Imported $CO_2$ (Mt $CO_2$) | Rank | Country | Exported $CO_2$ (Mt $CO_2$) |
| 1 | United States | 1,769 | 1 | China | 2,452 |
| 2 | China | 742 | 2 | United States | 597 |
| 3 | Japan | 634 | 3 | India | 489 |
| 4 | Germany | 443 | 4 | Russia | 416 |
| 5 | Hong Kong | 414 | 5 | Germany | 383 |
| 6 | United Kingdom | 393 | 6 | South Korea | 324 |
| 7 | France | 307 | 7 | Japan | 270 |
| 8 | South Korea | 296 | 8 | Canada | 198 |
| 9 | Italy | 258 | 9 | Indonesia | 194 |
| 10 | Canada | 236 | 10 | Malaysia | 193 |
| 11 | Russia | 211 | 11 | Mexico | 164 |
| 12 | Spain | 201 | 12 | Thailand | 160 |
| 13 | India | 196 | 13 | Taiwan | 157 |
| 14 | Brazil | 162 | 14 | South Africa | 145 |
| 15 | Singapore | 152 | 15 | Iran | 141 |
| | All Others | 3,101 | | All Others | 3,232 |

Note: Imports sum to about 200 Mt more than exports. One possible explanation is the incomplete accounting for bunkered marine and aviation fuel; other measurement issues may also play a role.

Source: "Eora Global Supply Chain Database," https://worldmrio.com.

result in numerous distortions that raise the cost of emissions reductions while undermining effectiveness. Political economy forces will only exacerbate those distortions.

Merging trade and climate policy will have important implications for various countries. Heterogeneity across countries, which has bedeviled international climate negotiations, is also likely to compound distortions from uncoordinated linkage of climate policy to trade. Some countries stand to gain far more than others, in large part due to different starting points with respect to trade. Imposing a BCA moves toward a consumption-based accounting of emissions. Table 2 shows the top fifteen importers and exporters of carbon in 2015, according to estimates compiled using a global input-output database. It is clear that many of the largest economies naturally trade large quantities of embodied $CO_2$. The leading countries account for nearly two-thirds of global trade in embodied emissions.

That only half of the countries appear on both lists suggests that size is not the only determinant. Specialization of production helps explain why some countries are large exporters. Conversely, the strong income effects associated with carbon emissions suggest that the largest and richest economies will attract emissions. On further inspection, it is clear that some countries export more carbon than they import, and vice versa. For merchandise trade, these relationships are summarized in a trade balance.

Table 3 identifies the countries with the largest carbon trade balances (in absolute value). China and the United States are outliers, albeit in opposite ways. China uses much more carbon emissions in production than it accounts for in its consumption, with the difference made up by large net exports. In contrast, in 2015 the United States consumed products with far more embodied emissions than it produced, using imports to make up the difference.

A second important difference is apparent between the pair. The last column in table 3 shows the $CO_2$ emissions from consumption in each country, normalized by GDP. Low values indicate low carbon intensity. The United States has about half the emissions intensity of consumption that China does. Comparing a similar measure in terms of produced $CO_2$ emissions per dollar of GDP, China's lead extends to about three times. As a general trend, the countries with carbon trade deficits are more emissions intensive on average, and those with carbon trade surpluses are less so.

Given a choice between a unilateral territorial climate policy and one with full border adjustment, a country with a positive carbon balance or surplus (exporting more than importing) should prefer the latter, while one with a negative balance or deficit (importing more than exporting) should prefer the former. This effect is secondary to the overall intensity of emissions in consumption. Countries

Table 3. Trade Balances in $CO_2$ Emissions and Carbon Intensity of GDP, 2015

| Rank | Country | Carbon Balance (Mt $CO_2$) | $CO_2$ Consumption/ GDP (g/$) |
|------|---------|---------------------------|-------------------------------|
| 1 | China | 1,710 | 0.88 |
| 2 | United States | −1,173 | 0.42 |
| 3 | Hong Kong | −390 | 1.37 |
| 4 | Japan | −364 | 0.34 |
| 5 | India | −269 | 1.05 |
| 6 | United Kingdom | −274 | 0.29 |
| 7 | Russia | 205 | 1.43 |
| 8 | France | −181 | 0.25 |
| 9 | Taiwan | 124 | 0.31 |
| 10 | Italy | −121 | 0.28 |
| 11 | Spain | −113 | 0.36 |
| 12 | Malaysia | 106 | 0.83 |
| 13 | Singapore | −105 | 0.60 |
| 14 | Algeria | 97 | 0.77 |
| 15 | South Africa | 90 | 1.45 |
|  | All Others | 97 | 0.61 |

*Note*: A negative value for the trade balance indicates a deficit, meaning consumed emissions are greater than produced emissions. A positive value indicates the country produces more embodied emissions than are consumed within its borders. The trade balance value for all other countries is a sum of the balance across all countries outside the top fifteen, which is the same value (with opposite sign) as the sum of the top fifteen. The carbon intensity is the weighted average of the remaining countries, using GDP as a weight. This calculation attaches zero contribution from countries without GDP estimates, such as North Korea and South Sudan.

*Sources*: "Eora Global Supply Chain Database," https://worldmrio.com; World Bank Databank, https://data.worldbank.org/; author's calculations.

able to achieve relatively low-cost reductions should be the least averse to further action. Countries with lower emissions intensity have already achieved some reductions that are potentially available to those with high emissions intensity.

## Balancing the Way Forward

Joseph Aldy explicitly recognizes the dynamic learning necessary to introduce thoughtful and effective climate policy in the United States.[53] The time necessary to implement policy counters the political urgency for climate action. Explicitly accounting for the costs of implementation provides a more realistic view of the effect of merging trade and climate policies. Imposing a BCA entails an increase in tariff barriers for nonexempt products but also a substantial increase in nontariff barriers, which have been a frustration for trading partners. Nontariff barriers currently account for half or more of total trade barriers around the world and substantially more in certain cases.[54]

Trade has been and remains a cornerstone of human affluence. The challenges of climate change confirm the value of trade as a tool in both the short and the long run. Baldos and Hertel contrast the value of trade on interannual and interdecadal bases.[55] Climate variability can lead to volatility in agricultural yields, and trade in food products is critical to alleviating shortages and distributing surpluses. Over a longer time period, climatic changes can alter comparative advantages and create new trading opportunities while also obviating existing ones. A hypothetical example is the evolution of comparative advantage from wheat to corn, while another country might require imported substitutes to offset failures of a staple grain crop due to lack of rainfall.

The capital goods integral to human adaptation also offer gains from trade. Air conditioners, and even more fundamentally the components of a functioning electric grid, are more easily and cheaply obtained via trade than domestic production, at least in many countries around the world. The ability to exploit comparative advantage and import tools for adaptation, whatever they may be, is a critical motivation for maintaining unencumbered trading relationships. BCAs are born of a linkage between trade and a strategy that relies entirely on climate mitigation. A strategy that embraces adaptation (and potentially amelioration) views trade as an opportunity, not a liability.

The appearance of coronavirus has pushed climate policy out of the policy pole position. If anything, the ability of the virus to thrive in a highly interconnected world has only strengthened the appetite for reducing reliance on international partners and weakened aversion to trade barriers as a matter of course. The macroeconomic relief packages implemented thus far have largely resisted calls to use the opportunity to reengineer parts of the economy in more climate-friendly ways. As the longer-term recovery from the virus shock takes shape, the desire to avoid letting "a good crisis go to waste" may embolden climate advocates.

International trade has plummeted in 2020 as individuals and governments struggle to find the best way forward. Whether trade patterns will ever return to their previous patterns is unknown, but policy makers are using the opportunity to introduce new ideas that effectively link climate and trade. The European Union, which has flirted with a BCA as part of its European Green Deal plan, has proposed coronavirus relief that pushes investment away from emissions-intensive sectors, irrespective of the value of progress in those sectors to economic recovery, resilience, or adaptation capacity.

## Conclusion

The historically bright lines between trade and climate policy are growing dimmer, creating opportunities for a merged policy that addresses climate and trade objectives. The same events might be interpreted as climate mitigation policy co-opting trade policy for ulterior motives. It is distinctly possible, if not probable, that a climate-infused trade policy will degenerate into protectionism.

Mitigation is not the only strategy available for climate policy. A second climate policy option is to invest in adaptation. Faced with uncertain and potentially large costs, this strategy focuses on increasing potential for adaptation by providing information and resources through economic growth. Free trade has long been an engine of economic growth, as the inexorable logic of comparative advantage increases economic surplus. Politically, this do-nothing approach also faces challenges thanks to a growing crescendo of political pressure for action on climate change. But the contrast is stark between a failed mitigation strategy trying to include and limit trade and an adaptation strategy that embraces the gains from trade.

Narrowing the focus of climate policy to only mitigation increases the tendency to try to induce greater results from that prong. Leakage resulting from differential values of emissions seems like a relatively easy problem to solve using a BCA. BCAs are, however, a second-best solution, bringing a whole collection of hidden costs, starting with substantial new monitoring and verification costs for traded products. The burden imposed on the trading regime, in the form of combined tariff and nontariff measures, will be greater than a simple Pigouvian equivalence suggests. Variation in firm performance, even within narrow sectors, offers gains from trade only if the verification and monitoring of embodied emissions can be built across a wide variety of products and countries. In addition, strategic incentives to raise protectionist barriers only compound the potential distortion. While there is some hope for voluntary plurilateral or club approaches, until the club encompasses all economies, there will always be concern about leakage. And by the same token, frictions will result from complex policies that are not fully synchronous. The strategic incentives of heterogeneous countries are compounded, not mitigated, by a choice to merge climate and trade policy.

## Notes

1. Marshall Burke et al., "Opportunities for Advances in Climate Change Economics," *Science* 352, no. 6283 (April 2016): 292–93.
2. Joseph E. Aldy and Richard Zeckhauser, "Three Prongs for Prudent Climate Policy," Harvard Kennedy School Faculty Research Working Paper Series, April 2020.
3. Although not limited strictly to carbon emissions, the practice of measuring the warming potential of various compounds relative to $CO_2$ or expressing

emissions as $CO_2$ equivalents is a common and useful measure. Summarizing those compounds under the umbrella of carbon emissions is convenient.

4. Aldy and Zeckhauser, "Three Prongs for Prudent Climate Policy."

5. Frédéric Branger, Philippe Quirion, and Julien Chevallier, "Carbon Leakage and Competitiveness of Cement and Steel Industries under the EU ETS: Much Ado about Nothing," *Energy Journal* 37, no. 3 (2016); Helene Naegele and Aleksandar Zaklan, "Does the EU ETS Cause Carbon Leakage in European Manufacturing?," *Journal of Environmental Economics and Management* 93 (2019): 125–47; Frédéric Branger and Philippe Quirion, "Would Border Carbon Adjustments Prevent Carbon Leakage and Heavy Industry Competitiveness Losses? Insights from a Meta-Analysis of Recent Economic Studies," *Ecological Economics* 99 (2014): 29–39.

6. United Nations Framework Convention on Climate Change (UNFCCC), "GHG Data," 2020, http://unfccc.int.

7. Aaron Cosbey et al., "Developing Guidance for Implementing Border Carbon Adjustments: Lessons, Cautions, and Research Needs from the Literature," *Review of Environmental Economics and Policy* 13, no. 1 (Winter 2019): 3–22.

8. Chad Bown and Melina Kolb, "Trump's Trade War Timeline: An Up-to-Date Guide," Peterson Institute for International Economics, March 13, 2020, https://www.piie.com/blogs/trade-investment-policy-watch/trump-trade-war-china-date-guide.

9. Linkage in a climate sense means that emissions reductions in two regions can substitute for one another. Linkage can take a number of forms. As an example, California and Quebec (to the considerable consternation of their respective federal governments) explicitly linked their emissions programs in 2014. Linkage is not necessarily permanent, as attested by the short-lived linkage of California's system to Ontario's in 2018.

10. Bruce Yandle, "Bootleggers and Baptists—the Education of a Regulatory Economist," *Regulation* 7, no. 3 (May/June 1983): 12.

11. Michael A. Mehling et al., "Beat Protectionism and Emissions at a Stroke," *Nature*, July 16, 2018.

12. Cosbey et al., "Developing Guidance for Implementing Border Carbon Adjustments."

13. Carol McAusland and Nouri Najjar, "Carbon Footprint Taxes," *Environmental and Resource Economics* 61, no. 1 (2015): 37–70

14. Joseph Shapiro, "The Environmental Bias of Trade Policy," working paper, University of California–Berkeley, 2020.

15. Jared C. Carbone, Carsten Helm, and Thomas F. Rutherford, "The Case for International Emission Trade in the Absence of Cooperative Climate Policy," *Journal of Environmental Economics and Management* 58, no. 3 (November 2009): 266–80.

16. Marisa Beck, Nicholas Rivers, Randall Wigle, and Hidemichi Yonezawa, "Carbon Tax and Revenue Recycling: Impacts on Households in British Columbia," *Resource and Energy Economics* 41 (August 2015): 40–69.

17. Joseph E. Aldy, "Frameworks for Evaluating Policy Approaches to Address the Competitiveness Concerns of Mitigating Greenhouse Gas Emissions," *National Tax Journal* 70, no. 2 (June 2017): 395–420.

18. Joseph E. Aldy and William A. Pizer, "The Competitiveness Impacts of Climate Change Mitigation Policies," *Journal of the Association of Environmental and Resource Economists* 2, no. 4 (September 2015): 565–95.

19. Brendan J. Casey et al., "How Does State-Level Carbon Pricing in the United States Affect Industrial Competitiveness?," National Bureau of Economic Research, NBER Working Paper 26629, January 2020.

20. Jared C. Carbone and Nicholas Rivers, "The Impacts of Unilateral Climate Policy on Competitiveness: Evidence from Computable General Equilibrium Models," *Review of Environmental Economics and Policy* 11, no. 1 (Winter 2017): 24–42.

21. Kate Crowley, "Up and Down with Climate Politics 2013–2016: The Repeal of Carbon Pricing in Australia," *Wiley Interdisciplinary Reviews: Climate Change* 8, no. 3 (May/June 2017): e458.

22. Thomas D. Crocker, "The Structuring of Atmospheric Pollution Control Systems," *Economics of Air Pollution* 61 (1966): 81–84; W. David Montgomery, "Markets in Licenses and Efficient Pollution Control Programs," *Journal of Economic Theory* 5, no. 3 (December 1972): 395–418.

23. William Nordhaus, "Climate Clubs: Overcoming Free-Riding in International Climate Policy," *American Economic Review* 105, no. 4 (2015): 1339–70.

24. Peter Egger et al., "The Trade Effects of Endogenous Preferential Trade Agreements," *American Economic Journal: Economic Policy* 3, no. 3 (August 2011): 113–43.

25. Eva Lyubich, Joseph Shapiro, and Reed Walker, "Regulating Mismeasured Pollution: Implications of Firm Heterogeneity for Environmental Policy," *AEA Papers and Proceedings* 108 (May 2018): 136–42.

26. Joseph E. Aldy, William A. Pizer, and Keigo Akimoto, "Comparing Emissions Mitigation Efforts across Countries," *Climate Policy* 17, no. 4 (2017): 501–15;

Keigo Akimoto et al., "Estimates of GHG Emission Reduction Potential by Country, Sector, and Cost," *Energy Policy* 38, no. 7 (July 2010): 3384–93.

27. Scott Barrett, "Self-Enforcing International Environmental Agreements," *Oxford Economic Papers* 46 (October 1994): 878–94.

28. Peter Holmes, Tom Reilly, and Jim Rollo, "Border Carbon Adjustments and the Potential for Protectionism," *Climate Policy* 11, no. 2 (2011): 883–900.

29. Dieter Helm, Cameron Hepburn, and Giovanni Ruta, "Trade, Climate Change, and the Political Game Theory of Border Carbon Adjustments," *Oxford Review of Economic Policy* 28, no. 2 (November 2012): 368–94.

30. Mary Amiti, Stephen J. Redding, and David E. Weinstein, "The Impact of the 2018 Tariffs on Prices and Welfare," *Journal of Economic Perspectives* 33, no. 4 (Fall 2019): 187–210; Pablo D. Fajgelbaum et al., "The Return to Protectionism," *Quarterly Journal of Economics* 135, no. 1 (February 2020): 1–55.

31. James R. Markusen, "International Externalities and Optimal Tax Structures," *Journal of International Economics* 5, no. 1 (February 1975): 15–29.

32. Christoph Böhringer, Edward J. Balistreri, and Thomas F. Rutherford, "The Role of Border Carbon Adjustment in Unilateral Climate Policy: Overview of an Energy Modeling Forum Study (EMF 29)," *Energy Economics* 34, no. S2 (December 2012): S97–S110.

33. Harrison Fell and Peter Maniloff, "Leakage in Regional Environmental Policy: The Case of the Regional Greenhouse Gas Initiative," *Journal of Environmental Economics and Management* 87 (January 2018): 1–23.

34. Niven Winchester, Sergey Paltsev, and John M. Reilly, "Will Border Carbon Adjustments Work?," *BE Journal of Economic Analysis and Policy* 11, no. 1 (January 2011): 1–29.

35. Christoph Böhringer, Jared C. Carbone, and Thomas F. Rutherford, "The Strategic Value of Carbon Tariffs," *American Economic Journal: Economic Policy* 8, no. 1 (February 2016): 28–51.

36. Helm, Hepburn, and Ruta, "Trade, Climate Change, and the Political Game Theory."

37. Baran Doda, Simon Quemin, and Luca Taschini, "Linking Permit Markets Multilaterally," working paper, 2019; Grischa Perino, Robert A. Ritz, and Arthur van Benthem, "Understanding Overlapping Policies: Internal Carbon Leakage and the Punctured Waterbed," National Bureau of Economic Research, NBER Working Paper 25643, March 2019.

38. Samuel Kortum and David Weisbach, "The Design of Border Adjustments for Carbon Prices," *National Tax Journal* 70, no. 2 (June 2017): 421.

39. Carolyn Fischer and Alan K. Fox, "Comparing Policies to Combat Emissions Leakage: Border Carbon Adjustments versus Rebates," *Journal of Environmental Economics and Management* 64, no. 2 (September 2012): 199–216.

40. Winchester, Paltsev, and Reilly, "Will Border Carbon Adjustments Work?"

41. Meredith Fowlie and Mar Reguant, "Challenges in the Measurement of Leakage Risk," *AEA Papers and Proceedings* 108 (May 2018): 124–29.

42. Junichiro Oda et al., "Diffusion of Energy Efficient Technologies and $CO_2$ Emission Reductions in Iron and Steel Sector," *Energy Economics* 29, no. 4 (July 2007): 868–88; Junichiro Oda et al., "International Comparisons of Energy Efficiency in Power, Steel, and Cement Industries," *Energy Policy* 44 (May 2012): 118–29.

43. Christoph Böhringer, Jared C. Carbone, and Thomas F. Rutherford, "Embodied Carbon Tariffs," *Scandinavian Journal of Economics* 120, no. 1 (January 2018): 183–210.

44. Thomas Cottier, Olga Nartova, and Anirudh Shingal, "The Potential of Tariff Policy for Climate Change Mitigation: Legal and Economic Analysis," *Journal of World Trade* 48, no. 5 (2014): 1007–37; Michael O. Moore, "Carbon Safeguard? Managing the Friction between Trade Rules and Climate Policy," *Journal of World Trade* 51, no. 1 (February 2017): 43–66; Joel P. Trachtman, "WTO Law Constraints on Border Tax Adjustment and Tax Credit Mechanisms to Reduce the Competitive Effects of Carbon Taxes," *National Tax Journal* 70, no. 2 (June 2017): 469–94.

45. Michael A. Mehling et al., "Designing Border Carbon Adjustments for Enhanced Climate Action," *American Journal of International Law* 113, no. 3 (July 2019): 433–81.

46. Cosbey et al., "Developing Guidance for Implementing Border Carbon Adjustments."

47. Edward J. Balistreri, Daniel T. Kaffine, and Hidemichi Yonezawa, "Optimal Environmental Border Adjustments under the General Agreement on Tariffs and Trade," *Environmental and Resource Economics* 74, no. 3 (November 2019): 1037–75.

48. Yandle, "Bootleggers and Baptists."

49. Steven J. Davis and Ken Caldeira, "Consumption-Based Accounting of $CO_2$ Emissions," *Proceedings of the National Academy of Sciences* 107, no. 12 (March 2010): 5687–92.

50. Misato Sato, "Embodied Carbon in Trade: A Survey of the Empirical Literature," *Journal of Economic Surveys* 28, no. 5 (December 2014): 831–61.

51. This metric depends on both the *share* and *value* of the product being traded. Many products are widely traded, but they lack the size of the global marketplace. Automobiles are a very valuable traded product but are not as widely traded after final assembly. Considering the entire supply chain for automobiles further increases the value but also the breadth of products considered.

52. British Petroleum, *BP Statistical Review of World Energy 2019*, https://www.bp.com/content/dam/bp/business-sites/en/global/corporate/pdfs/energy-economics/statistical-review/bp-stats-review-2019-full-report.pdf.

53. Joseph E. Aldy, "Carbon Tax Review and Updating: Institutionalizing an Act-Learn-Act Approach to US Climate Policy," *Review of Environmental Economics and Policy* 14, no. 1 (Winter 2020).

54. Council of Economic Advisers, *Economic Report of the President* (Washington, DC: Government Printing Office, 2018).

55. Uris Lantz C. Baldos and Thomas W. Hertel, "The Role of International Trade in Managing Food Security Risks from Climate Change," *Food Security* 7, no. 2 (2015): 275–90.

# 5

# Subsistence in Alaska Native Villages

## Adapting in the Face of Climate Change and Government Regulations

E. Barrett Ristroph

It is 9 p.m. on October 2, 2019, in the tiny, quiet village of Allakaket in Interior Arctic Alaska, and I am thinking about going to bed. My hostess, a Koyukon Athabascan Indian in her mid-seventies, tells me that tonight may be the night that the Koyukuk River finally freezes over for the winter. In past years, the river would have frozen over months before. But with climate change, everything is different. While I lazily shuffle off to bed, she and her husband, a man near eighty, take their boat down the river. They spend much of the night pulling their subsistence fishing nets out of the frigid waters under the light of the full moon. In the morning everything is frozen. The nets have come out just in time.

This couple along the Koyukuk River is not alone. There are still many indigenous people (as well as some nonindigenous people) practicing subsistence traditions in Alaska Native Villages (ANVs), which are both communities and federally recognized tribes. Given the high costs of flying commercial foods into remote villages off the road system, subsistence helps ensure food security.[1]

But this lifeway faces challenges, including the rapid climate change that has been occurring since the late twentieth century.[2] Climate change has contributed to species shifts: changes in species abundance or migration routes that affect ANV subsistence practices.[3] Not only are species shifting, but access to species has become more difficult.[4] During the summer, low river water levels impede boat travel.[5] During the fall and winter, snow-machine travel can be complicated and dangerous due to less snow coverage and rivers that remain unfrozen late in the season.[6]

In addition to shifting species and impeding access to these species, climate change complicates food preservation.[7] For example, on Alaska's North Slope, melting permafrost has complicated food storage in traditional ice cellars.[8] As soil temperatures rise, the cellars are less likely to protect food from pathogens that cause food-borne illness.[9]

Of course, climate change is not the only challenge to ANV subsistence. Social and economic changes associated with colonization and westernization have eased life in some ways but have threatened the core of ANV lifeways in others.[10] In particular, Western laws intended to promote fair access by Alaska residents to healthy fish and game populations have complicated ANV subsistence. It is difficult for an ANV like Allakaket to overcome these obstacles, given its remote location with a tiny population (130 people) and lacking road access, a local economy, or political influence on institutions that could assist with adaptation.[11]

This chapter focuses on the intersection of climate change and the federal and state laws governing subsistence. I draw on two previous articles documenting the effects of climate change and law on Alaska Native subsistence. The first article, written in the mid-2000s, called attention to ways in which laws and climate change constrain Alaska Natives' subsistence opportunities and rights.[12] The second article was based on dissertation research conducted in the mid-2010s, including communications with more than

150 research participants and a review of community plans relevant to the fifty-nine ANVs from which I selected participants.[13]

This chapter updates previously cited research and laws and incorporates additional research findings. Sequentially, sections explain the importance of subsistence to Alaska Natives; explain how Alaska Natives have adapted their subsistence over time; provide a simplified overview of the complex state and federal subsistence regime and how it complicates Alaska Native subsistence; and propose some incremental legal changes and discuss strategies for adapting in spite of restrictions. At the same time, this chapter recognizes the limits to adaptation for communities that lack the capacity to influence or even navigate the institutions that affect adaptation.

## The Nature of Subsistence

Alaska law defines *subsistence uses* as "the noncommercial, customary, and traditional uses of wild, renewable resources by a resident domiciled in a rural area of the state for direct personal or family consumption as food, shelter, fuel, clothing, tools, or transportation, for the making and selling of handicraft articles out of non-edible by-products of fish and wildlife resources taken for personal or family consumption, and for the customary trade, barter, or sharing for personal or family consumption."[14]

This definition does not convey the significance of subsistence for many Alaska Natives, who value it as a fundamental part of their culture.[15] In addition to providing food security, subsistence enables families to spend time together and pass down knowledge and values.[16] Alaska Native culture has traditionally been based on communal sharing of subsistence foods to satisfy individual and community needs.[17] Communities dependent on subsistence consider it a collective or cultural right (and duty) rather than an individual right, since a limited number of individuals usually provide for a larger community.[18]

Economic development has allowed most Alaska Native communities to shift from a "pure" subsistence economy into a mixed economy, in which hunting is more efficient, comfortable, and humane. But subsistence has remained a critical part of Alaska Native culture and persists even in communities with the financial means to exist in a pure market economy.[19] For example, in Utqiagvik (Barrow), where the average household income is $78,804, the most recent subsistence harvest estimate found that 90 percent of households share in the subsistence harvest (even if they are not all hunting), with an average of 362 pounds of subsistence foods consumed each year.[20] Estimates for Allakaket, a less wealthy community, suggest that *all* households in the ANV share in the subsistence harvest, with an average of 525 pounds consumed each year.[21] In the words of one subsistence hunter from Utqiagvik, "If we couldn't go whaling . . . if nobody were speaking Inupiaq . . . I might just relocate to Anchorage. . . . The reason I want to live here is because I can get on my snow machine, drive five minutes away, and hunt caribou. Or I can take my kids out on the ice and teach them whaling. . . . If you don't [get out on land], what's the point of living here?"

The harm caused by not participating in subsistence is existential as well as physical. Reductions in participation have been associated with health problems due to increased consumption of commercial Western foods, reduced physical exertion, and increased stress.[22] Reduced subsistence participation may result in a loss of community knowledge associated with traditional subsistence practices.[23]

## Adaptation Strategies

Like other indigenous peoples, Alaska Natives have a long history of adapting their subsistence practices to climate change and other challenges.[24] Given Alaska's vastness and the broad range of geographies, cultures, and subsistence practices, only a very general history is described in this section.[25] Prior to contact with Western civilization and until the mid-twentieth century, many groups of Alaska Natives moved seasonally to harvest the resources available in various locations.[26] Hunters and fishers relied on a wide range of resources that were available in abundance for short time frames in localized areas. Territory and property rights were governed by successful hunters and fishers who had achieved leadership in their communities.[27] With small migratory populations posing little risk of overharvesting, rules provided for how to hunt and fish rather than how much should be taken.[28] Adaptation generally took the form of moving and harvesting different species with specialized techniques involving tools and accumulated knowledge.[29]

In the mid-twentieth century, colonization led to permanent settlements, reducing the ability to adapt through relocation.[30] For some time, many families maintained seasonal hunting and fishing camps, but today most hunting and fishing take the form of short trips near villages.[31] Still, many traditional adaptation strategies have persisted, including the use of flexible hunting practices (i.e., hunting in different times or places or for different species), preserving and storing food, using traditional environmental knowledge, and sharing and trading.[32] These traditional strategies have been supplemented with modern technology, illegal hunting, and more reliance on store-bought food.[33]

As with other economic systems, flexibility is an important component of subsistence adaptation. This flexibility involves "doing what you can when you can."[34] Modern Western technology contributes to flexibility by increasing hunting ranges and reducing travel and processing time. As one Alaska Native elder told me, "With modern tools you do certain things easier but you still do the same things they did way back." Hunters may use more fuel or bigger snow machines and boats that are safer and can travel farther, though this results in greater dependency on fossil fuels and greater susceptibility to fluctuations in the market economy.[35] Since the sale of the subsistence harvest is illegal, hunters typically must engage in occupations unrelated to subsistence to earn the income that facilitates subsistence. Hunters are anchored in their permanent communities, which represent millions of dollars of infrastructure investment and provide jobs and schools.[36] These communities have become the center of many subsistence activities that used to take place at the harvest site, including butchering and sharing food.

Beyond the individual and household level of adaptation, some ANVs are considering how to adapt as communities. Many ANV community plans refer to the importance of preserving subsistence lifeways, though not as many have specific measures to adapt. An example of a plan with specific measures is the Nome adaptation plan, which calls for adapting food preservation techniques, reconnecting families to subsistence resources, and increasing tribal representation in subsistence management.[37] Action items from other plans include seeking regulatory change, raising food locally, conserving and creating habitats, improving trails to access subsistence areas, and storing food.[38]

Outside of planning, a number of ANVs and their residents are participating in federal and state agency rulemaking processes in an effort to change restrictions on hunting and fishing limits and seasons. This participatory approach is more common among ANVs that have more funding and can afford to have Western scientists (who tend to be non-Native) on their staff, since state and federal boards may not accept traditional knowledge as a basis for changing rules. Other community-level adaptation measures that have been put into action include improving and maintaining trails to subsistence areas, improving food storage (e.g., building community ice cellars), and subsidizing the cost of fuel and ammunition for residents.[39]

While the aforementioned strategies demonstrate that ANVs and their residents are clearly capable of adapting, the magnitude of today's rapid climate change, along with the restrictions posed by the Western legal system and socioeconomic pressures, present bigger adaptation challenges to Alaska Native subsistence than ever before.[40] A number of individuals and families feel pressured to move to cities, where there is better access to jobs, education, and lower costs of energy and store-bought food.[41] This migration not only takes Alaska Natives away from customary hunting grounds, it relocates them in areas where their subsistence is not protected.[42] It also dilutes their legislative representation.[43] Adaptive capacity may be reduced even further as fewer people carry on subsistence hunting practices and some traditional knowledge is lost.[44]

## How State and Federal Regimes Hinder Adaptation to Climate Change

This section outlines some of the major state and federal laws that affect how most ANV residents engage in subsistence, starting with the laws that wrested management responsibilities from ANVs and placed them in the hands of state and federal agencies. While there have been efforts to involve ANVs in agency decision making and to adjust rules in response to changing climate conditions, ANVs and Alaska Natives have less ability to adapt under the current legal regime than they did prior to colonization.

### Limited Jurisdiction and Opportunities for Meaningful Comanagement by ANVs

While the hunting and fishing rights of many tribes in the lower forty-eight states are protected by treaties, Alaska Natives have no such treaties.[45] The 1971 Alaska Native Claims Settlement Act (ANCSA) purported to extinguish aboriginal hunting and fishing rights in Alaska.[46] As one Alaska Native commented, "The local people did not cede the land or fight for it. They did not vote in favor of ANCSA."

Congress attempted to address ANCSA's effects on subsistence through the Alaska National Interest Lands Conservation Act (ANILCA) in 1981.[47] ANILCA prioritizes subsistence over other consumptive uses of fish and game and gives rural subsistence users priority over urban users.[48] The federal government determines which communities are rural based on population as well as community characteristics, such as economy and integration with urban centers.[49]

ANILCA has been a disappointment to Alaska Natives who feel that the preference should have been "Native" rather than "rural."[50] As Natives have moved toward urban areas and the percentage of non-Natives in rural areas has increased, the rural preference has been less beneficial to Alaska Natives as a whole.[51]

Various laws do allow for some shared management responsibilities in the form of comanagement, which can facilitate adaptation and power sharing between agencies and ANVs by integrating community knowledge into decision making.[52] But in Alaska and elsewhere, the lack of trust between parties, lack of technical and financial resources to carry out agreements, and lack of appreciation for community knowledge have hindered effective comanagement.[53] As one Alaska Native said, "There are laws and court orders requiring agencies to work with tribes, government to government, but they don't happen." That said, the handful of ANVs that have been able to adapt to agency expectations of Western-science-based management have achieved greater control over subsistence.

## Dual Management by State and Federal Government

Another institutional challenge to adaptation is the fragmentation and complexity of the state and federal subsistence regimes. As one former state regulator described these systems,

A person fishing for sockeye salmon in the Copper River might fish under state regulations for commercial, resident sport, non-resident sport, subsistence, or personal use, or under federal regulations for subsistence use. Now consider that Alaska's management system must accommodate harvests of five species of salmon, not to mention halibut, whitefish, king crab, moose, caribou, sheep, and many more species, in every corner of the state. While a person who harvests in one area for one purpose can avoid most of the complications, fish and wildlife management in Alaska is necessarily complicated.

ANILCA was originally intended to be implemented by the State of Alaska, through the Alaska Department of Fish and Game, throughout the entire state.[54] Consistent with ANILCA, the State of Alaska adopted laws that provided for a subsistence priority over other consumptive uses, and later for a "rural" (rather than a "Native" or ANV) priority over urban subsistence participants.[55] But after the Alaska Supreme Court determined that the rural priority established under ANILCA violated the Alaska Constitution, Alaskans were instead left with a dual state and federal management system.[56] The rural priority under ANILCA and federal laws specific to federal agencies applies to most federal lands and waters within Alaska, while state subsistence laws govern elsewhere. Many other federal acts govern subsistence in the waters offshore of Alaska.

In one sense, subsistence regulations in Alaska are adaptive, since rules are tailored to the particular circumstances of the species in each area and regularly updated. But it is challenging for subsistence participants trying to adapt their practices to understand all these externally imposed, ever-changing rules. And there are significant penalties for noncompliance, including forfeiture of their catch and gear.[57]

## Obstacles to the Participation of ANV Citizens
## in Agency Decision Making

As challenging as it can be to understand the state and federal subsistence regime, it can be even more challenging for participants to
change the system for their benefit. Despite rules allowing proposals for regulatory change to come from the public, citizens of some
ANVs feel disenfranchised. One village elder from Western Alaska
explained the difficulty of participating in rulemaking processes: "A
lot of regulations are made far away, it's very hard to go there and
testify. It can cost $180 to get to Nome, and then $500–$600 to get
to Anchorage, and you have to get a hotel. Then you only get three
minutes to testify. It's not effective to talk on the phone. Face to face
is more effective to convey feelings and get the point across. It's bad,
because we can't see each other on equal footing."

Even when ANV citizens are present in decision-making forums,
they often find that their views and knowledge are not meaningfully
considered.[58] Community knowledge regarding hunting and fishing
activity does not always meet agency standards. Agencies sometimes
incorporate only the data associated with the knowledge, leaving out
context that is important to the community. Agency decisions are
often made in forums with language and procedures that can mar-
ginalize ANV knowledge and participation.[59] A southeastern tribal
leader referred to the gaps in knowledge that come with failure to
consider community knowledge: "The combination of so-called science and indigenous science can be useful. If you're really a scientist,
why would you leave any knowledge out? It's essential to incorporate
local people into research, not just if you happen to have funding. To
not include them would be like leaving out beakers from a lab experi-
ment. All of this has to be planned at the beginning. Elders can't be
hired as an afterthought. This is not good science."

Yet bridging community knowledge with Western science
continues to be more aspirational than realistic, as described by

a lower-level agency manager: "Agencies talk about how valuable [community knowledge] is but don't really use it. All biologists have done is casually ask people if there are more or less of a species. I proposed using it once three years ago and got shot down." There is no easy answer for increasing ANV participation in state and federal agency decision making regarding subsistence. Incorporating community, traditional, and indigenous knowledges in state and federal agency decisions is important but clearly difficult.[60]

## Lack of Flexibility

Even when laws provide for ANV subsistence and participation in decision making, they can be problematic if they cannot timely change in response to climate change. As climate change shifts habitats and species across the United States, there has been recognition that wildlife and natural resource laws are overly stationary.[61] In Alaska, stationary laws can reduce the flexibility of subsistence participants to adapt by adjusting the time, manner, and place of their practice.[62] This is especially problematic if the times when hunting and fishing are legally allowed are inconsistent with the times when fish and game appear.[63]

State and federal fish and game regulatory boards have mechanisms in place to revise regulations in response to species changes. Both provide for proposed revisions to go through advisory boards prior to consideration at board meetings, and both allow emergency petitions to be reviewed outside of the normal meeting process.[64] But boards often make determinations well before anyone could anticipate local weather conditions during the hunting season, such that advance regulations are frequently inconsistent with actual weather patterns.[65] In addition, the state "board[s] may decline to act on a subsistence proposal for any reason."[66] There is a perception among ANVs that emergency petitions to the state and federal boards are not often granted.[67]

## Inconsistencies between Regulations and Traditional Rules

As discussed above, Alaska Natives have embraced Western technology as a way to adapt subsistence lifeways to the many legal limitations as well as the institutional limitations of permanent settlements. Still, many want to continue the traditions that transcend social and economic change, such as holding a customary potlatch to memorialize a community death. Many Alaska Natives believe that subsistence laws (particularly those of the State of Alaska) conflict with or unnecessarily burden Native hunting traditions.[68]

An example is the requirement to get a license or permit to practice traditional hunting and fishing.[69] In subsistence surveys, Alaska Native Villages may underreport what they catch because they refuse to acquire licenses or permits or fear being cited with violations.[70] Failure to comply with state and federal permit and reporting requirements may result in ineligibility to receive these permits the following year.[71]

Despite the potential penalties, there are subsistence participants that "do what they need to do" (i.e., hunt out of season or beyond the legal limit) to continue their lifeway, regardless of the law.[72] One ANV resident said, "I would venture to say that 90 percent of our lifestyle is illegal in some fashion or another." Another said, "There's a difference between 'hunting-hunting' and 'feeding-our-families-hunting,'" implying that the latter was illegal but necessary. Illegal hunting has been a long-term strategy for coping with the complicated regulatory scheme and its limitations on hunting.[73]

Resentment of the requirement to purchase a federal duck stamp to hunt waterfowl led to amendments made in 2014 to the federal Migratory Bird Hunting and Conservation Stamp Act. As a result, permanent rural residents who are eligible for subsistence under ANILCA no longer need a stamp where the spring/summer migratory bird subsistence harvest is allowed.[74] But a state waterfowl stamp (and license) is still required.[75] State and federal law do accommodate some out-of-season traditional/cultural hunts associated with funerals or cultural celebrations, although permits and reporting requirements may still apply.[76] In some instances, the reporting burden has been eased through allowance of online reporting rather than requiring a signed, written report.[77]

Limitations on who exactly can hunt and how much hunters can take are another inconsistency with traditional rules. Historically (and in many parts of Alaska today), an ANV's subsistence needs have often been met by a small group of hunters who provide for the entire community.[78] Essentially, this group of hunters serves as a proxy for other community members who are not as well positioned to hunt. But in many cases under both state and federal law, subsistence hunters and fishers are subject to bag limits and permits or licenses for each individual hunter.[79] Limits under the federal and state systems generally cannot be added together to increase individual entitlement.[80] Both the state and federal systems provide for proxy hunting and fishing to a limited degree that is inconsistent with traditional subsistence practices.[81]

## Maximizing ANV Adaptation under Existing Law and the Potential for Legal and Institutional Change

ANVs are experiencing challenges to their subsistence lifeways not only from climate change but also from laws that constrain adaptation, industrial development, and increased competition for fish and game from a growing population. There is no turning back the clock to precolonial times, when ANVs had the liberty to fully control subsistence. Nor is climate change going to stop in the near future, and the changes will be irreversible for millennia.[82]

While legal and institutional change to increase the ANV role in decisions about subsistence would be ideal from the standpoint of ANVs, such change is not easy. ANVs lack political influence, and state and federal decision makers lack the will to address ANV lifeway disruptions.[83] ANVs with tiny populations have limited human resources or educational opportunities and may grapple with historical trauma, all of which can limit adaptive capacity.[84] This section evaluates subsistence adaptation strategies in the context of these political limitations and offers modest recommendations that may be more likely to garner political acceptance than those requiring greater change. The analysis is focused on strategies for ANVs and state and federal agencies to increase ANV participation in planning processes and reduce restrictions to adaptation that are not necessary to conserve subsistence resources.

## Addressing the Dual Regulatory Regime

It is unlikely that ANILCA would be amended to provide a Native rather than rural preference, or that the state would implement a Native or rural priority. This subsection examines alternatives to address complications related to the dual regulatory regime.

A relatively feasible legal change would be to adjust federal board rules specifying which communities are rural, and thus entitled to the federal rural subsistence preference, as well as state board rules specifying which areas are urban, such that they get no preference for subsistence over other types of hunting. Expanding the definition of *rural* and limiting *urban* could increase participation of Alaska Natives and ANVs closer to urban centers who still have a subsistence lifeway. On the other hand, such a change could increase competition from non-Native urban users. Whether the change benefits a particular ANV depends on whether the board considers the ANV in question to have a more rural character than non-Native communities in the area.

Assuming the dual regime stays in place, there are ways to reduce the current confusion. The state has already developed a program for making custom hunting maps to print or use on a mobile device, showing what animals can be hunted on what lands under different types of hunts.[85] One must still refer to the *Alaska Hunting Regulations* booklet for hunting limits, seasons, and additional regulations concerning this hunt. The state should incorporate this additional information into the maps, if possible. Ideally, hunters and fishers could see, based on their GPS location, what rules apply based on the target species and type of hunt. The state and federal governments should cooperate to create a joint system rather than maintaining separate ones, particularly since a separate federal system has yet to be developed.

As climate change brings more species changes and greater difficulties in accessing species used for subsistence, there may be a need for more rule changes to reflect environmental circumstances. Ensuring that subsistence participants understand what rules apply can help the subsistence management system as a whole better adapt.

### Increasing ANV Participation

As long as the state and federal regimes persist, increasing ANV participation in these regimes is essential. The Federal Subsistence Board has made an effort by reserving two seats on the board for rural subsistence users. As of this writing, the Federal Subsistence Board is chaired by the mayor of the ANV of Hydaburg and includes two additional ANV citizens. Implementing a similar requirement for state boards could be difficult, since these boards allocate game among *all* hunters, not just subsistence users. Even in the absence of a requirement, however, ANVs should encourage their citizens to seek these positions.

Another way to support ANV input is to give deference to findings made by local advisory committees. Under ANILCA section 805(c), the Federal Subsistence Board must defer to committee findings unless they are unsupported by substantial evidence, violate recognized principles of fish and wildlife conservation, or would be detrimental to the satisfaction of subsistence needs. A similar provision for the state boards could be useful.

There are a number of ways for ANVs to increase their participation in decision making even without legal changes. These include entering into agreements with agencies under laws that allow for comanagement, participating in agency decisions as a "cooperating agency" under the National Environmental Policy Act, and engaging in government-to-government consultation.[86] That said, the reality in Alaska is that comanagement and related strategies are expensive and time consuming, and the ANV voice may not be heard if it is not supported by some form of Western science.[87]

It is important to note that ANVs and Native entities with strong environmental management programs often have non-Native Western scientists on their staff or as consultants, and these people may not live in ANVs. An example is the ANV of St. Paul, which successfully petitioned the National Marine Fisheries Service to modify subsistence use regulations for fur seals to liberalize the hunt and eliminate some duplicative regulations.[88] While it might be idealistic to incentivize Natives with master's degrees to return to ANVs, a second-best alternative may be to have urban-based scientists willing to work for ANVs and take seriously their community knowledge and values. Where ANVs cannot afford Western scientists and higher levels of participation, they are at least entitled to government-to-government consultation (at the agency's expense for federally sponsored or permitted activities that affect tribal resources).[89]

ANVs should not be saddled with the entire burden for increasing their participation in the state and federal regimes; agencies should also do their part. Some of the disconnection and mistrust between agencies and ANVs could be addressed by having outside decision makers spend more time in the villages.[90] This is particularly important for upper-level agency officials who, unlike some of the lower-level staff, have not spent any time in ANVs and do not understand the concerns about food security or the importance of the subsistence lifeway.

As outlined above, while some legal changes could allow greater deference to ANV perspectives, laws providing for more ANV authority may not be helpful if ANVs lack the capacity (from a Western point of view) to administer subsistence management. ANVs may need to resort to hiring non-ANV staff if they are not able to get local staff with the capacity needed for comanagement. In turn, state and federal agencies should support capacity-building efforts, including funding for ANVs, and at the very least spend more time in ANVs to better understand their subsistence concerns.

## Increasing Flexibility

Responding to climate change may require the law to provide decision makers, communities, and individuals with greater flexibility so that they have options when environmental conditions change.[91] There is more than one way to approach this.

One possibility is a change to the laws that govern land mammal hunting and fishing to allow for more flexibility, similar to that of ocean mammals and fish. An example is the Alaska Eskimo Whaling Commission's (AEWC) cooperative agreement with the National Oceanic and Atmospheric Administration to manage the annual bowhead whale hunt in Alaska.[92] The International Whaling Commission allocates a certain amount of bowhead whale strikes to AEWC, which in turn allocates the strikes among Alaska's eight whaling villages. Each strike at a whale that a hunter takes counts against that village's quota for that year, whether or not the whale is successfully landed.[93] One village may share its quota with another village, and AEWC has previously shared its quota with Siberian Yupik Eskimos. There are no government-imposed seasonal limits to whaling. This has allowed St. Lawrence Island whalers to take advantage of a later fall freeze-up to pursue bowhead whales later in the year, offsetting some of the difficulties they have experienced during the traditional period for whaling.[94]

Another example of flexibility in regulation of ocean mammals and fish is the Community Development Quota, which is designed to give Western Alaska and Aleutian ANVs a stake in commercial Bering Sea fisheries.[95] The coastal system allows fishers to meet their ground-fish quotas at any time during an extended fishing period. Coastal subsistence fishers have described the benefits of the longer open seasons, which reduce the incentive to undertake unsafe, risky actions to obtain adequate catch within a short season.[96]

A third example of flexibility is NOAA's Community Harvest Permit. The program allows certain coastal and rural communities and tribes to appoint individuals from their communities or tribes to harvest subsistence halibut from a single vessel under reduced gear and harvest restrictions.[97]

Ideally, the principles of community quotas that have been successful with marine mammals and offshore fishing could apply to land animals. The State Board of Game previously established a program to hunt moose and caribou that allowed for community (rather than individual) permits.[98] But the program had unintended consequences: as it became more attractive, it went from six to seventy-three groups, and applicants teamed up to apply for permits without even knowing each other. The state could improve the program by assigning an annual quota directly to each ANV within a limited range, whereby each ANV could develop its own system for allocating the hunt among village residents. An ANV could trade or share a quota with another ANV. Rather than implementing a fixed end date for a season, the season could close when the community has met its quota. Such a program is easier said than done: potential pitfalls include competition from subsistence participants outside of the limited range, interjurisdictional issues, and the potentially limited capacity of the participating village to fulfill tracking and reporting requirements of the program.[99] If shifting quotas from individuals to communities proves too politically difficult, a simpler change could involve liberalizing the proxy system to better enable hunting and fishing on behalf of others. One should not have to be blind, elderly, or disabled to receive a proxy hunting license, as is required under the current system.[100]

Aside from community quotas and proxies, another approach to increase flexibility is to grant lower-level staff greater authority to make adjustments and exceptions. Regulatory managers could work with weather and climate forecasters and subsistence specialists to anticipate and respond to both climate conditions and village harvest success during each season.[101] This may already be occurring to some degree, as managers for both the state and the federal government have occasionally lengthened a season or expanded a usage area for fishing and hunting in the absence of specific regulatory authorization.[102]

Another way to increase flexibility relates to the timing of seasons. Alaska regulates vehicular travel across the tundra on a flexible basis, based on the occurrence of an event (sufficient snow thickness and temperature) rather than a calendar date.[103] Ideally, such logic could be applied to establish thresholds for opening and closing hunting seasons for prey and fish, rather than relying on calendar dates or emergency petitions. Hunting and fishing seasons could be opened and closed when agency biologists, in cooperation with ANV residents, document certain activities occurring, such as the presence of a population of a certain size in a particular area.

Another option regarding timing would be to allow for a longer regulatory open season (e.g., May 1 to September 1) and limit a user to a certain number of consecutive days (e.g., sixty within one season). In this example, if the species does not arrive until June 1, a hunter could start on that day and continue until the end of July.

In short, agencies already possess the tools to facilitate flexibility by expanding quotas to include more hunters and providing for longer seasons. In using these tools, the aim is not necessarily to increase the overall harvest but to ensure that users can obtain harvest levels to which they are legally entitled in the face of climate change and other obstacles. Further, empowering subsistence participants to exercise more control over their practices may create greater buy-in to the rules and help avoid illegal harvest.[104] Agencies should explore pilot projects using existing tools for more flexible management.

## Reducing Regulatory Burden

In an era when tribes are no longer able to easily migrate (so as to reduce take in a concentrated area) and must compete with many others for the same resource, it is difficult to imagine a system in which no form of harvest tracking (be it permits, licenses, tags, or after-the-fact reporting) would occur. The end of the federal duck stamp requirement in 2014 was politically achievable perhaps because it did not eliminate concurrent tracking mechanisms and did not substantially deprive wildlife management agencies of needed revenue. There may be other opportunities to eliminate redundant tracking mechanisms, such as the need for both a permit and license from the same agency, through amendments to regulations. At the same time, there may be benefits to tracking redundancy if it gives a more complete view of harvests so as to improve management and increase the data needed to implement an adaptive management scheme. Both federal and state agencies should consider whether the redundancy is beneficial, or whether some requirements for permits, licenses, tags, or after-the-fact reporting could be eliminated with no loss of information.

Given that penalties for failure to obtain the proper permits or license have not always been effective, it may make sense to include some sort of incentive for those who do consistently obtain the proper permissions (i.e., waiver of fees after a certain number of years of compliance).

The state's movement toward electronic reporting may be a step in the right direction, if it provides more flexibility to subsistence participants trying to comply with reporting requirements. It could be helpful for both federal and state agencies to develop a smartphone app that allows participants to photograph harvests and upload information on location, number of animals taken, and so on. The app would need to work when out of cell range and sync to the relevant agency's system once back in cell range. Certainly this suggestion (which could be improved by more knowledgeable people in the relevant agencies) is not traditional. But it is consistent with the modernization of equipment that hunters and fishers have sought in order to adapt (e.g., the use of GPS and weather forecasts as weather becomes more unpredictable). And it could reduce barriers to hunting and fishing associated with a highly bureaucratized system that is difficult for users to understand and comply with.

## Other ANV Actions

Since ANVs' sovereignty over their citizens continues to be recognized (even if jurisdiction over lands is not), ANV councils can pass ordinances governing citizens' subsistence actions. This can be effective in regulating resource access if there is no competition from those outside the community.[105] For example, in 2008, the Tribal Council of Point Lay adopted its own bylaws to protect and manage the traditional community beluga hunts.[106] The bylaws aim to regulate resident hunters, visitors (including visiting hunters, journalists, photographers, and scientists), and aircraft flying near Point Lay during the hunt period.

Other examples include harvest limits placed by the ANVs of Nanwalek and Port Graham on bidarki (a mollusk) and eelgrass. The State of Alaska had no regulations dealing with these resources, so it did not object to the ANV laws.[107] Yet another example was an agreement by people in Unalakleet to stop hunting moose for three years, then ease back into hunting gradually over five years. A resident from Unalakleet who explained the agreement to me said, "The strategy is, don't wait for the state to take action, take it yourself."

ANVs can develop other community-level strategies to support subsistence, such as subsidizing fuel and ammunition, as some ANVs have done, or creating a community space for food processing and storage.

## Conclusion

The combination of climate change, externally imposed rules, and other challenges hinder ANV subsistence lifeways. There is some flexibility at the household level to legally adapt subsistence practices to climate change and other constraints. Adaptations at the community level can be more difficult, given the limited jurisdiction and financial capacity of ANVs. But indigenous people both in and out of ANVs should recognize that the federal and state governments are unlikely to reverse climate change trends. Nor are these governments likely to assemble comprehensive programs to assist communities with adaptation.[108] There is a need to build the capacity to both manage subsistence within the parameters of tribal sovereignty and influence the direction of federal and state rulemaking through Western science and well-documented community knowledge.

Each ANV, and each sovereign indigenous government, is different. As one ANV resident told me, "Some adaptation strategies are going to be shared broadly among villages, but there's quite a bit of local differences that only a local would know about. There's no blanket fix for climate change issues." A solution that an ANV government leads for itself may be more likely to succeed.

While each ANV may be different, there are broader implications for this study. One is the need for the regulated community to have a strong voice in the institutions that design and enforce regulations. Lack of voice can result in disenfranchisement and encourage illegal activity. Another implication is the power of individuals with high adaptive capacity and communities with strong leadership to find ways to adapt within the existing legal institutions, so long as they have the resources to do so. A final implication is that there are inherent inequities in adaptation. Those with more financial resources, education, and political influence may be better able to navigate the complex laws that affect adaptation. Communities that lack adaptive capacity and have no way to build this capacity may be doomed to population decline and, ultimately, extinction.

It is June 2020 as I finish writing this chapter, and I am back in the village of Allakaket. This community, like all others, has suddenly had to adapt to a new challenge on top of climate change: COVID-19. Fortunately for the subsistence lifeway, there is little risk of contagion for families that go out in the open air to hunt and fish as they have for thousands of years. With the relatively higher risk associated with traveling to urban centers for food and supplies and the lack of jobs, residents may depend more heavily on subsistence than they did in previous years. All are watching the Koyukuk River, waiting for it to lower to just the right level, when fishers will once again immerse their nets.

## Notes

1. Patricia Cochran et al., "Indigenous Frameworks for Observing and Responding to Climate Change in Alaska," *Climatic Change* 120, no. 3 (October 2013): 557–67; Davin Holen, "Fishing for Community and Culture: The Value of Fisheries in Rural Alaska," *Northern Fisheries* 50, no. 4 (October 2014): 403–13; Shannon Michele McNeeley, "Seasons out of Balance: Climate Change Impacts, Vulnerability, and Sustainable Adaptation in Interior Alaska" (PhD diss., University of Alaska, Fairbanks, 2009), http://www.cakex.org

/sites/default/files/project/documents/McNeeley_Dissertation_2009.pdf; Philip A. Loring et al., "Ways to Help and Ways to Hinder: Governance for Effective Adaptation to an Uncertain Climate," *Arctic* 64, no. 1 (March 2011): 73–88.

2. Carl J. Markon et al., "Alaska," in *Impacts, Risks, and Adaptation in the United States: Fourth National Climate Assessment*, vol. 2, ed. D. R. Reidmiller et al. (Washington, DC: US Global Change Research Program, 2018), 1185–1241; Intergovernmental Panel on Climate Change, *Climate Change 2014: Impacts, Adaptation, and Vulnerability, Contribution of Working Group II to the Fifth Assessment Report of the Intergovernmental Panel on Climate Change* (Cambridge: Cambridge University Press, 2014).

3. Markon et al., "Alaska"; Shannon M. McNeeley, "Examining Barriers and Opportunities for Sustainable Adaptation to Climate Change in Interior Alaska," *Climatic Change* 111, nos. 3–4 (April 2012): 835–57; Nicole J. Wilson, "The Politics of Adaptation: Subsistence Livelihoods and Vulnerability to Climate Change in the Koyukon Athabascan Village of Ruby, Alaska," *Human Ecology* 42, no. 1 (February 2014): 87–101.

4. Todd J. Brinkman, Winslow D. Hansen, F. Stuart Chapin III, Gary Kofinas, Shauna BurnSilver, and T. Scott Rupp, "Arctic Communities Perceive Climate Impacts on Access as a Critical Challenge to Availability of Subsistence Resources," *Climatic Change* 139, nos. 3–4 (December 2016): 413–27.

5. Markon et al., "Alaska"; McNeeley, "Examining Barriers and Opportunities."

6. Corrine N. Knapp et al., "Parks, People, and Change: The Importance of Multistakeholder Engagement in Adaptation Planning for Conserved Areas," *Ecology and Society* 19, no. 4 (December 2014): 16; Gary P. Kofinas et al., "Resilience of Athabascan Subsistence Systems to Interior Alaska's Changing Climate," *Canadian Journal of Forest Research* 40, no. 7 (July 2010): 1347–59.

7. McNeeley, "Examining Barriers and Opportunities"; N. Kettle, J. Martin, and M. Sloan, *Nome Tribal Climate Adaptation Plan*, Nome Eskimo Community and the Alaska Center for Climate Assessment and Policy, Fairbanks, Alaska, September 2017, https://www.necalaska.org/PDF/6.%20Tribal_Resources/Nome%20Tribal%20Climate%20Adaptation%20Plan%20(Final-LowRes).pdf.

8. E. Barrett Ristroph, "Alaska Tribes' Melting Subsistence Rights," *Arizona Journal of Environmental Law and Policy* 1 (Fall 2010): 47–101.

9. Michael Brubaker et al., "Climate Change in Point Hope, Alaska: Strategies for Community Health," Alaska Native Tribal Health Consortium, 2010, https://www.cidrap.umn.edu/sites/default/files/public/php/26952/Climate%20Change%20HIA%20Report_Point%20Hope_0.pdf.

10. E. Barrett Ristroph, "Addressing Climate Change Vulnerability in Alaska Native Villages through Indigenous Community Knowledge," *Sociology Study* 9, no. 1 (January 2019): 1–19.

11. Ristroph, "Addressing Climate Change Vulnerability."

12. Ristroph, "Alaska Tribes' Melting Subsistence Rights."

13. E. Barrett Ristroph, "Still Melting: How Climate Change and Subsistence Laws Constrain Alaska Native Village Adaptation," *University of Colorado Natural Resources, Energy, and Environmental Law Review* 30, no. 2 (2019): 245–86.

14. Alaska Stat. § 16.05.940 (33).

15. Ristroph, "Alaska Tribes' Melting Subsistence Rights."

16. Mark Nuttall et al., "Hunting, Herding, Fishing and Gathering: Indigenous Peoples and Renewable Resource Use in the Arctic," in *Arctic Climate Impact Assessment* (Cambridge: Cambridge University Press, 2005), 649–90; Holen, "Fishing for Community and Culture."

17. Linda O. Smiddy, "Responding to Professor Janda—the U.S. Experience: The Alaska Native Claims Settlement Act (ANCSA) Regional Corporation as a Form of Social Enterprise," *Vermont Law Review* 30 (2006): 823–54; Sophie Theriault et al., "The Legal Protection of Subsistence: A Prerequisite of Food Security for the Inuit of Alaska," *Alaska Law Review* 22, no. 1 (June 2005): 35.

18. Shauna BurnSilver et al., "Are Mixed Economies Persistent or Transitional? Evidence Using Social Networks from Arctic Alaska," *American Anthropologist* 118, no. 1 (March 2016): 121–29, https://doi.org/10.1111/aman.12447.

19. Ristroph, "Alaska Tribes' Melting Subsistence Rights."

20. Alaska Division of Community and Regional Affairs (DCRA), DCRA Information Portal, Utqiagvik, Alaska, 2018, https://dcced.maps.arcgis .com/apps/MapJournal/index.html?appid=2393d4e4452448c4a55af959a3 c7c817#; Alaska Department of Fish and Game, "Harvest Information for Community," Barrow, 2014, http://www.adfg.alaska.gov/sb/CSIS/index.cfm ?ADFG=harvInfo.harvest.

21. Alaska Department of Fish and Game, "Harvest Information for Community," Allakaket, 2011, http://www.adfg.alaska.gov/sb/CSIS/index.cfm?ADFG =harvInfo.harvest.

22. Ristroph, "Alaska Tribes' Melting Subsistence Rights"; Brubaker et al., "Climate Change in Point Hope, Alaska."

23. T. M. Bull Bennett et al., "Indigenous Peoples, Lands, and Resources," in *Climate Change Impacts in the United States: The Third National Climate Assessment* (Washington, DC: US Global Change Research Program, 2014), 297–317; E. Barrett Ristroph, "Integrating Community Knowledge into

Environmental and Natural Resource Decision-Making: Notes from Alaska and Around the World," *Washington and Lee Journal of Energy, Climate, and the Environment* 3, no. 1 (2012): 81–132.

24. Ristroph, "Still Melting."

25. Don E. Dumond, "A Chronology of Native Alaskan Subsistence Systems," *Senri Ethnological Studies* 4 (1980): 23–47.

26. S. J. Langdon, "Increments, Ranges and Thresholds: Human Population Responses to Climate Change in Northern Alaska," in *Human Ecology and Climate Change: People and Resources in the Far North*, ed. David L. Peterson and Darryll R. Johnson (Washington, DC: Taylor and Francis, 1995); Robin Bronen, *Climate-Induced Displacement of Alaska Native Communities* (Washington, DC: Brookings Institution, 2013), http://www.Brookings.Edu /Research/Papers/2013/01/30-Arctic-Alaska-Bronen.

27. Langdon, "Increments, Ranges and Thresholds."

28. C. S. Holling, Fikret Berkes, and Carl Folke, "Science, Sustainability and Resource Management," in *Linking Social and Ecological Systems: Management Practices and Social Mechanisms for Building Resilience*, ed. Fikret Berkes, Carl Folke, and Johan Colding (Cambridge: Cambridge University Press, 1998), 342–62.

29. Langdon, "Increments, Ranges and Thresholds"; Dumond, "A Chronology of Native Alaskan Subsistence Systems"; C. Osgood, *Contributions to the Ethnography of the Kutchin* (New Haven, CT: Yale University Press, 1936).

30. Langdon, "Increments, Ranges and Thresholds"; Elizabeth Marino, "The Long History of Environmental Migration: Assessing Vulnerability Construction and Obstacles to Successful Relocation in Shishmaref, Alaska," *Global Environmental Change* 22, no. 2 (May 2012): 374–81; Bronen, *Climate-Induced Displacement.*

31. Annette McFadyen Clark, *Koyokuk River Culture: National Museum of Man* (Ottawa: National Museums of Canada, 1974); Erin Carey, "Building Resilience to Climate Change in Rural Alaska: Understanding Impacts, Adaptation, and the Role of TEK" (master's thesis, University of Michigan, 2009).

32. Carey, "Building Resilience"; Ristroph, "Still Melting"; Kenneth L. Pratt, Joan C. Stevenson, and Phillip M. Everson, "Demographic Adversities and Indigenous Resilience in Western Alaska," *Études/Inuit/Studies* 37, no. 1 (2013): 35; Jon Rosales and Jessica Chapman, "Perceptions of Obvious and Disruptive Climate Change: Community-Based Risk Assessment for Two Native Villages in Alaska," *Climate* 3, no. 4 (December 2015): 812–32; McNeeley, "Seasons out of Balance"; Fikret Berkes and Dyanna Jolly, "Adapting to Climate Change: Social-Ecological Resilience in a Canadian Western Arctic Community," *Conservation Ecology* 5, no. 2 (January 2002): 18.

33. Ristroph, "Still Melting."
34. Ristroph, "Still Melting."
35. Ristroph, "Addressing Climate Change Vulnerability."
36. Ristroph, "Alaska Tribes' Melting Subsistence Rights."
37. Kettle, Martin, and Sloan, *Nome Tribal Climate Adaptation Plan.*
38. Ristroph, "Still Melting."
39. Ristroph, "Still Melting."
40. Marino, "The Long History of Environmental Migration"; Ristroph, "Alaska Tribes' Melting Subsistence Rights."
41. Ristroph, "Addressing Climate Change Vulnerability."
42. Ristroph, "Alaska Tribes' Melting Subsistence Rights"; Alaska Stat. § 16.05.258(c).
43. Pat Forgey, "Natives Losing Political Influence," *Juneau Empire*, March 24, 2010, http://juneauempire.com/stories/032410/sta_595649976.shtml.
44. Ristroph, "Alaska Tribes' Melting Subsistence Rights."
45. Ristroph, "Alaska Tribes' Melting Subsistence Rights."
46. 43 U.S.C. § 1603(b).
47. 16 U.S.C. § 3101 et seq.
48. 16 U.S.C. § 3114.
49. 36 C.F.R. § 242.15.
50. John Sky Starkey, "Protection of Alaska Native Customary and Traditional Hunting and Fishing Rights through Title VIII of ANILCA (Alaska National Interest Lands Conservation Act)," *Alaska Law Review* 33, no. 2 (2016): 315; Robert T. Anderson, "Sovereignty and Subsistence: Native Self-Government and Rights to Hunt, Fish, and Gather after ANCSA (Special Issue on the Forty-Fifth Anniversary of the Alaska Native Claims Settlement Act)," *Alaska Law Review* 33, no. 2 (2016): 187.
51. Clive S. Thomas, Laura Savatgy, and Kristina Klimovich, eds., *Alaska Politics and Public Policy: The Dynamics of Beliefs, Institutions, Personalities, and Power* (Fairbanks: University of Alaska Press, 2016).
52. E. Barrett Ristroph, "Strategies for Strengthening Alaska Native Village Roles in Natural Resource Management," *Willamette Environmental Law Journal* 4 (Spring 2016): 57–124; 16 U.S.C. § 1388, 3119; 25 U.S.C. §§ 5361–5638.
53. Ristroph, "Still Melting"; Laurie Richmond, "Incorporating Indigenous Rights and Environmental Justice into Fishery Management: Comparing Policy Challenges and Potentials from Alaska and Hawai'i," *Environmental Management* 52, no. 5 (November 2013): 1071–84.
54. 16 U.S.C. § 3115(d).

55. Ch. 151, Alaska Session Laws 1978; Alaska Stat. § 16.05.90 (1986).

56. *McDowell v. State*, 785 P.2d 1, 9 (Alaska 1989).

57. See, e.g., Alaska Admin. Code tit. 5 §§ 39.002, 92.002, 92.049, 92.050(a)(8), 92.072(f); 36 C.F.R. §§ 242.25(h)(5), 242.8; 50 C.F.R. §§ 100.25(h)(5), 100.8.

58. Starkey, "Hunting and Fishing Rights"; Ristroph, "Still Melting."

59. Philip H. Jos and Annette Watson, "Privileging Knowledge Claims in Collaborative Regulatory Management: An Ethnography of Marginalizaton," *Administration & Society* 51, no. 3 (2016) 13; Ristroph, "Still Melting."

60. Ristroph, "Integrating Community Knowledge."

61. Robert L. Fischman and Jillian R. Rountree, "Adaptive Management," in *The Law of Adaptation to Climate Change: U.S. and International Aspects*, ed. Michael Gerrard and Katrina Fischer Kuh (Chicago: American Bar Association, Section of Environment, Energy, and Resources, 2012), 19–47; F. Stuart Chapin III, Carl Folke, and Gary P. Kofinas, "A Framework for Understanding Change," in *Principles of Ecosystem Stewardship: Resilience-Based Natural Resource Management in a Changing World*, ed. F. Stuart Chapin III, Gary P. Kofinas, and Carl Folke (New York: Springer, 2009), 3–28; Robin Kundis Craig, "'Stationarity Is Dead'—Long Live Transformation: Five Principles for Climate Change Adaptation Law," *Harvard Environmental Law Review* 34, no. 1 (2010): 9–75.

62. Pratt, Stevenson, and Everson, "Demographic Adversities and Indigenous Resilience."

63. Ristroph, "Alaska Tribes' Melting Subsistence Rights"; McNeeley, "Examining Barriers and Opportunities."

64. Alaska Stat. § 44.62.230; 36 C.F.R. § 36.19(a); 50 C.F.R. § 100.19(a).

65. Loring et al., "Ways to Help and Ways to Hinder."

66. Alaska Admin. Code tit. 5 § 96.615(c).

67. McNeeley, "Examining Barriers and Opportunities"; Ristroph, "Still Melting."

68. Theriault et al., "The Legal Protection of Subsistence"; Ristroph, "Still Melting."

69. E.g., 36 C.F.R. § 242.6/50 C.F.R. § 100.6; Alaska Admin. Code tit. 5, Art. 2.

70. Kofinas et al., "Resilience of Athabascan Subsistence Systems"; McNeeley, "Seasons out of Balance"; Melanie B. Jacobs and Jeffery J. Brooks, "Alaska Native Peoples and Conservation Planning: A Recipe for Meaningful Participation," *Native Studies Review* 20, no. 2 (2011): 91–135.

71. E.g., Alaska Admin. Code tit. 5 § 92.050(a)(8); 36 C.F.R. §242.25(h)(5)/ 50 C.F.R. § 100.25(h)(5).

72. Ristroph, "Still Melting."

73. Kofinas et al., "Resilience of Athabascan Subsistence Systems."

74. 16 U.S.C. § 718a(a)(2)(D).

75. AS 16.05.340(a)(17); Alaska Admin. Code tit. 5 § 92.018.

76. E.g., Alaska Admin. Code tit. 5 §§ 92.017, 92.053, 92.055.

77. Alaska Admin. Code tit. 5 § 92.010.

78. BurnSilver et al., "Are Mixed Economies Persistent or Transitional?"; Mouhcine Guettabi et al., "Evaluating Differences in Household Subsistence Harvest Patterns between the Ambler Project and Non-Project Zones," Natural Resource Report NPS/GAAR/NRR—2016/1280, National Park Service, Fort Collins, Colorado, 2016.

79. E.g., Alaska Admin. Code tit. 5 § 92.130.

80. 36 C.F.R. § 242.27(a)/50 C.F.R. § 100.27(a).

81. E.g., Alaska Stat. § 16.05.405(b); Alaska Admin. Code tit. 5, § 92.011(a), (d); 36 C.F.R. § 242.25(a)/50 C.F.R. § 100.25(a).

82. Susan Solomon et al., "Irreversible Climate Change Due to Carbon Dioxide Emissions," *Proceedings of the National Academy of Sciences* 106, no. 6 (February 10, 2009): 1704–9; Thomas L. Frolicher and Fortunat Joos, "Reversible and Irreversible Impacts of Greenhouse Gas Emissions in Multi-Century Projections with the NCAR Global Coupled Carbon Cycle-Climate Model," *Climate Dynamics* 35, nos. 7–8 (December 2010): 1439–59.

83. E. Barrett Ristroph, "Fulfilling Climate Justice and Government Obligations to Alaska Native Villages: What Is the Government Role?," *William & Mary Environmental Law and Policy Review* 43, no. 2 (2019): 501–39.

84. Ristroph, "Addressing Climate Change Vulnerability."

85. Alaska Department of Fish and Game (ADFG), *Hunting Maps by Hunt Type, Search Results for Tier II Hunts*, http://www.adfg.alaska.gov/index.cfm?adfg=huntingmaps.byhunttype.

86. 42 U.S.C. § 4331; Ristroph, "Strategies for Strengthening Alaska Native Village Roles."

87. Ristroph, "Still Melting."

88. National Oceanic and Atmospheric Administration (NOAA), Subsistence Taking of Northern Fur Seals, 84 Fed. Reg. 52372 (Oct. 2, 2019); 50 C.F.R. Part 216.

89. Exec. Order No. 13175.

90. Ristroph, "Still Melting."

91. McNeeley, "Examining Barriers and Opportunities"; F. Stuart Chapin III and Patricia Cochran, "Community Partnership for Self Reliance and Sustainability, Final Report to Communities from the Alaska Native Science Commission and the University of Alaska Fairbanks" (working paper, 2014).

92. NOAA, Cooperative Agreement between the National Oceanic and Atmospheric Administration and the Alaska Eskimo Whaling Commission (2013), https://www.fisheries.noaa.gov/webdam/download/64417380.

93. Alaska Eskimo Whaling Commission, Bowhead Harvest Quota, http://www.aewc-alaska.com/bowhead-quota.html.

94. Cochran et al., "Indigenous Frameworks."

95. 16 U.S.C. § 1855 (i)(2)(B)(iii); Loring et al., "Ways to Help and Ways to Hinder"; Richmond, "Incorporating Indigenous Rights."

96. Loring et al., "Ways to Help and Ways to Hinder."

97. 50 C.F.R. § 300.65 (i).

98. Alaska Admin. Code tit. 5 § 92.072.

99. Ristroph, "Still Melting."

100. E.g., Alaska Stat. § 16.05.405(b).

101. McNeeley, "Seasons out of Balance."

102. Ristroph, "Still Melting."

103. Alaska Department of Natural Resources, "Fact Sheet, Off-Road Travel on the North Slope on State Land," 2015, http://dnr.alaska.gov/mlw/factsht/land_fs/off-road_travel.pdf.

104. Elinor Ostrom, *Understanding Institutional Diversity* (Princeton, NJ: Princeton University Press, 2005); Evelyn Pinkerton, "Coastal Marine Systems: Conserving Fish and Sustaining Community Livelihoods with Co-Management," in *Principles of Ecosystem Stewardship: Resilience-Based Natural Resource Management in a Changing World*, ed. F. Stuart Chapin III, Carl Folke, and Gary P. Kofinas (New York: Springer, 2009), 241–57; Chapin et al., "A Framework for Understanding Change."

105. Ostrom, *Understanding Institutional Diversity*.

106. Point Lay Native Village, Bylaws for the Traditional Beluga Hunt by the Tribal Village of Point Lay, June 27, 2008.

107. Ristroph, "Still Melting."

108. Ristroph, "Fulfilling Climate Justice."

# 6

# Improving Price Discovery to Accelerate Adaptation to Climate Change

Gregory W. Characklis, Benjamin T. Foster,
and Matthew E. Kahn

Variation in weather conditions imposes financial and economic costs on individuals, firms, and governments.[1] Extreme events are particularly costly, with droughts, floods, extreme temperatures, and violent storms causing global losses of nearly $500 billion per year.[2] Climate scientists posit, and an increasing amount of data suggests, that rising greenhouse gas levels are changing the incidence, spatial distribution, and severity of these events, raising costs and driving demand for actions that will limit these losses.[3] These actions often fall into two general categories: mitigation designed to reduce the emissions (primarily carbon dioxide) that drive climate change, and adaptation to limit the effects of climate

The authors are grateful to Terry Anderson and Andrew Hamilton, who contributed thoughtful comments and suggestions that improved this work greatly. This paper also benefited from discussion at the Financial Risk in Environmental Systems: Efficient and Sustainable Adaptation in the Face of Global Change Conference held by the Hoover Institution in May 2019 and with members of the Center on Financial Risk in Environmental Systems at the University of North Carolina at Chapel Hill.

change. Both types will ultimately be required, but the relative role that each should play is the subject of debate.

Currently, the United Nations Environment Programme estimates that in 2017–18 global expenditures on mitigation were roughly $570 billion, while funding for adaptation, which is mostly public, came in at only $30 billion.[4] Meanwhile, the Global Commission on Adaptation estimates that the payoff for adaptation could be substantial, with a global investment of $1.8 trillion over the period 2020–30 yielding $7.1 trillion in net benefits.[5] Accelerating adaptation is important, because regulatory efforts at mitigation are economically and politically challenging, any transition to a carbon-free energy system will take time, and we are locked into an existing durable capital stock, such as vehicle fleets, power plants, and buildings that will contribute to the future flow of greenhouse gas emissions. Finally, because much of the greenhouse gas already emitted is likely to remain in the atmosphere for many years, increasing the rate of adaptation will allow for a more efficient response to the near- and medium-term effects of climate change and provide time to mitigate carbon emissions.[6]

Framing the problem in economic terms, mitigation and adaptation strategies must be utilized in an efficient combination that will require complex coordination. Market forces, and by extension the use of prices to influence choices, will be a critical part of this endeavor, but the information and institutions that would allow for the development of both are currently inadequate.

Nonetheless, the information and the institutions to disseminate it have begun to evolve. Concerns over climate risk have led to an explosion of entrepreneurial activity related to providing information that better describes the increased vulnerability of many activities to weather-related losses.[7] An expanding array of financial tools and markets, such as catastrophe bonds and parametric insurance, can transfer or share the risks of extreme events among different parties. Furthermore, an increasing number of institutional agents are working to improve methods to more fully incorporate climate-related risks into decisions related to lending and investing (e.g., credit rating agencies and institutional investors).[8] Finally, there is a growing push to phase out subsidies for risky behavior (government crop and flood insurance programs, for example), such that individual decision makers more accurately experience the costs and benefits of their actions. While all of this will hasten the process of price discovery as related to climate change adaptation, much more is needed.

## Background

Both mitigation and adaptation are motivated by the risk of losses, which are the product of the hazard and its consequences, for example the financial losses resulting from more frequent and severe storms. Wolfgang Kron describes the consequences as the product of values exposed to the hazard and their vulnerability to damage from the hazard.[9] While scientists focus primarily on characterizing the hazard, engineers and economists work to develop solutions for reducing the consequences, especially via adaptation.

Building a sea wall, moving houses to higher ground, and developing a new insurance product are all potential adaptive actions, but how can markets or governments produce the right amount of each, particularly when actions are taken by both individuals and groups of individuals? When adaptation actions are taken by individuals especially, it is crucial that prices, for both assets and risk, reflect the values of each. Typically, prices provide information to the individual property owner that should encourage adaptation that increases asset values. In some cases, the adaptation will be a physical resilience investment for reducing the expected economic loss suffered from climate shocks. In others it will be nonphysical risk management that transfers risky outcomes to parties better able to withstand them. These measures that pool or reduce risk via contracts such as insurance, however, are less than perfect as a result of insurance price regulations, subsidies, and government catastrophe payments. Removing impediments to risk pricing contracts allows parties willing to accept more risk to absorb it, thereby lowering the financial cost when damages occur. Risk prices should also help groups of individuals make better collective decisions around physical resilience investments.

Dating back at least to Friedrich Hayek, economists have recognized the key information embedded in market prices.[10] High prices signal scarcity, and this encourages behavioral change and innovation. Identifying the "correct" price for assets and risk requires that market participants have accurate information with respect to the costs and benefits that will accrue to them as a result of their choices. When it comes to the effects of climate change—particularly those occurring well into the future—uncertainty in estimating the costs and benefits of adaptation can be particularly vexing.

Without improved information on climate change, neither consumers' demand for adaptation nor producers' willingness to supply it will be well substantiated. Data that will inform decisions will evolve as climate change progresses, as will the institutions that translate and communicate this information to individuals and firms. This chapter focuses on the challenges to and opportunities for improving price discovery related to climate change adaptation.

## Theory

Despite the fact that there are millions of markets in our modern economy, there remain many missing markets. Missing markets limit the ability of people to transact and generate prices. This is particularly true for risk markets.

Kenneth Arrow, a corecipient of the 1972 Nobel Prize for economics, conceived of a system of risk sharing such that there are complete markets. In an economy featuring complete markets, one can purchase securities that offer a payoff at every date and in every "state of the world." For example, a person who wants to be able to receive $400 in the year 2032 if a major pandemic occurs would be able to purchase this asset, the price of which would be dependent on different perceptions of the probability that a pandemic will occur. If there are sufficient parties interested in arbitraging this risk, a market will evolve in which the risk will be transferred to the agent able to manage risk at the lowest cost.

Markets for sharing risk effectively separate exposure from the productivity of assets. For example, in the case of vulnerability to fire, an insurer takes on the fire risk while the property owner manages the property. Unlike fire risk, for which there is much more information about the causes and consequences, the risks of climate change are less well known. For a climate risk market to evolve, many points of information must be better known: the relationship between climate change and asset values, the relationship between the actions of asset owners and asset risk due to climate change, and the costs of developing contracts delineating risk sharing obligations between asset owners and risk bearers, to mention a few.

One cause and consequence of the incomplete risk-transfer markets is the involvement of public institutions in the backing and mitigation of risk, such as public flood mitigation infrastructure and provision of flood insurance. Arrow recognized that moving risk management out of markets would lead to less-efficient management: "What we observe is that the failure of the price system to handle risk-bearing adequately leads to a diminished use of prices even in contexts where they would be most useful in bringing about a careful and flexible confrontation of needs and resources."[11]

To understand how risk markets develop, start with Arrow's complete risk market, whose mechanics might be described thus: risky outcomes are supplied to the market by the owner of a risky asset and are acquired by an agent who has a comparative advantage in managing that particular risk. Although Arrow notes that transacted risks are neither a material good nor a service, he never fully resolves why some risks are transacted, while others are not, and who has the comparative advantage in managing them. The answers to those questions come from Yoram Barzel in his *Economic Analysis of Property Rights*. Barzel conceives of risks as the attributes of an asset's value that are not captured in its physical characteristics. For example, a beach house is valuable because of its structure, view, and access to the beach but is less valuable due to weather risks such as tidal flooding and hurricane winds. Barzel refers to these external risk attributes of assets as "risk residuals."[12]

To illustrate the power of this insight, Barzel discusses the fire-risk attribute of a building. In his example, the building owner purchases an insurance contract that transfers the building's fire-risk attribute to an insurer. The transaction occurs because the fire-risk attribute of a building can be well defined and the insurer is a more efficient holder of the risk than the building owner. The insurer has both the expertise and the resources to minimize the expected loss from fire. She also faces lower financial costs of losses because she holds a larger and more diversified balance sheet relative to the individual building owner.

Of course, the building owner typically faces a deductible on his insurance policy. The deductible ensures that the building owner retains a small portion of the fire risk, a contractual clause typically justified because, fully insured, he could have an incentive to engage in activity that increases fire risk—a moral hazard problem. Barzel explains the presence of a deductible in different terms: "Both parties . . . contribute to the mean effect of fire hazard, and both are expected to bear some of the effect."[13] In other words, a deductible is simply a mechanism for splitting the fire-risk attribute such that the building owner retains a portion commensurate with his influence over expected losses. The building owner can take many low-cost actions to reduce the incidence of fire, such as turning off the oven, or the costs if one should occur, such as replacing batteries in smoke alarms so inhabitants are notified quickly, and he is therefore the most efficient owner of that portion of the risk attribute.

Combining Barzel's property rights framework with Arrow's conception of an ideal risk allocation process generates a rich model for understanding how climate change risk might be transferred. We identify three conditions that are important determinants of where, when, and how risk residuals are transferred.

1. The barbed-wire condition. The risk to be transferred is well defined. If the risk is not clearly defined, ownership will also be unclear, thus complicating its transfer. This condition is named for the role barbed wire played in defining land ownership in the American West.[14]
2. The efficiency condition. There is a more efficient holder of the risk residual. This would be a risk holder with a comparative advantage in management or mitigation. An example is a reinsurer who has a large diversified balance sheet enabling him to absorb certain risky outcomes at lowest cost. This efficient risk bearer could also be a government that can invest in public infrastructure that mitigates risk and lowers risk exposure over a large population.
3. The bargaining condition. Transaction costs are low enough to facilitate bargaining and trade.

These conditions provide a useful framework for analyzing the ways new information, innovation, policy, and market shocks affect the evolution of risk markets so as to move closer to Arrow's complete risk market world. They also help explain the role asset prices play in mitigating, managing, and adapting to risks related to climate change.

Ideally, government rules strengthen the price system through a commitment to the rule of law and help price discovery by transmitting information, providing key public goods such as satellites, and funding basic research. Conversely, government place-based policies play spatial favorites by subsidizing insurance in flood- and wildfire-prone areas, thus discouraging the private sector from researching and pricing useful insurance products. Such increasingly costly subsidies must eventually lead to higher taxes, and this distorts capital market and labor market decisions.

To provide a preview of how information, incentives, and risk markets can come together to produce enhanced adaptation, consider coastal real estate that faces elevated flood risk from a combination of sea level rise and the increased frequency of extreme storms. In this setting, information represents the emerging climate science predictions concerning changes in both of these environmental processes, but this information alone is not enough. This information needs to be translated into prices, such as higher mortgage rates that reflect increased flood risk, which will, in turn, incentivize the real estate owner to adapt, perhaps by elevating the structure to reduce risk. Physical adaptation can also be combined with products from risk markets, including traditional indemnity insurance, parametric insurance, weather derivatives, and catastrophe bonds. The starting point for this chain of events is, however, accurate information.

## Supply and Demand for Information and Price Discovery

Market prices signal scarcity. In the case of climate change, scarcity arises as a result of limited capacity to reduce climate change and its effects, whether this capacity comes in the form of mitigation or adaptation. While more extreme arguments have been made in favor of near sole reliance on approaches in one area or the other, it seems clear that combating climate change will require a mix of both: a combination of mitigation activities that reduce the probability of large-scale environmental disruption (and related human impacts) and adaptation activities that take full advantage of human ingenuity to reduce short-term effects and bridge the gap to a less carbon-intensive economy. This integrated approach is likely to provide the most practical and efficacious path to a climate change strategy.

Early recognition of emerging spatial climate patterns and their subsequent impacts on weather will play a key role in helping us to understand how to build up an economy's adaptive capacity. If a new spatial pattern is recognized, such as an increased frequency of severe drought, this new information will be noted and disseminated through the modern information technology infrastructure (e.g., Google, Twitter, Facebook). Prices will adjust as buyers and sellers react to this new information.

Consider the example of a coastal property facing increased flood risk. All other conditions remaining static, as flood risk increases, the price of the property will likely be affected by a number of risk-related factors, including the price of flood insurance, the mortgage interest rate assigned to the property, and perhaps even the price of the mortgage-backed security containing that property.[15] Thus, in this case, an efficient outcome requires not only the new information generated by scientists and engineers on both flood hazard (i.e., the frequency and severity of flooding) and flood consequence (i.e., losses), but also new or modified institutions capable of translating increased flood risk into market prices for property, mortgages, and securitization—the purview of economists.

Returning to Kenneth Arrow's complete markets paradigm, the case of real estate facing increased flood risk highlights the *incompleteness* of existing markets. There are no available contingent securities that offer a payoff if a change in flood risk occurs. Instead, a lender holding the mortgage on the home likely experiences an increased probability of default, just as a homeowner who has paid off her mortgage would be exposed to all of this risk. In the case of the latter, if there is new information that a home faces greater flood risk in the near future, the future rental income stream of this asset declines, and the home's price—which reflects the present discounted value of this expected cash flow—is reduced.

There are several reasons why real estate prices may not reflect the full emerging risk.[16] For one, the risk may be fully or partially unknown. In the context of our motivating example, we know it is not trivial to accurately assess flood risk at the property level, especially a decade or more in the future. Flood insurance instruments might incorporate information on flood risk, but flood insurance is dominated by the federally backed National Flood Insurance Program (NFIP). The NFIP premiums are both subsidized (in certain circumstances) and a function of flood hazard maps that are often incomplete and infrequently updated to account for changes in land use or climate that can significantly affect flood risk.[17] Further, insurance is only required if a property has a federally backed mortgage and is within the hundred-year floodplain. This depends on a FEMA-calculated 1-in-100 chance of flooding in any given year, a calculation that is based on an arbitrary threshold that may not represent true risk. This is an information problem.

Even if a risk is accurately assessed, the institutional mechanisms for translating this risk into a risk price, and thus providing the appropriate incentives to react, may be flawed. We know that premiums as calculated by the NFIP do not represent true risk.[18] There is some evidence that flood risk is capitalized into property values, though the effect can be difficult to distinguish from other contributors to property value.[19] Ideally flood risk would be separated from the property, allowing the risk to be priced independently. In practice flood risk is rarely considered in determining mortgage rates, much less in the pricing of mortgage-backed securities.[20] Recent concerns over climate risk have motivated increased scrutiny of flooding (and related risks) by credit rating agencies and investors, a trend that suggests that these risks are slowly becoming monetized in a manner that will facilitate a move toward price discovery.[21]

If this risk information is not available, potential buyers of assets will pursue purchasing those assets, whose other attributes (such as coastal beauty) are so attractive. Behavioral economic research suggests that there are many such investors.[22] If this is the case, then market price signals transmitted by insurance rates and interest rates are even more important for sending signals to these investors to consider the full consequences of the investment opportunity. There is a small but increasing number of markets in which climate risk is playing a growing role, such that price signals will begin to communicate risk to buyers in the form of lower property values, higher mortgage rates, and increased insurance premiums for at-risk assets.

The demand for climate information creates a profit opportunity for suppliers to deliver quality information, but such private-sector efforts often piggyback on government public goods. The government's monitoring networks (e.g., satellites, streamflow gauges) and its financing of data collection and research provide key ingredients for private entities to process, organize, and disseminate relevant information to buyers and sellers. In some cases, the information is in a raw form (e.g., probabilities of extreme drought or flood, temperatures, wind speeds), while in others it is transformed into outcomes that can be directly incorporated into decisions, such as credit ratings provided to lenders and investors by organizations such as Moody's and Standard and Poor's. This information is increasingly being provided in the private sector by firms such as Jupiter and Four Twenty Seven, but the process of making the information actionable is in the nascent stages of development, and we anticipate that a new industry of climate ratings will be introduced.

There has been a recent push from both the private and non-profit sectors to improve parcel-level assessments of both current and future flood risk. One nonprofit, the First Street Foundation, through its Flood Lab program, has pulled together industry-leading models and information to assess current and future flood risk for every property parcel in the United States. The goal is for this information to spur a recognition of flood risk that can be incorporated into decisions related to property value, the purchase of flood insurance, setting of mortgage rates, and others, all of which will facilitate greater price discovery. Ultimately, more organizations (nonprofit and for-profit) with goals similar to First Street's will be needed to characterize risks related to extremes in hydrology, temperature, wind speed, and other weather-related phenomena affected by climate change, with these groups focused on collecting, storing, modeling, and analyzing data that reflect conditions in both natural and human systems.

The emergence of such organizations is becoming a reality in the era of big data. Advances in data-storage technologies and innovations in instrumentation that enable remote sensing (e.g., satellites, drones) of climate and weather conditions have lowered the cost of collecting vast amounts of information. These advances have been leveraged to unlock a wealth of data related to the state of the environment. For example, a NASA-funded program called Air Quality Citizen Science is using low-cost sensors dispersed to everyday people to improve air quality monitoring, and low-cost drones have enabled farmers to monitor field conditions (e.g., moisture, crop growth) at the millimeter scale, allowing them to more efficiently use resources like water and fertilizer.

The existence of data alone is not sufficient, however, to improve information about specific environmental risks. These data have to be connected, interpreted, and translated into a meaningful form. The first approach to understanding these linkages is often statistical. Machine-learning techniques have improved these analyses, enabling us to find and characterize statistical relationships across many variables. Overreliance on statistical correlations based on past conditions, however, can lead to overconfidence about the strength of those relationships in the future. This is particularly problematic when we expect the future to look different from the past, as we do for many environmental financial risks in the face of climate change.

A systems-based approach, on the other hand, offers a number of advantages, as it uses both big-data techniques and a structured understanding of the relationships between linked natural-engineered-economic systems that collectively give rise to financial risks. For example, characterizing the risk of drought-related financial losses for a hydropower generator requires understanding the probability of low streamflow as well as the consequences of both the reduced hydropower generation (engineered system) and the market price of the forgone electricity (economic system).[23] A systems-based understanding of this risk and the relationships that underlie it allows for accurate assessments of financial risk to the hydropower producer even if one or more of the inputs change.[24] This type of integrated analysis supports a better understanding of risk by those exposed as well as innovation of tools and strategies for managing that risk.[25]

## Incentives Induced by Information and Price Dynamics

Creation of risk markets will depend on the degree of risk exposure and of risk management options. Economic actors who believe they are confronted with climate risk will be more proactive in seeking solutions to reduce their risk exposure. Imagine if insurance prices, interest rates, and real estate prices reflected up-to-date climate risk information. Price information in insurance and mortgage contracts would provide incentives for adaptation and heighten the demand for local infrastructure investments. The net effect of these actions would be fewer exposed real estate assets, leading to higher resale values, lower mortgage rates, and reduced insurance premiums. This dynamic requires up-to-date climate risk information.

An increasing amount of data and research describes the current and future effects of climate change and is being combined with a nascent but improving ability to adapt based on this information.[26]

Insurers and reinsurers have a direct, obvious financial interest in quantifying climate risk because improved information leads to more accurate risk pricing, as well as the potential to develop new risk management products.[27] In an open letter to CEOs in 2020, Larry Fink, the chairman of BlackRock (the world's largest asset manager, with over $7 trillion under management), wrote, "The evidence on climate risk is compelling investors to reassess core assumptions about modern finance." He explained that climate change is the top concern investors raise with BlackRock and concluded, "In the near future—and sooner than most anticipate—there will be a significant reallocation of capital."[28]

Similar concern over climate risk has been voiced by institutional investors, including the California Public Employees' Retirement System (CalPERS), the largest public fund manager in the United States, with roughly $380 billion in assets under management. In December 2019, CalPERS issued a report on climate change estimating 20 percent of its investment portfolio to be subject to physical or transition-related climate change risks.[29] In both cases, investors consistently describe the need for more actionable information on current climate risks, as well as the importance of reducing uncertainty over future projections. Both investors and insurers are increasingly pushing organizations to become more transparent in evaluating and communicating their financial vulnerability to climate risks.

Credit rating agencies, such as Moody's and Standard and Poor's, are rising to the occasion by discovering and producing data relevant to climate risks. By quantifying climate change risks, these agencies are incorporating such risks into creditworthiness. Here are three examples of investments where these data are being used in financial analyses:

- Irrigation districts, which provide the infrastructure to deliver water to member farmers in many regions around the country, experience considerable reductions in their revenue stream when drought reduces water deliveries and the fees that come with them, thus jeopardizing their ability to service their debt.[30]

- Power utilities represent a similarly capital-intensive sector, with those having significant hydropower capacity experiencing a significant decline in revenues during drought, a risk that is exacerbated if they have firm power delivery contracts that necessitate their purchasing additional (more expensive) power from external sources to fulfill these obligations.[31] The Bonneville Power Administration (BPA), for example, uses hydropower to supply most of the Pacific Northwest with electricity. It recently had its credit rating downgraded, largely as a result of concerns over increased hydrologic variability and the company's inability to manage the financial implications, with the resulting increase in interest rates projected to cost BPA hundreds of millions over the coming years.[32]

- Urban water utilities are another infrastructure-intensive sector that borrows heavily from the bond market. The expectation has historically been that predictable consumer demand and hydrologic patterns lead to revenues that will be sufficiently stable to ensure high confidence in debt service (and thus higher credit ratings and lower interest rates). Similar to irrigation districts, these utilities suffer significant revenue reductions (and sometimes cost increases) during drought. The increased incidence of dry periods, as well as greater reliance on conservation to combat it, have led credit rating agencies to put these utilities on notice that their exposure to hydrologic (i.e., climate) risk will be an important criterion going forward.[33]

The public sector could also play a role in providing improved incentives for adaptation, but that would require changing policies that reduce the incentive of private actors to invest in adaptation. Prime examples include insurance subsidies for wildfire and flood risk. The federal government's National Flood Insurance Program offers subsidized insurance for communities that comply with

FEMA's rules, thus attracting more people to move to flood-prone areas and increasing the deficit of the NFIP.[34] Similarly, the federal government's provision of wildfire-fighting services reduces the risk of building in high hazard zones of the American West.[35]

The US government is also actively involved in providing backstop finances for mortgage lending through government-sponsored enterprises such as Fannie Mae and Freddie Mac, with these GSEs in turn assuming some portion of the risk of default on the mortgages.[36] Amine Ouazad and Matthew Kahn document that lenders issue more loans that meet the specifications required by the GSEs in the immediate aftermath of major natural disasters.[37] Such loans have reduced the bank's incentive to conduct detailed research on whether a home buyer seeking a loan for a location subject to climate risk is more likely to default.

Large-scale infrastructure projects by the US Army Corps of Engineers and the Bureau of Reclamation also partially shield investors from climate risk. The question is whether large-scale infrastructure to protect against climate change risk crowds out more individualized adaptation measures. In certain dimensions, public investment in adaptation represents a substitute for private actions that might lead to risk pricing. Public infrastructure may, for example, attract additional private investment to areas, and this could have its own consequences. Carolyn Kousky and her colleagues show that public investments in risk reduction attract more private sector investment in places that receive protection.[38] It is an open question whether these investments crowd out private adaptation, and whether that private adaptation would be more efficient.

In summary, public decisions to build infrastructure to reduce climate risk should account for the possibility that such investments could be partially replaced by smaller-scale adaptive actions. These could be either physical or nonphysical and would have the benefit of bringing about risk pricing and thereby providing information that would support more effective adaptation choices. In the absence of protection infrastructure, demand for risk information may be enough to incentivize private provision of this information.

## Adaptation Tools

Information is important not only because it is the engine driving incentives, but because it supports decisions regarding how the risk might be most efficiently managed. Risk management alternatives, whether physical or nonphysical, fall into two categories. The first is actions that reduce the consequences of an event before it happens. This includes most physical adaptations, whether at a large or individualized scale (e.g., a seawall versus storm-proofing a house), and some nonphysical actions, such as a tax that discourages building in flood-prone areas. These actions lower expected losses. The second category includes actions that are designed to compensate for losses after an event occurs. These actions reduce the financial impact of losses and are almost exclusively nonphysical actions. Examples are reserve funds that can be drawn on to cover unexpected losses and financial instruments ranging from common insurance contracts to complex weather derivatives.

Risk management strategies involving both traditional actions and new tools, as well as improved methods for designing these strategies, offer significant opportunities for improving the efficiency of adaptation to climate change. This points to one of the areas currently most ripe for innovation: the development of novel financial instruments. While the methods for developing infrastructure alternatives, and perhaps physical actions in general, are mostly well established, recent years have seen growth in the development of new financial instruments. One indication of this is the growth in the catastrophe bond market, which has nearly tripled in size from $14 to $39 billion over the last decade.[39] It should be noted, however, that to facilitate efficient adaptation, the costs of these financial contracts must be sufficiently low so as to encourage their use. One primary means of lowering these costs is by reducing uncertainty regarding the size and magnitude of the payouts, thereby allowing providers to offer them at a lower price. This can be achieved by either improving the quantification of the risk or lowering concerns over moral hazard or fraud.

Financial instruments involve either shifting risks to a third party better positioned to manage the risk or pooling (mostly) uncorrelated risks across a number of similarly exposed parties. Payouts from these instruments can be indemnity based (linked directly to losses) or index based (linked to some observed metric or combination of metrics—rainfall, wind speed, electricity price—that is highly correlated with losses). The price of financial instruments is the sum of the expected payouts and an amount ("loading") consistent with compensating the party assuming the costs of managing a very uncertain stream of payouts (e.g., maintaining large capital reserves), as well as taking on related factors such as moral hazard.

There is a long history of financial instruments that indemnify the buyer against losses stemming from environmental events (e.g., flooding), as well as examples of index-based contracts designed to do the same. But the latter have typically been limited to cases in which there are obvious strong correlations between a single environmental metric and losses, as in the case of property damage caused by high winds. There is, however, a growing demand for more sophisticated index-based instruments, the development of which can be facilitated by increased data collection and improved modeling of the systems that give rise to the financial risk, systems often involving natural, engineered, and economic elements.

Compared to physical strategies, terms of financial and insurance contracts have the advantage of flexibility because their terms can be adjusted annually or sooner to accommodate new information on climate change. Physical action, on the other hand, involves long-lived infrastructure for which long-term uncertainty regarding climate risk can be confounding to decision makers. Committing to an investment in which the long-term benefits will be highly contingent on climate change can lead to regret over what later appear to be bad investments. Integrating both physical and nonphysical actions can lead to more flexible and efficient adaptation strategies. To advance this idea just a bit further, infrastructure that can be designed with the potential for successive increases in capacity (e.g., to reduce drought or increase flood protection) creates a real option that could be coupled with nonphysical financial instruments to develop very flexible adaptation strategies. One of the challenges in designing these combined strategies is how to jointly evaluate the net benefits of physical and nonphysical actions in a consistent way that allows them to be integrated efficiently.

## Financial Instruments for Risks Associated with Drought

The combination of physical and nonphysical risk management strategies for climate change is evolving to optimize the benefits of the two regarding drought-related losses. An example can be seen in the roles of dredging and index insurance for managing the risks to Great Lakes shipping from variability in water levels.[40] During low-water periods ships must reduce their draft in order to enter shallow harbors and locks. This means reducing cargos and hence revenues. Alternatively, shipping channels can be dredged to accommodate heavier cargos during low flows. A combined strategy using an insurance contract indexed to lake level and dredging can reduce the total cost of managing low-water risks by over 20 percent relative to dredging or insurance alone.

Low water levels on the Mississippi River also disrupt navigation, leading to lower cargo loads (and thus lower revenues) for shippers and higher costs for firms that contract with them, as they must pay higher barge rates or resort to more expensive alternatives like truck or rail.[41] A new financial instrument indexed to Mississippi River water levels could assist in managing the risk of low water levels for both shippers and those firms that rely on them to transport their goods. Recent research goes even further to demonstrate that drought-related impairments to commercial navigation on the Mississippi affect the market price of corn, a good often transported via barge. That risk is poorly recognized by the forward and futures markets, suggesting that such an index-based instrument could be used by any participant in the corn market to reduce the financial risk of increased drought frequency and severity.[42]

With respect to new opportunities for efficiently sharing risks, the low level of spatial correlation in drought over large areas (e.g., the continental United States) offers an opportunity to develop risk pools that can efficiently share risk. A study of roughly 150 water utilities distributed across the United States finds that pooling drought-related financial risks via index insurance based on drought severity (as determined by the Palmer Hydrologic Drought Index, or PHDI) could have tremendous advantages. In this case, the (mostly) independent nature of the drought risks allows the utilities to collectively reach an equivalent level of risk management with only one-third the level of reserve funds that would be required if each utility were to manage its risk via its own reserve fund.[43] This reduction in reserves substantially lowers the opportunity costs of capital, leading to smaller loadings, and thus lower prices, on the contracts. Given the wide range of circumstances that dictates each utility's drought-related financial risk, however, some face considerably greater basis risk than others when relying on PHDI-based index insurance. New research suggests that machine-learning techniques can be used to quickly tailor multifactor indices (e.g., PHDI, streamflow, snowpack) to individual utilities, lowering basis risk and increasing buyers' willingness to pay, without reducing the advantages of risk pooling.[44]

## Financial Instruments for Environmental Risks

Another example of combining physical and financial risk management strategies is the environmental impact bond (EIB) of DC Water (the public water utility for Washington, DC). DC Water raised private capital to fund green infrastructure projects whose purpose was to reduce specific storm water runoff events called combined sewer overflows.[45] These events are costly for the water utility, but the green infrastructure projects have an uncertain effect on combined sewer overflows, making investment in projects risky. The EIB's key innovation is a mechanism that specifically shifts some performance risk to investors, protecting DC Water financially if the projects do not generate a certain level of reduction in combined sewer overflows. Similarly, forest resilience bonds are used to fund forest management in the Tahoe National Forest and reduce wildfire risk.[46]

One critical challenge of designing these financing mechanisms is measuring and calculating benefits of the physical intervention, because those outcomes often determine who pays. In DC Water's case, the target outcome of improved water quality is easy to observe, but in the forest resilience bond case, the outcome is more complex because of difficulty in quantifying the reduction in wildfire risk attributable to forest management interventions. The ability, or inability, to accurately connect interventions to benefits will determine the success of these tools.

In all of these instances, developing financial instruments is facilitated by the information provided by modeling the linked natural-engineered-economic systems that underlie the risk. The new information generated by these models can also bring insights to the multiple factors that give rise to risk, as well as the level of correlation between similar risks, information that can be used to develop broader risk management strategies that include not only financial instruments but infrastructure, pricing policies, reserve funds, and a range of other tools. As information regarding the risks of climate change improves, it is likely that more financial instruments will be developed to allow private adaptation to flooding, extreme temperatures, low snowpack, wind speed variability, and solar irradiance.

## The Role of Government in Private Adaptation

Private adaptation to climate change will involve both new infrastructure and better information about climate-related financial risks. The latter includes (1) acquiring more and better data on climate change impacts; (2) improving the ability to translate climate impacts into decision-relevant end points; (3) developing new tools or instruments for managing climate risks; and (4) designing more efficient institutions that provide appropriate incentives for adaptation. All of these actions have the ability to better quantify the financial effects of climate change, thereby leading to advances that improve price discovery (such as insurance rates, mortgage rates, and credit ratings) and provide broad incentives for innovation and adaptation.

Government will have a role to play in all aspects of adaptation. One way to move toward more and better adaptation is to realistically price risk by moving the government out of subsidies to incentivize business and have it focus more on producing information. Government often has a comparative advantage in collecting broad-scale, highly resolved data related to climate change. This includes remote sensing platforms (satellites and drones, for example) that can monitor temperature, wind speed, precipitation, vegetation, and many other factors at the continental scale, as well as nationwide networks of terrestrial sensors (e.g., streamflow gauges, weather stations) and mapping efforts (as for flooding). These would be difficult for the private sector to replicate. Yet the private sector can, and does, use this information as a foundation for innovation.

Similarly, basic and applied research within the National Science Foundation, National Institutes of Health, and various federal agencies (e.g., National Oceanic and Atmospheric Administration, Department of Energy) support efforts to understand and quantify the complex natural-engineered-economic systems through which climate change effects are transmitted to decision makers. Let the private sector take this information, find new ways to capitalize it into prices, and then drive tool innovation and organize (incentivize) risk management actions, including public infrastructural investments. In this way, we suggest that government resources aid the development of risk characterization efforts (through data collection, verification, and storage), because those investments are big and have benefits that are hard for a single economic agent to capture.

With respect to climate adaptation via infrastructure, government will surely continue to play a role. Both major US political parties say they favor increased infrastructure investment, but this can distort price discovery by crowding out efforts at private self-protection.[47] This weakens incentives to search for better risk management strategies or information, while also creating opportunities for state and local governments to try to capture value from this risk absorption. For example, government might use infrastructural investments to encourage development in high-risk areas—also high-amenity areas—to preserve or increase property tax revenues.

As a result, we propose two general remedies for situations in which infrastructure-based adaptation is considered. First, the consequences of distorting risk prices through this protection should be estimated and used to develop incentives that lead to more efficient risk management choices. Second, the design of an infrastructure-based adaptation should consider integration with nonphysical measures (e.g., financial instruments) during the planning stage, as opposed to considering them after the infrastructure is already in place. This will facilitate more flexibility (as with a real option approach) in the face of climate uncertainty, which is likely to be a factor in long-lived infrastructure, and therefore will provide greater long-term efficiency with respect to these large, permanent investments.

Finally, there are adaptation activities in which the government should play a smaller role, or perhaps no role at all. Nobel laureate Gary Becker argued that as the social cost of inefficient policies increases, interest groups are more likely to pursue the efficient policy.[48] Such logic suggests that a silver lining of the rising inefficiency from today's policies is that reform is on the horizon. These issues matter for our analysis because adaptation will accelerate if more risks are priced.

## Conclusion

At its heart, climate change adaptation is Arrow's "careful confrontation of needs and resources." Prices, of both risk and assets, will play a critical role in organizing the "careful confrontation." As a consequence, it is critical that we consider how our institutions encourage or disrupt risk pricing mechanisms. In an increasingly uncertain climate world, our ability to incorporate new information quickly into market prices will be a critical determinant of adaptation success. One important contribution to this puzzle is improved risk information, which will require private effort to synthesize publicly provided fundamental data in order to make it relevant for decision making. This new information can lead to tools that transfer, and importantly lead to prices on, new and emerging risks by lowering the costs of meeting the three risk transfer criteria: the barbed-wire, efficiency, and bargaining conditions. The price discovery process will also improve as risk decisions migrate to the risk manager with the comparative advantage in coping with new risks helping align incentive structures. It will also encourage the development of new risk transfer tools and accelerate efficient adaptation. The federal government can accelerate adaptation through markets by withstanding the urge to provide public insurance and continuing to provide support in the form of data collection. The net effect of embracing the price discovery process will be an economy that is far more resilient to climate change.

## Notes

1. Maximilian Auffhammer, "Quantifying Economic Damages from Climate Change," *Journal of Economic Perspectives* 32, no. 4 (November 2018): 33–52.
2. Jeffrey K. Lazo et al., "U.S. Economic Sensitivity to Weather Variability," *Bulletin of the American Meteorological Society* 92, no. 6 (June 2011): 709–20.
3. Intergovernmental Panel on Climate Change, *Climate Change 2014: Impacts, Adaptation, and Vulnerability* (Cambridge: Cambridge University Press, 2014).
4. Bella Tonkonogy, Federico Mazza, and Valerio Micale, "Understanding and Increasing Finance for Climate Adaptation in Developing Countries," *Climate Policy Initiative*, December 13, 2018.
5. "Softening the Blow: Climate Adaptation Policies Are Needed More Than Ever," *The Economist*, 2020 Schools Brief, May 30, 2020, https://www .economist.com/schools-brief/2020/05/30/climate-adaptation-policies-are -needed-more-than-ever.
6. Nicole Glanemann, *The Optimal Climate Policy of Mitigation and Adaptation: A Real Options Theory Perspective* (Hamburg: WiSo-Forschungslabor, 2014).
7. Daniel Cusick, "Climate Change a Boon for Analytics Firms," *Climatewire*, April 23, 2019, https://www.eenews.net/climatewire/2019/04/23/stories /1060201479.
8. Jessica Williams, "How Environmental and Climate Risks and Opportunities Factor into Global Corporate Ratings—an Update," S&P Global, Nov. 9, 2017, https://www.spglobal.com/en/research-insights/articles/environmental-and -climate-risks-factor-into-ratings; Philipp Krueger, Zacharias Sautner, and Laura T. Starks, "The Importance of Climate Risks for Institutional Investors," *Review of Financial Studies* 33, no. 3 (March 2020): 1067–111.
9. Wolfgang Kron, "Flood Risk = Hazard • Values • Vulnerability," *Water International* 30, no. 1 (2005): 58–68.
10. Friedrich A. Hayek, "The Use of Knowledge in Society," *American Economic Review* 35, no. 4 (September 1945): 519–30.
11. Kenneth J. Arrow, "Insurance, Risk and Resource Allocation," in *Essays in the Theory of Risk Bearing* (Amsterdam: North-Holland, 1974), 141.

12. Yoram Barzel, *Economic Analysis of Property Rights* (Cambridge: Cambridge University Press, 1997).

13. Barzel, *Property Rights*, 61.

14. Terry L. Anderson and Peter J. Hill, "The Evolution of Property Rights: A Study of the American West," *Journal of Law and Economics* 18, no. 1 (April 1975): 163–79.

15. Asaf Bernstein, Matthew T. Gustafson, and Ryan Lewis, "Disaster on the Horizon: The Price Effect of Sea Level Rise," *Journal of Financial Economics* 134, no. 2 (November 2019): 253–72; Francesc Ortega and Süleyman Taşpınar, "Rising Sea Levels and Sinking Property Values: Hurricane Sandy and New York's Housing Market," *Journal of Urban Economics* 106 (July 2018): 81–100; Markus Baldauf, Lorenzo Garlappi, and Constantine Yannelis, "Does Climate Change Affect Real Estate Prices? Only If You Believe in It," *Review of Financial Studies* 33, no. 3 (March 2020): 1256–95.

16. For a longer discussion, see the review of this issue in Howard Kunreuther et al., "Flood Risk and the US Housing Market," SSRN 3426638.

17. National Research Council, *Tying Flood Insurance to Flood Risk for Low-Lying Structures in the Floodplain* (Washington, DC: National Academies Press, 2015).

18. National Research Council, *Tying Flood Insurance to Flood Risk.*

19. Bernstein, Gustafson, and Lewis, "Disaster on the Horizon"; Okmyung Bin, Thomas W. Crawford, Jamie B. Kruse, and Craig E. Landry, "Viewscapes and Flood Hazard: Coastal Housing Market Response to Amenities and Risk," *Land Economics* 84, no. 3 (August 2008): 434–48.

20. Carolyn Kousky and Howard Kunreuther, "Addressing Affordability in the National Flood Insurance Program," *Journal of Extreme Events* 1, no. 1 (August 2014); Amine Ouazad and Matthew E. Kahn, "Mortgage Finance in the Face of Rising Climate Risk," National Bureau of Economic Research, NBER Working Paper 26322, September 2019.

21. Karl Mathiesen, "Rating Climate Risks to Credit Worthiness," *Nature Climate Change* 8, no. 6 (June 2018): 454–56; Piet Eichholtz, Eva Steiner, and Erkan Yönder, "Where, When, and How Do Sophisticated Investors Respond to Flood Risk?," SSRN, https://dx.doi.org/10.2139/ssrn.3206257.

22. Richard H. Thaler, "From Cashews to Nudges: The Evolution of Behavioral Economics," *American Economic Review* 108, no. 6 (June 2018): 1265–87.

23. Benjamin T. Foster, Jordan D. Kern, and Gregory W. Characklis, "Mitigating Hydrologic Financial Risk in Hydropower Generation Using Index-Based Financial Instruments," *Water Resources and Economics* 10 (April 2015): 45–67, doi:10.1016/j.wre.2015.04.001; Jordan D. Kern, Gregory W. Characklis,

and Benjamin T. Foster, "Natural Gas Price Uncertainty and the Cost-Effectiveness of Hedging against Low Hydropower Revenues Caused by Drought," *Water Resources Research* 51, no. 4 (April 2015): 2412–27.

24. Jordan D. Kern and Gregory W. Characklis, "Evaluating the Physical and Financial Vulnerability of Power Systems to Drought under Climate Uncertainty and an Evolving Generation Mix," *Environmental Science & Technology* 51, no. 15 (August 1, 2017): 8815–23, doi:10.1021/acs.est.6b05460.

25. Andrew L. Hamilton, Gregory W. Characklis, and Patrick M. Reed, "Managing Financial Risk Tradeoffs for Hydropower Generation Using Snowpack-Based Index Contracts," *Water Resources Research* (forthcoming).

26. Dawn Lim and Julie Steinberg, "BlackRock to Hold Companies and Itself to Higher Standards on Climate Risk," *Wall Street Journal*, January 14, 2020.

27. Geneva Association, "Managing Physical Climate Risk: Leveraging Innovations in Catastrophe Risk Modelling," https://www.genevaassociation .org/sites/default/files/research-topics-document-type/pdf_public/ga_risk _modelling_18112018.pdf; Geneva Association, "Climate Change and the Insurance Industry, Taking Action as Risk Managers and Investors," https:// www.genevaassociation.org/sites/default/files/research-topics-document -type/pdf_public//climate_change_and_the_insurance_industry_-_taking _action_as_risk_managers_and_investors.pdf.

28. Larry Fink, "A Fundamental Reshaping of Finance," BlackRock, accessed June 4, 2020, https://www.blackrock.com/corporate/investor-relations/larry -fink-ceo-letter.

29. California Public Employees' Retirement System (CalPERS), "Addressing Climate Change Risk," accessed June 4, 2020, https://www.calpers.ca.gov /docs/forms-publications/addressing-climate-change-risk.pdf.

30. Standard and Poor's, "Delano-Earlimart Irrigation District," Ratings Direct Analysis, January 6, 2017.

31. Kern and Characklis, "Evaluating the Physical and Financial Vulnerability of Power Systems to Drought under Climate Uncertainty and an Evolving Generation Mix," *Environmental Science & Technology* 51, no. 15 (August 1, 2017): 8815–23, doi:10.1021/acs.est.6b05460.

32. Moody's Investor Services, "Moody's Assigns Aa1 to Energy Northwest (WA) Columbia Generating Station Revenue Bonds; Affirms BPA and Its Supported Debt Obligations at Aa1; Outlook Revised to Negative from Stable," https:// www.moodys.com/research/Moodys-assigns-Aa1-to-Energy-Northwest-WA -Columbia-Generating-Station--PR_905774475#; Moody's Investor Services, "Moody's Downgrades BPA (OR) to Aa2 from Aa1; Assigns Aa2 Rating to

Morrow (Port of) OR's Transmission Revenue Bonds; Outlook Is Stable," February 12, 2020.

33. Theodore A. Chapman and James M. Breeding, *U.S. Public Finance Waterworks, Sanitary Sewer, and Drainage Utility Systems: Methodology and Assumptions* (New York: S&P Global Market Intelligence, 2016); Mary Wyatt Tiger, Jeff Hughes, and Shadi Eskaf, *Designing Water Rate Structures for Conservation and Revenue Stability* (Chapel Hill: Environmental Finance Center at the University of North Carolina at Chapel Hill, 2014).

34. Terry Dinan, Perry Beider, and David Wylie, "The National Flood Insurance Program: Is It Financially Sound?," *Risk Management and Insurance Review* 22, no. 1 (March 2019): 15–38.

35. Patrick Baylis and Judson Boomhower, "Moral Hazard, Wildfires, and the Economic Incidence of Natural Disasters," National Bureau of Economic Research, NBER Working Paper 26550, December 2019.

36. For a more detailed discussion of GSE-held risks, see David Finkelstein, Andreas Strzodka, and James I. Vickery, "Credit Risk Transfer and De Facto GSE Reform," *Economic Policy Review* 24, no. 3 (December 2018).

37. Ouazad and Kahn, "Mortgage Finance in the Face of Rising Climate Risk."

38. Carolyn Kousky, Erzo F. Luttmer, and Richard J. Zeckhauser, "Private Investment and Government Protection," *Journal of Risk and Uncertainty* 33, nos. 1–2 (September 2006): 73–100.

39. Artemis, "Catastrophe Bonds and ILS Issued and Outstanding by Year," https://www.artemis.bm/dashboard/catastrophe-bonds-ils-issued-and -outstanding-by-year.

40. Eliot S. Meyer et al., "Integrating Physical and Financial Approaches to Manage Environmental Financial Risk on the Great Lakes," *Water Resources Research* 56, no. 5 (May 2020): e2019WR024853.

41. US Army Corps of Engineers, Event Study: 2012 Low-Water and Mississippi River Lock 27 Closures, August 2013.

42. Benjamin T. Foster, Gregory W. Characklis, and W. Thurman, "Hedging Performance of Corn Futures and Forwards Contracts during Drought on the Mississippi River" (forthcoming).

43. Rachel Baum, Gregory W. Characklis, and Marc L. Serre, "Effects of Geographic Diversification on Risk Pooling to Mitigate Drought-Related Financial Losses for Water Utilities," *Water Resources Research* 54, no. 4 (April 2018): 2561–79.

44. Rachel Baum, Jonathan D. Herman, and Gregory W. Characklis, "Designing Index Insurance Contracts to Manage Hydrologically-Driven Financial Risks Using Machine Learning," *Water Resources Research* (forthcoming).

45. Environmental Protection Agency, "DC Water's Environmental Impact Bond: A First of Its Kind U.S. EPA Water Infrastructure and Resiliency Finance Center," April 2017, https://www.epa.gov/sites/production/files/2017-04/documents/dc _waters_environmental_impact_bond_a_first_of_its_kind_final2.pdf.

46. Blue Forest Conservation, "Fighting Fire with Finance: A Roadmap for Collective Action," 2017, https://static1.squarespace.com/static /556a1885e4b0bdc6f0794659/t/59c1157f80bd5e1cd855010e/1505826201656 /FRB+2017+Roadmap+Report.pdf.

47. Kousky, Luttmer, and Zeckhauser, "Private Investment and Government Protection."

48. Gary S. Becker, "Public Policies, Pressure Groups, and Dead Weight Costs," *Journal of Public Economics* 28, no. 3 (December 1985): 329–47; Gary S. Becker, "A Theory of Competition among Pressure Groups for Political Influence," *Quarterly Journal of Economics* 98, no. 3 (August 1983): 371–400.

# 7

# Can Fire Insurance Manage Wildfire Risks in California?

Ronald Bailey

In California, from January through mid-October 2020, wildfires burned more than 4 million acres—an area larger than the state of Connecticut.[1] In just the eight weeks between August 15 and mid-October, the state's fires killed at least thirty-one people and destroyed more than 9,200 structures. The amount of the state's forestland that burned over the first nine months of 2020 has been described as "unprecedented" and "record-breaking."[2]

The area annually burned by wildfires has been zigzagging upward since 1950. Figure 1 displays data through 2017; subsequently, Cal Fire reports, the wildfires consumed 1.6 million acres in 2018 and 260,000 in 2019 respectively.[3]

The latest area burned may not be as unprecedented on a longer time scale. For example, a 2007 study in *Forest Ecology and Management* suggests that the area in California burned by Native Americans to manage landscapes, as well as those sparked by lightning before the era of European settlement and active fire suppression, may have fallen between 4.5 and 12 million acres annually.

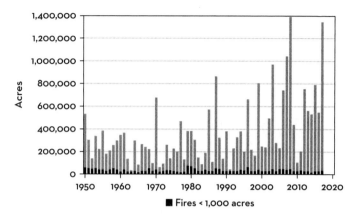

Figure 1. California Statewide Annual Acres Burned, 1950–2017.
*Source:* CalFire 2018, located at California Office of Environmental Health Hazard Assessment, "Wildfires," February 11, 2019, https://oehha.ca.gov/epic/impacts-biological -systems/wildfires.

"The idea that US wildfire area of approximately two million hectares (about 5 million acres) annually is extreme is certainly a 20th or 21st century perspective," wrote the researchers. "Skies were likely smoky much of the summer and fall in California during the pre-historic period."[4]

In the twentieth century, the National Interagency Fire Center reports that the area annually burned by wild land fires in the United States (not just California) may have exceeded 50 million acres in 1930 and 1931. But the agency cautions that the less rigorous methods for collecting and compiling these early-twentieth-century data mean that "figures prior to 1983 should not be compared to later data."[5] For example, the data from the 1930s may well include fires intentionally set in the Southeast to clear agricultural land.[6]

A 2009 study in *Ecological Applications* identified a U-shaped trend in eleven western US states, in which fires burned more space at the beginning of the last century, less in the middle decades, and more again recently (figure 2, updated to include data through 2020 [provisional]).[7]

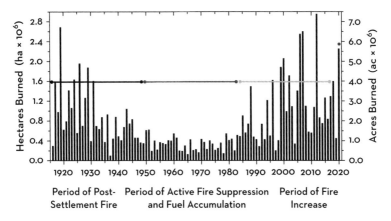

Figure 2.  Area Burned in Eleven Western States.

*Note:* Data for 2020 are provisional.

*Source:* Graph courtesy of J. S. Littell, US Geological Survey, after methods in Jeremy S. Littell, Donald McKenzie, David L. Peterson, and Anthony L. Westerling, "Climate and Wildfire Area Burned in Western US Ecoprovinces, 1916–2003," *Ecological Applications* 19, no. 4 (2009): 1003–1021.

What is causing the upward trend in the area burned by wildfires in the western United States? During a visit to California in September 2020, President Donald Trump suggested that bad forest management is the chief cause. During the briefing, California governor Gavin Newsom gingerly suggested that "the science is in, and observed evidence is self-evident that climate change is real, and that is exacerbating this."[8] In fact, both have played a role, as has the complicating circumstance that millions of Californians have moved to fire-prone wildlands.

A 2009 report from researchers associated with California Polytechnic State University observed that bad forest management, including active fire suppression and restrictions on timber harvests, have "resulted in an unnatural accumulation of fuels on many California forestlands." The report further noted: "Where 50–70 trees per acre stood before the Gold Rush, California forests now average over 400 trees per acre. When fire enters these ecosystems

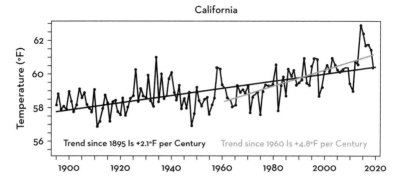

Figure 3. Average Temperature for All Weather Stations in California, 1895–2020.
*Source:* Clark Weaver, Eugene Cordero, Nilay Shah, Erica DeJoannis, Scott Weaver, and Jacob Reed, Congressional Temperature Trends: Thermometer Records from Weather Stations, https://temperaturetrends.org/state.php?state=CA.

the resulting high-intensity wildfires are as unnatural as the accumulated fuels that they consume."[9]

Meanwhile, California's climate has been heating up, and periods of drought have been deepening and lengthening. Using surface temperature data, a team led by University of Maryland atmospheric chemist Clark Weaver calculates that California, since 1895, has been growing warmer at a rate of about 2.1°F per century (figure 3).[10] The warming sped up over that time: from 1960 to 2020, the rate was 4.8°F per century.

An August 2020 study in *Environmental Research Letters* finds that since 1979, a combination of rising temperatures and falling average precipitation has increased the likelihood of extreme autumn wildfire conditions across California.[11] The researchers report trends for the months of September, October, and November in both temperatures (up about 1°C) and precipitation (down an average of 30 percent), doubling the risk of fire weather conditions statewide over the four-decade period (figure 4).

The researchers find that from 1984 to 2018, the trends toward a hotter and drier California correlate with an increase of about

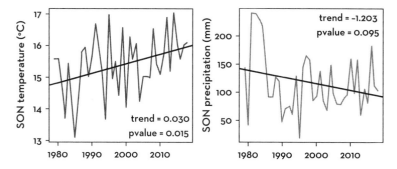

Figure 4. Average Temperatures (in Celsius) and Precipitation (in Millimeters) for September, October, and November (SON), 1979–2018.

*Source:* Michael Goss, Daniel L. Swain, John T. Abatzoglou, Ali Sarhadi, Crystal A. Kolden, A. Park Williams, and Noah S. Diffenbaugh, "Climate Change Is Increasing the Likelihood of Extreme Autumn Wildfire Conditions across California," *Environmental Research Letters* 15, no. 9 (August 2020), https://iopscience.iop.org/article/10.1088/1748-9326/ab83a7/pdf.

40 percent per decade in the size of the statewide autumn-burned area.

As all this was happening, more people were heading into the woods, that is, making their homes in the "wildland-urban inter-face" (WUI) areas where houses and wildland vegetation meet and intermingle. Some go there because they can't afford to live in pricey urban areas with strict restrictions on new building, while other, more fortunate, people move to the woods to enjoy the scenery, wildlife, and outdoor activities.[12]

A 2007 report in the *International Journal of Wildland Fire* found that by 2000, some 3.5 million California housing units were located in WUI areas, with another 1.5 million intermixed within and surrounded by wild landscapes. On top of that, 62 percent of net California housing growth from 1990 to 2000 occurred in WUI zones.[13] A 2018 study in the *Proceedings of the National Academy of Sciences* reported that America's wildland-urban interface "grew rapidly from 1990 to 2010 in terms of both number of new houses (from 30.8 to 43.4 million; 41 percent growth) and land area (from 581,000 to 770,000 km²; 33 percent growth), making it the

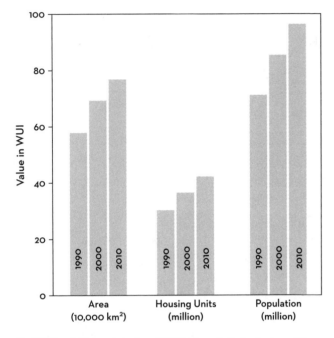

Figure 5. Wildland-Urban Interface (WUI) Growth Rates in Area, Houses, and People during the 1990s and the 2000s.

*Source:* Volker C. Radeloff, David P. Helmers, H. Anu Kramer, Miranda H. Mockrin, Patricia M. Alexandre, Avi Bar-Massada, Van Butsic, et al., "Rapid Growth of the US Wildland-Urban Interface Raises Wildfire Risk," *Proceedings of the National Academy of Sciences* 115, no. 13 (March 27, 2018): 3314–19, https://www-pnas-org.stanford.idm.oclc.org/content/115/13/3314.

fastest-growing land use type in the conterminous United States."[14] In other words, more and more Americans have moved into areas where the wildfire risk is higher (figure 5).

The measure that could make a big difference with respect to California wildfire risk is, as the president advised, better and more proactive forest management. As it happens, the federal government, which the president oversees, owns 57 percent of California's forests, whereas state and local governments own around 3 percent. (The rest is in private hands.)[15]

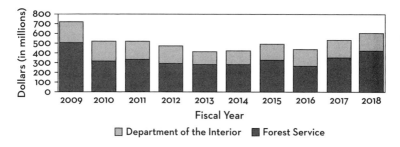

Figure 6. Forest Service and Department of the Interior Fuel Reduction Appropriations, Fiscal Years 2009–18.

*Source:* United States Government Accountability Office, "Wildland Fire: Federal Agencies' Efforts to Reduce Wildland Fuels and Lower Risk to Communities and Ecosystems," GAO-20-52 (December 2019), https://www.gao.gov/assets/710/703470.pdf.

Better forest management to reduce wildfire risk chiefly involves reducing the fuel load in overgrown fire-suppressed forests using mechanical harvesting and prescribed burns. A 2019 Government Accountability Office report found that federal agencies spent around $5 billion on reducing wildland fuels from 2009 to 2018 (figure 6).[16]

The Forest Service and the Bureau of Land Management estimate that more than one hundred million acres of federal lands are at high risk from wildfire, but in 2018 the agencies managed to treat only about three million acres.

An intriguing 2019 study in *Fire* notes that 70 percent of all prescribed burns between 1998 and 2018 were completed by nonfederal entities in the southeastern United States. In other words, private owners and state agencies in the Southeast have completed more than twice as many prescribed burns as the entire remainder of the country. "This may be one of many reasons why the Southeastern states have experienced far fewer wildfire disasters relative to the Western U.S. in recent years," the researcher observes.[17] It is worth noting that the federal government owns just a small percentage of the land in most southeastern states.[18]

A 2020 study in *Nature Sustainability* estimated that 20 million acres of California forestland—about 20 percent of the state's land area—would benefit from prescribed burning to cut the risks of catastrophic wildfires.[19] Yet California intentionally burned just 50,000 acres in 2017.[20] The costs for prescribed burns range from $100 to $500 per acre. That suggests that it would take roughly $2 billion to $10 billion to treat 20 million acres. For comparison, in its latest budget request, the US Forest Service says it has a backlog of 80 million acres in need of active management but plans to reduce fuel loads on just over one million acres in 2021.[21] The US Department of Agriculture, which oversees the Forest Service, suggested in a July 2020 report that "restoration of national forests comes with an estimated price tag of $65 billion."[22]

The insurance risk analytics firm Verisk assesses the primary factors that contribute to wildfire risk—fuel, slope, and road access—to determine a property's individual wildfire hazard score. The company finds that more than 2 million properties in California are at high and extreme risk from wildfire. (Nationwide, about 4.5 million properties are at high wildfire risk.)[23] The Insurance Information Institute reports that annual insured wildfire losses in the United States generally hovered below $1 billion from 2004 until 2017. In 2017 and 2018, insured wildfire losses escalated to around $15 and $17 billion, respectively, before dropping back down in 2019 to around $1 billion.[24] US insured wildfire losses in the first nine months of 2020 are estimated at around $8 billion.[25]

After the spectacular wildfire losses in 2017 and 2018, insurance companies have revised their risk models and are now pulling out of the California market. Why? Because the premiums that state regulators allow insurers to charge don't cover their projected wildfire risks.[26] By one calculation, insurers covering California wildfire losses paid out more than $2 for every $1 in premiums in 2017 and $1.70 for every $1 in premiums in 2018.[27] With that dynamic, it is not surprising that insurance companies have dropped wildfire coverage for nearly 350,000 California homeowners since 2015.[28] Property owners who can still buy insurance in the market have seen their premiums increase recently by as much as 300 to 500 percent.[29]

In the wake of 2018's disastrous fires, the California legislature passed Senate Bill 824, which prohibits cancellation or nonrenewal of homeowners' policies within a year of a declared state of emergency if a structure is either in an area where a wildfire occurred or adjacent to a fire perimeter.[30] In December 2019, California Insurance Commissioner Ricardo Lara imposed a mandatory one-year moratorium on insurance companies' refusing to renew certain policies; this applies to at least eight hundred thousand homes in California wildfire disaster areas.[31]

As more Californians lose their standard wildfire insurance coverage, they have been turning to the state's Fair Access to Insurance Requirements (FAIR) plan to protect their properties. The FAIR plan is basically a high-risk insurance pool that offers last-resort, bare-bones coverage, chiefly for fire losses, to property owners who cannot obtain a policy in the regular market. It was established in 1968, in the wake of urban riots and brush fires, when the California legislature required insurance companies offering property policies in the state to create and contribute to the plan. It is not taxpayer financed, and plan premiums are statutorily required to be actuarially sound.[32]

The FAIR plan's premiums have been increasing at a rate of 8 percent per year since 2016.[33] This year, the program got regulators' permission to raise its rates by 15.6 percent—after trying to hike them by 35 percent.[34] Being unable to obtain insurance means, of course, that owners will find it much harder to sell, since banks will not issue mortgages for uninsurable properties.

Recognizing that his one-year nonrenewable mandate forcing insurance companies to maintain fire policies was coming to its end, Insurance Commissioner Lara announced convening an investigatory hearing in October 2020 to focus on ways to protect California residents against increasing wildfire risks. "Our current reality of increasing insurance premiums and non-renewals hurts those who can least afford it, including working families and retirees on fixed incomes," said Commissioner Lara in a press release. "We can lower the insurance risk by incentivizing people to bring down the fire risk on their properties and in their communities with clear, science-based home-hardening standards."[35]

Home hardening could help, but not perhaps as much as the commissioner and property owners may think. A 2019 *Fire* article analyzed the factors associated with structure loss in the California areas burned by wildfire from 2013 to 2018. Examining how more than forty thousand structures exposed to wildfire fared, the researchers found that "in most regions home structural characteristics are far more important in determining home survival than defensible space." (Defensible space generally means cutting back brush and trees as much as one hundred feet to establish a perimeter around a house.) They added that many "destroyed structures could be characterized as 'fire-safe,' such as having >30 meters of defensible space or fire-resistant building materials."[36]

So why would one of the most frequently referenced protection measures—expanding defensible space—have so little impact on whether a house survives a wildfire? Because flying embers that precede the fire front by a mile or two often waft over the cleared perimeter to set houses alight. Measures that do somewhat increase the chances that a house will survive a wildfire are having enclosed (or no) eaves, multiple-pane windows, and screened vents. These tend to exclude embers from gaining entry into more combustible parts of a structure.

If this study is right, the home-hardening measures that Commissioner Lara wants insurance companies to take into account when setting premiums will probably not have much impact on whether Californians who live in fire-prone areas can obtain coverage or reduce what those who can get coverage pay for their policies.

Whatever is sparking the upsurge in wildfires, California regulators and residents should take market signals seriously when deciding where to live. As the Pomona College environmental historian Char Miller recently put it in the *New York Times*, insurance companies ask themselves: "Why am I insuring something that I know is going to be destroyed?"[37] Homeowners should certainly be asking themselves a similar question.

Meanwhile, a 2007 analysis in the *Journal of Real Estate Finance and Economics* found that repeated fires in any given area of Southern California brought down property values. "The first fire reduces house prices by about 10 percent," they calculated, "while the second fire reduces house prices by nearly 23 percent."[38] Both insurance rates and resell prices are signals that living in the woods is costly. Many people may be willing to take the risk of losing their property to wildfire, but insurance policyholders or taxpayers may not want to be compelled to subsidize that choice. Charging people the full cost of their fire risks could well incline them to build and live in safer areas.[39]

A fascinating 2016 *Stanford Law Review* article highlights that point. The authors, legal scholars Omri Ben-Shahar and Kyle Logue, observe that insurance can serve "as a form of private regulation of safety—a contractual device controlling and incentivizing behavior *prior to the occurrence of losses*." Their focus is on flood insurance, but the point is valid for fire coverage too:

> In the U.S., insurance is denied its potential role as an efficient regulator of pre-storm conduct. It does not induce rational precautions by individuals, cost-justified community development by localities, or efficient infrastructure investment. American insurance fails to achieve these straightforward and enormously important roles for a reason that can be stated in one sentence: insurance policies for

weather related losses are not priced to reflect the real risk. As a result of government intervention in property insurance markets, through either rate regulation or direct government provision of subsidized insurance, private markets no longer generate price signals regarding the cost of living in severe weather regions. The cost of insurance is suppressed, thus failing to alert private parties who purchase property insurance to the true risk of living dangerously. It allows these private parties to (rationally) assume excessive risk and dump the cost of living in the path of storms on others. Indeed, much of the development of storm-stricken coastal areas is due to insurance subsidies and would likely not have happened at the same magnitude otherwise.[40]

Insurance could contribute at least modestly toward mitigating California's rising wildfire risks. Although it is way too bureaucratically complex and slow, the Federal Emergency Management Agency (FEMA) has a severe repetitive loss program that hints at a way forward.[41] That voluntary program buys out homeowners whose property has been flooded numerous times and encourages them to relocate to higher ground.[42] FEMA has acquired more than forty-three thousand such flood-prone properties since 1989.[43] A streamlined buyout program for structures destroyed by wildfire, ideally run by private insurers, could give residents of high-risk areas a stronger incentive to relocate and rebuild elsewhere.

One preliminary idea, based on what has been happening with many FEMA buyouts, is that insurers might pay the pre-fire value for burnt-out properties and communities, then turn the now-vacant land over to local land trusts to oversee and manage.[44]

Another innovative measure that would help homeowners reduce their wildfire risks is to issue forest resilience bonds (FRBs).[45] These raise private capital to fund forest restoration efforts, such as mechanical harvesting and prescribed burning, that reduce the chances of wildfire. Smaller fires mean lower costs. The bond issuers—who could be government entities but also could be utility companies or other private parties—reimburse the investors over time. For example, a $4.6 million FRB was issued in 2018 to treat and lower the fire risks on fifteen thousand acres of forestland in the North Yuba River watershed via tree thinning and prescribed burning.[46] Instead of waiting for action and fickle funding from distant federal and state agencies, local communities at high risk of wildfire could issue such bonds and begin forest restoration sooner. Insurance companies might even invest in such bonds and could also factor the lower fire risk into their premiums for that community's homeowners.

An alternative to state and federal wildfire suppression is privately provided wildfire fighting. The Montana-based Wildfire Defense Systems (WDS) has been offering just such services since 2013.[47] Insurance companies contract with WDS to evaluate the wildfire risks of policyholders and advise them on how to lower those risks. WDS also offers insurers access to private firefighting services that are on call across twenty states.[48]

The Trump administration is right to complain about poor forest management, but it has been offering no credible plans for fixing it. And California's insurance regulators seem dead set on policies that will eventually drive private insurance companies out of the state. Meanwhile, forests burn, thousands flee their homes, and millions choke on smoke.

## Notes

A version of this chapter originally appeared as "Can Fire Insurance Manage Wildfire Risks in California?," *Reason*, September 18, 2020, https://reason.com /2020/09/18/can-fire-insurance-manage-wildfire-risks-in-california/.

1. All statistics are as of this writing in mid-October 2020: Cal Fire, "California Statewide Fire Summary October 9, 2020," https://www.fire.ca.gov/daily -wildfire-report.

2. Diana Leonard and Andrew Freeman, "Western Wildfires: An 'Unprecedented,' Climate Change–Fueled Event, Experts Say," *Washington Post*, September 11, 2020, https://www.washingtonpost.com/weather/2020/09/11/western-wildfires-climate-change/; Yasemin Saplakoglu, "Record-Breaking 2.2 Million Acres Burned by California Wildfires," *Live Science*, September 9, 2020, https://www.livescience.com/california-wildfires-record-breaking.html.

3. Cal Fire, "Stats and Events," accessed October 1, 2020, https://www.fire.ca.gov/stats-events.

4. Scott L. Stephens, Robert E. Martin, and Nicholas E. Clinton, "Prehistoric Fire Area and Emissions from California's Forests, Woodlands, Shrublands, and Grasslands," Division of Ecosystem Science, Department of Environmental Science, Policy, and Management, University of California–Berkeley, June 2007, https://nature.berkeley.edu/stephenslab/wp-content/uploads/2015/04/Stephens-et-al.-CA-fire-area-FEM-2007.pdf.

5. National Interagency Fire Center, "Total Wildland Fires and Acres (1926–2019)," https://www.nifc.gov/fireInfo/fireInfo_stats_totalFires.html, retrieved October 1, 2020.

6. Zeke Hausfather, "Factcheck: How Global Warming Has Increased US Wildfires," *Carbon Brief*, August 9, 2018, https://www.carbonbrief.org/factcheck-how-global-warming-has-increased-us-wildfires; William M. Ciesla and John Coulston, "Report of the United States on the Criteria and Indicators for the Sustainable Management of Temperate and Boreal Forests of the United States" (2003), https://www.fs.fed.us/research/sustain/docs/national-reports/2003/data/documents/Indicator%2015/Indicator%2015.pdf.

7. Jeremy S. Littell, Donald McKenzie, David L. Peterson, and Anthony L. Westerling, "Climate and Wildfire Area Burned in Western U.S. Ecoprovinces, 1916–2003," *Ecological Applications* 19, no. 4 (June 2009): 1003–21; data updated by Jeremy Littell in "Fire Management, Fire Science, and Climate Change: Where Do We Go from Here?," Alaska Climate Science Center, https://www.frames.gov/documents/alaska/webinars/AFSC_webinar_20131125_FireMgmtFireScienceClimateChangeWhereDoWeGoFromHere.pdf.

8. Peter Baker, Lisa Friedman, and Thomas Kaplan, "As Trump Again Rejects Science, Biden Calls Him a 'Climate Arsonist,'" *New York Times*, September 14, 2020, https://www.nytimes.com/2020/09/14/us/politics/trump-biden-climate-change-fires.html.

9. Christopher Dicus, "Fire on the Landscape: Current Policies and a Changing Climate Lead toward Higher Costs, More Severe Wildfire," *California Forests*

12, no. 2 (Fall 2009), https://digitalcommons.calpoly.edu/cgi/viewcontent.cgi
?article=1023&context=nrm_fac.

10. Clark Weaver, Eugene Cordero, Nilay Shah, Erica DeJoannis, Scott Weaver,
and Jacob Reed, Congressional Temperature Trends: Thermometer Records from Weather Stations, https://temperaturetrends.org/state.php?state
=CA; source data from National Oceanic and Atmospheric Administration,
National Centers for Environmental Information, "Climate at a Glance:
Statewide Time Series," published September 2020, https://www.ncdc.noaa
.gov/cag/statewide/time-series/4/tavg/12/9/1895-2020?base_prd=true&beg
baseyear=1901&endbaseyear=2000.

11. Michael Goss, Daniel L. Swain, John T. Abatzoglou, Ali Sarhadi, Crystal
A. Kolden, A. Park Williams, and Noah S. Diffenbaugh, "Climate Change Is
Increasing the Likelihood of Extreme Autumn Wildfire Conditions across
California," *Environmental Research Letters* 15, no. 9 (August 2020), https://
iopscience.iop.org/article/10.1088/1748-9326/ab83a7/pdf.

12. Annie Lowrey, "California Is Becoming Unlivable," *The Atlantic*, October 30,
2019, https://www.theatlantic.com/ideas/archive/2019/10/can-california
-save-itself/601135.

13. Roger B. Hammer, Volker C. Radeloff, Jeremy S. Fried, and Susan I. Stewart,
"Wildland-Urban Interface Housing Growth during the 1990s in California,
Oregon, and Washington," *International Journal of Wildland Fire* 16 (2007):
255–65, https://www.fs.fed.us/pnw/pubs/journals/pnw_2007_hammer001
.pdf.

14. Volker C. Radeloff, David P. Helmers, H. Anu Kramer, Miranda H. Mockrin,
Patricia M. Alexandre, Avi Bar-Massada, Van Butsic, et al., "Rapid Growth
of the US Wildland-Urban Interface Raises Wildfire Risk," *Proceedings of the
National Academy of Sciences* 115, no. 13 (March 27, 2018): 3314–19, https://
www-pnas-org.stanford.idm.oclc.org/content/115/13/3314.

15. Little Hoover Commission, "Fire on the Mountain: Rethinking Forest
Management in the Sierra Nevada," Report #242 (February 2018), https://lhc
.ca.gov/sites/lhc.ca.gov/files/Reports/242/Report242.pdf.

16. United States Government Accountability Office, "Wildland Fire: Federal
Agencies' Efforts to Reduce Wildland Fuels and Lower Risk to Communities
and Ecosystems," GAO-20-52 (December 2019), https://www.gao.gov/assets
/710/703470.pdf.

17. Crystal A. Kolden, "We're Not Doing Enough Prescribed Fire in the Western
United States to Mitigate Wildfire Risk," *Fire* 2, no. 2 (June 2019), https://www
.mdpi.com/2571-6255/2/2/30/htm?dom=prime&src=syn.

18. "Federal Land Ownership by State," Ballotpedia, accessed October 1, 2020, https://ballotpedia.org/Federal_land_ownership_by_state.

19. Rebecca K. Miller, Christopher B. Field, and Katharine J. Mach, "Barriers and Enablers for Prescribed Burns for Wildfire Management in California," *Nature Sustainability* 3, no. 2 (February 2020): 101–9, https://www.nature.com/articles/s41893-019-0451-7.

20. Brad Plumer and John Schwartz, "These Changes Are Needed Amid Worsening Wildfires, Experts Say," *New York Times*, September 20, 2020 (updated September 22, 2020), https://www.nytimes.com/2020/09/10/climate/wildfires-climate-policy.html.

21. Forest Service (US Department of Agriculture), *FY2021 Budget Justification* (February 2020), https://www.fs.usda.gov/sites/default/files/2020-02/usfs-fy-2021-budget-justification.pdf.

22. Nathalie Woolworth and Zack Knight, "Innovative Finance Model Accelerates Forest Restoration," US Department of Agriculture, https://www.usda.gov/media/blog/2020/07/09/innovative-finance-model-accelerates-forest-restoration.

23. Verisk, "Wildfire Risk Analysis," accessed October 1, 2020, https://www.verisk.com/insurance/campaigns/location-fireline-state-risk-report.

24. Insurance Information Institute, "Facts + Statistics: Wildfires," accessed October 1, 2020, https://www.iii.org/fact-statistic/facts-statistics-wildfires.

25. "Moody's Says Property/Casualty Insurers Face Significant Losses from Western Wildfires," *Insurance Journal*, September 17, 2020, https://www.insurancejournal.com/news/west/2020/09/17/582984.htm.

26. Christopher Flavelle, "Wildfires Hasten Another Climate Crisis: Homeowners Who Can't Get Insurance," *New York Times*, September 10, 2020, https://www.nytimes.com/2020/09/02/climate/wildfires-insurance.html.

27. Don Jergler, "Industry Representative Puts Fire Insurance Availability at Feet of Commissioner," *Insurance Journal*, December 6, 2019, https://www.insurancejournal.com/news/west/2019/12/06/550633.htm.

28. "California Fires Could Accelerate Home Insurance Crisis in Wildfire Zones," Insurance News Net, reprinted from *Sacramento Bee*, September 12, 2020, https://insurancenewsnet.com/oarticle/fires-across-california-could-accelerate-home-insurance-crisis-in-wildfire-zones#.X3db-5NKhBw.

29. Tony Cignarale, Joel Laucher, Kenneth Allen, and Lisbeth Landsman-Smith, "The Availability and Affordability of Coverage for Wildfire Loss in Residential Property Insurance in the Wildland-Urban Interface and Other High-Risk Areas of California: CDI Summary and Proposed Solutions," California Department

of Insurance (2018), http://www.insurance.ca.gov/0400-news/0100-press -releases/2018/upload/nr002-2018AvailabilityandAffordabilityofWildfire Coverage.pdf.

30. Stephen C. Clarke, "California Wildfires Spark State Insurance Legislation," *Visualize* (Verisk), September 27, 2018, https://www.verisk.com/insurance /visualize/california-wildfires-spark-state-insurance-legislation.

31. California Department of Insurance, "Wildfire Insurance Crisis Leads Commissioner to Call for First-Ever Statewide Non-Renewal Moratorium," press release, December 5, 2019, http://www.insurance.ca.gov/0400-news /0100-press-releases/2019/release092-19.cfm.

32. California FAIR Plan Property Insurance, accessed October 1, 2020, https:// www.cfpnet.com.

33. "California FAIR Plan Review," *Young Alfred*, August 20, 2020, https:// youngalfred.com/homeowners-insurance/california-fair-plan-review.

34. Paul Carroll, "An Early Taste of Climate Change Disrupting Insurance," *Insurance Thought Leadership*, September 3, 2020, https://www.insurancethoughtleadership .com/tag/wildfires.

35. California Department of Insurance, "Commissioner Lara Takes Action to Protect Consumers, Stabilize Insurance Market Following Wildfires," press release, September 16, 2020, http://www.insurance.ca.gov/0400-news/0100 -press-releases/2020/release088-2020.cfm.

36. Alexandra D. Syphard and Jon E. Keeley, "Factors Associated with Structure Loss in the 2013–2018 California Wildfires," *Fire* 2, no. 3 (September 2019), https://www.mdpi.com/2571-6255/2/3/49.

37. Flavelle, "Wildfires Hasten Another Climate Crisis."

38. Julie Mueller, John Loomis, and Armando González-Cabán, "Do Repeated Wildfires Change Homebuyers' Demand for Homes in High-Risk Areas? A Hedonic Analysis of the Short and Long-Term Effects of Repeated Wildfires on House Prices in Southern California," *Journal of Real Estate Finance and Economics* 38, no. 2 (February 2009): 155–72, https://doi.org/10.1007/s11146 -007-9083-1.

39. Lloyd Dixon, Flavia Tsang, and Gary Fitts, "The Impact of Changing Wildfire Risks on California's Residential Insurance Market," report for California's Fourth Climate Change Assessment, California Natural Resources Agency (August 2018), https://www.rand.org/pubs/external_publications/EP67670 .html.

40. Omri Ben-Shahar and Kyle D. Logue, "The Perverse Effects of Subsidized Weather Insurance," *Stanford Law Review* 68, no. 3 (March 2016): 571, https://

chicagounbound.uchicago.edu/cgi/viewcontent.cgi?article=12498&context =journal_articles.

41.  Linda Poon, "As Flooding Worsens, Home Buyouts Move at a Snail's Pace," *Bloomburg CityLab*, September 17, 2019, https://www.bloomberg.com/news /articles/2019-09-17/most-post-flood-buyouts-take-more-than-5-years.

42.  Federal Insurance and Mitigation Administration, "Frequently Asked Questions: Property Acquisitions for Open Space," accessed October 1, 2020, https://www.fema.gov/media-library-data/1487973067729-d34bd451527229 a45bad0ef5ac6ddf93/508_FIMA_Acq_FAQs_2_24_17_Final.pdf.

43.  Poon, "As Flooding Worsens."

44.  Marina Schauffler, "Enhancing Natural Protections Against Rising Waters," *Saving Land* (Land Trust Alliance) (Winter 2019), https://www.landtrustalliance .org/news/enhancing-natural-protections-against-rising-waters.

45.  Todd Gartner, "Investing in Wildfire Risk Reduction," Property and Environment Research Center, November 2, 2018, https://www.perc.org /2018/11/02/investing-in-reducing-wildfire-risk.

46.  "Forest Resilience Bond," Calvert Impact Capital, accessed October 1, 2020, https://www.calvertimpactcapital.org/portfolio/list/forest-resilience-bond.

47.  Wildfire Defense Systems, accessed October 1, 2020, https://wildfire-defense .com/index.html.

48.  Monique Dutkowsky, "A Private Solution to Wildfire Risk," Property and Environment Research Center, September 14, 2020, https://www.perc.org /2020/09/14/a-private-solution-to-wildfire-risk.

# Epilogue
## Adaptation—Simple but Effective

Bjorn Lomborg

Adaptation is crucial in tackling climate change. Of course, there are also other policies we need to consider, as I discuss in my book, *False Alarm*. A well-conceived carbon tax can help us avoid the worst climate change damage, although political reality can make that harder (see chapters 3 and 4). A large investment in innovation can bring forward the day when the global economy ends its reliance on fossil fuels, although that day may yet be far off (see chapter 2). Poverty alleviation and prosperity make everyone more resilient and reduce vulnerability, but climate policy often forgets those most vulnerable to the effects of climate change (see chapter 5), while research into geoengineering is a useful backup plan. But even with all of these policies, the temperature will continue to rise, at least for some time, as the data in *False Alarm* verifies.

This is why we need to adapt to a warmer planet over the coming decades, and fortunately, humanity has remarkable adaptive capacity. There are people living in the icy extremes of Siberia and northern Canada, in the burning hot Sahel and the Australian outback, in the dry Atacama desert plateau of South America, and in the rain-soaked Meghalaya state of India. Not only do people withstand significant variations in temperature and rainfall, but falling per-capita death rates from natural disasters show that we have more resilience today than ever before.[1]

At its simplest, adaptation simply means that people react sensibly to a changing climate: as it gets warmer, more people will adapt by turning on their air conditioners (and fewer will use their heaters).[2] If they don't yet have an air conditioner, more people will buy one (and more people will be able to buy one as global prosperity increases). Similarly, tourists will adapt to a warming world by changing their travel destinations. Warm places like Sri Lanka will host fewer tourists. On the other hand, more visitors will choose Finland and Canada for their next holiday, while fewer Finns and Canadians will travel abroad.[3]

Cutting emissions has significant costs but helps everyone in the world a little, albeit a half century down the line. By contrast, adaptation often has immediate and very localized benefits.[4] Indeed, most adaptation happens naturally and needs little public focus or investment.[5]

Businesses often don't need to be forced to invest in adaptation, because it makes sound financial sense. There are plenty of examples of this already happening. In the rich world, the chemical giant BASF has installed additional water pumps in the Rhine, so that even if climate change lowers water levels, there is enough water for production.[6] Finance and insurance markets are developing innovative ways of incorporating the new risks of climate change into private decisions (see chapter 6).

In poorer countries, farmers also adapt to a changing climate. In South America, a study shows that farmers already tailor what they grow to the climate; farmers grow fruit and vegetables in warmer locations and wheat and potatoes in cooler locations. Where it is wetter, they grow rice, fruits, and potatoes, and in drier locations they grow corn and wheat.[7] As climate change drives up temperatures, farmers will adapt by switching toward more fruits and vegetables, and depending on whether it gets wetter or drier (the models are still not sure), they will add potatoes or squash.

But not all adaptation will happen without specific adaptation policies. Clearly, governments should reconsider policies that can make private adaptation harder. Levying high taxes on air conditioners or the electricity required to run them means fewer people can stay cool during heat waves. Subsidizing insurance for people who build on seashores or in floodplains makes private adaptation less relevant.

Governments could implement policies that make adaptation easier. Across the world, agricultural adaptation is easier if you are better educated, if you are better off (for instance, if you have a tractor), and if you have better access to agricultural information.[8] So governments would do well to make sure there is better access to education, agricultural information—and tractors.

In Ethiopia, a study found that farmers with access to credit can better adapt to a changing climate, and they end up with higher food productivity.[9] This is not surprising: if you can get extra resources to overcome difficult times, you will be much more likely to do well. So governments should make sure that credit opportunities are as widely available as possible. This doesn't mean subsidizing actual loans but rather ensuring a well-functioning legal and institutional framework that will make it easier for individuals to access the necessary funds to adapt.

Individuals seem to be adapting housing construction to sea level rise, but mitigating the effect of rising sea levels and storm surges often requires collective action—government action. Governments need to step up with flood defenses and early-warning systems. And while air conditioning can help in heat waves, the right infrastructure can make whole cities cool. Moreover, while many people can adapt on their own, the most vulnerable groups often can't. Public policy can be especially useful in helping elderly and marginalized people when heat waves hit.

Pursuing policies that enable adaptation seems like common sense. Yet, weirdly, for a long time it was considered bad form in climate change policy discussions to even mention adaptation.[10] Climate change campaigners have tended to view the idea of adaptation as distracting from cutting carbon dioxide emissions. Perhaps they also believe that acknowledging the need for adaptation is an admission of defeat in the battle against climate change.

To the contrary: if we are to fix climate change, we need to put adaptation at the heart of our policy response.

There is perhaps no better example of the need to adapt—and to include adaptation in any description of the future—when it comes to rising seas. Sea level rise gets a huge amount of attention, and it is often portrayed as uncharted territory for humanity. In fact, sea levels have risen about a foot over the past 150 years.[11] Around the world, when you ask anyone what important events happened over that century and a half, they will talk about wars, medical breakthroughs that saved lives, perhaps the moon landing—but they won't tell you that rising sea levels were a big deal. Why? Because we adapted to them by protecting our coastlines.

One of the clearest results from adaptation studies around the world is that coastal protection for populations and valuable land is a great investment.[12] It turns out that global coastal protection costing tens of billions of dollars can avoid tens of trillions of dollars in flood damages.

That is why a recent overview shows that the cost of sea level adaptation almost everywhere will be much lower than the cost of not adapting. The study shows that even if the seas were to rise an improbable 6 feet 7 inches (2 meters) by 2100—vastly more than the United Nations expects—it would be economically advantageous to protect at least 90 percent of the global coastal floodplain population along with 96 percent of all assets.[13]

For more than half of the global population in the coastal floodplains, each dollar spent on protection will avoid more than one hundred dollars of damage. The total cost of protection *and* all remaining flooding damage across the century, even in the absolute worst-case scenario, will cost the United States just 0.037 percent of its GDP, and possibly one-fifth of that.[14]

Coastal defense in many cases will mean dikes (a long wall or embankment built to prevent flooding), but softer approaches, often without government support, such as artificial nourishment (meaning adding sand to beaches), can be even more effective in dealing with the impacts of sea level rise and storm surges.[15] In an overview of nineteen studies, dikes on average reduce damages by $40 for each dollar spent, but artificial nourishment can avoid $111 in damages for each dollar spent.

More natural defenses, such as restoration of mangroves, can help, too. As well as providing a buffer against tidal storm surges, mangroves provide critical habitat to sustain local fisheries. Planting (or reestablishing) mangrove forests, as is being done in Indonesia and elsewhere, is a fraction of the expense of building flood protection infrastructure. The benefits of mangrove preservation and restoration are worth up to ten times the cost, including not just avoided losses from coastal flooding but also the benefits associated with fisheries, forestry, and recreation.[16] Clearly, poorer people have fewer resources to spend on adaptation (see chapter 5). When a hurricane hits poor shanty towns, many people die. When a hurricane hits rich Florida, it might have a severe economic impact, but the human devastation is far less, because most can afford to invest in much more adaptation.

Perhaps the most remarkable fact about adaptation is that most of its benefits can be achieved fairly cheaply within days or a few years. Compare this speed to the delayed impact of worldwide carbon taxes. Adaptive actions can typically deliver much more, faster and more cheaply than any realistic climate policy.

As this book amply attests, we should invest far more in planning and infrastructure to provide protection from natural disasters, rising sea levels, and changes in temperatures. We must do all of this with a clear understanding that adaptation is an effective and necessary climate policy.

## Notes

1. Giuseppe Formetta and Luc Feyen, "Empirical Evidence of Declining Global Vulnerability to Climate-Related Hazards," *Global Environmental Change* 57 (July 2019), https://doi.org/10.1016/j.gloenvcha.2019.05.004.
2. Maximilian Auffhammer and Erin T. Mansur, "Measuring Climatic Impacts on Energy Consumption: A Review of the Empirical Literature," *Energy Economics* 46 (November 2014): 522–30, https://doi.org/10.1016/j.eneco.2014.04.017.
3. Maria Berrittella, Andrea Bigano, Roberto Roson, and Richard S. J. Tol, "A General Equilibrium Analysis of Climate Change Impacts on Tourism," *Tourism Management* 27, no. 5 (October 2006): 913–24, https://doi.org/10.1016/j.tourman.2005.05.002.
4. Rico Kongsager, "Linking Climate Change Adaptation and Mitigation: A Review with Evidence from the Land-Use Sectors," *Land* 7, no. 4 (December 2018): 8, https://doi.org/10.3390/land7040158.
5. Sam Fankhauser, "Adaptation to Climate Change," *Annual Review of Resource Economics* 9, no. 1 (October 2017): 215, https://doi.org/10.1146/annurev-resource-100516-033554.
6. Shardul Agrawala et al., "Private Sector Engagement in Adaptation to Climate Change: Approaches to Managing Climate Risks," OECD Environment Working Papers no. 39 (November 2011): 29, https://doi.org/10.1787/5kg221jkf1g7-en.
7. S. Niggol Seo and Robert Mendelsohn, "An Analysis of Crop Choice: Adapting to Climate Change in South American Farms," *Ecological Economics* 67, no. 1 (August 2008): 109–16. https://doi.org/10.1016/j.ecolecon.2007.12.007.
8. Minjie Chen et al., "Diversification and Intensification of Agricultural Adaptation from Global to Local Scales," *PLOS ONE* 13, no. 5 (May 2018): e0196392, https://doi.org/10.1371/journal.pone.0196392; Melese Gezie, "Farmer's Response to Climate Change and Variability in Ethiopia: A Review," *Cogent Food & Agriculture* 5, no. 1 (May 2019), https://doi.org/10.1080/23311932.2019.1613770; Khuda Bakhsh and M. Asif Kamran, "Adaptation to Climate Change in Rain-Fed Farming System in Punjab, Pakistan," *International Journal of the Commons* 13, no. 2 (October 2019): 833–47, https://doi.org/10.5334/ijc.887.

9. Salvatore Di Falco, Marcella Veronesi, and Mahmud Yesuf, "Does Adaptation to Climate Change Provide Food Security? A Micro-Perspective from Ethiopia," *American Journal of Agricultural Economics* 93, no. 3 (March 2011): 829–46. https://doi.org/10.1093/ajae/aar006.

10. Kongsager, "Linking Climate Change Adaptation and Mitigation," 158.

11. Sea level rise of 31 cm or 1.01 ft from an average of 1850–70 up to 2010. S. Jevrejeva, J. C. Moore, A. Grinsted, A. P. Matthews, and G. Spada, "Trends and Acceleration in Global and Regional Sea Levels since 1807," *Global and Planetary Change* 113 (February 2014): 11–22, https://doi.org/10.1016/j.gloplacha.2013.12.004.

12. Jochen Hinkel et al., "Coastal Flood Damage and Adaptation Costs under 21st Century Sea-Level Rise," *Proceedings of the National Academy of Sciences* 111, no. 9 (Mar. 2014): 3292–97, https://doi.org/10.1073/pnas.1222469111; Daniel Lincke and Jochen Hinkel, "Economically Robust Protection against 21st Century Sea-Level Rise," *Global Environmental Change—Human and Policy Dimensions* 51 (July 2018): 67–73, https://doi.org/10.1016/j.gloenvcha.2018.05.003; Ambika Markanday, Ibon Galarraga, and Anil Markandya, "A Critical Review of Cost-Benefit Analysis for Climate Change Adaptation in Cities," *Climate Change Economics* 10, no. 4 (November 2019), https://doi.org/10.1142/S2010007819500143.

13. Lincke and Hinkel, "Economically Robust Protection against 21st Century Sea-Level Rise."

14. Lincke and Hinkel, "Economically Robust Protection against 21st Century Sea-Level Rise," table S1.

15. Markanday, Galarraga, and Markandya, "A Critical Review of Cost-Benefit Analysis," 19.

16. Global Commission on Adaptation, *Adapt Now: A Global Call for Leadership on Climate Resilience* (2019), 14, 31, https://gca.org/global-commission-on-adaptation/report.

# Bibliography

Agrawala, Shardul, Maëlis Carraro, Nicholas Kingsmill, Elisa Lanzi, Michael Mullan, and Guillaume Prudent-Richard. "Private Sector Engagement in Adaptation to Climate Change: Approaches to Managing Climate Risks." OECD Environment Working Papers no. 39, November 2011. https://doi.org /10.1787/5kg221jkf1g7-en.

Akimoto, Keigo, Fuminori Sano, Takashi Homma, Junichiro Oda, Miyuki Nagashima, and Masanobu Kii. "Estimates of GHG Emission Reduction Potential by Country, Sector, and Cost." *Energy Policy* 38, no. 7 (July 2010): 3384–93.

Alaska Department of Fish and Game (ADFG). "Harvest Information for Community." Allakaket, 2011. http://www.adfg.alaska.gov/sb/CSIS/index.cfm ?ADFG=harvInfo.harvest.

———. "Harvest Information for Community." Barrow, 2014. http://www.adfg .alaska.gov/sb/CSIS/index.cfm?ADFG=harvInfo.harvest.

———. *Hunting Maps by Hunt Type, Search Results for Tier II Hunts.* http://www .adfg.alaska.gov/index.cfm?adfg=huntingmaps.byhunttype.

Alaska Department of Natural Resources (ADNR). "Fact Sheet, Off-Road Travel on the North Slope on State Land," 2015. http://dnr.alaska.gov/mlw/factsht /land_fs/off-road_travel.pdf.

Alaska Division of Community and Regional Affairs (DCRA). DCRA Information Portal, Utqiagvik, Alaska, 2018. https://dcced.maps.arcgis.com /apps/MapJournal/index.html?appid=2393d4e4452448c4a55af959a3c7c817#.

Alaska Eskimo Whaling Commission. Bowhead Harvest Quota. http://www.aewc -alaska.com/bowhead-quota.html.

Aldy, Joseph E. "Carbon Tax Review and Updating: Institutionalizing an Act-Learn-Act Approach to US Climate Policy." *Review of Environmental Economics and Policy* 14, no. 1 (Winter 2020): 76–94.

———. "Frameworks for Evaluating Policy Approaches to Address the Competitiveness Concerns of Mitigating Greenhouse Gas Emissions." *National Tax Journal* 70, no. 2 (June 2017): 395–420.

Aldy, Joseph E., and William A. Pizer. "The Competitiveness Impacts of Climate Change Mitigation Policies." *Journal of the Association of Environmental and Resource Economists* 2, no. 4 (September 2015): 565–95.

Aldy, Joseph E., William A. Pizer, and Keigo Akimoto. "Comparing Emissions Mitigation Efforts across Countries." *Climate Policy* 17, no. 4 (2017): 501–15.

Aldy, Joseph E., and Richard Zeckhauser. "Three Prongs for Prudent Climate Policy." Harvard Kennedy School Faculty Research Working Paper Series, April 2020.

Amiti, Mary, Stephen J. Redding, and David E. Weinstein. "The Impact of the 2018 Tariffs on Prices and Welfare." *Journal of Economic Perspectives* 33, no. 4 (Fall 2019): 187–210.

Anderson, Robert T. "Sovereignty and Subsistence: Native Self-Government and Rights to Hunt, Fish, and Gather after ANCSA. (Special Issue on the Forty-Fifth Anniversary of the Alaska Native Claims Settlement Act)." *Alaska Law Review* 33, no. 2 (2016): 187.

Anderson, Terry L., and Peter J. Hill. "The Evolution of Property Rights: A Study of the American West." *Journal of Law and Economics* 18, no. 1 (April 1975): 163–79.

Anderson, Terry L., and Donald R. Leal. *Free Market Environmentalism: For the Next Generation.* New York: Palgrave Macmillan, 2015.

Anderson, Terry L., and Gary D. Libecap. *Environmental Markets: A Property Rights Approach.* New York: Cambridge University Press, 2014.

Arrow, Kenneth J. "Insurance, Risk and Resource Allocation." In *Essays in the Theory of Risk Bearing*, 134–43. Amsterdam: North-Holland, 1974.

Artemis. "Catastrophe Bonds and ILS Issued and Outstanding by Year." https://www.artemis.bm/dashboard/catastrophe-bonds-ils-issued-and-outstanding-by-year/, accessed May 5, 2019.

Auffhammer, Maximilian. "Quantifying Economic Damages from Climate Change." *Journal of Economic Perspectives* 32, no. 4 (November 2018): 33–52.

Auffhammer, Maximilian, and Erin T. Mansur. "Measuring Climatic Impacts on Energy Consumption: A Review of the Empirical Literature." *Energy Economics* 46 (November 2014): 522–30. https://doi.org/10.1016/j.eneco.2014.04.017.

Bailey, David, and David Bookbinder. "The Conservative Case against Market-Oriented Climate Policy." Niskanen Center, July 5, 2015. https://www.niskanencenter.org/the-conservative-case-against-market-oriented-climate-policy.

Bakhsh, Khuda, and M. Asif Kamran. "Adaptation to Climate Change in Rain-Fed Farming System in Punjab, Pakistan." *International Journal of the Commons* 13, no. 2 (October 2019): 833–47. https://doi.org/10.5334/ijc.887.

Baldauf, Markus, Lorenzo Garlappi, and Constantine Yannelis. "Does Climate Change Affect Real Estate Prices? Only If You Believe in It." *Review of Financial Studies* 33, no. 3 (March 2020): 1256–95.

Baldos, Uris Lantz C., and Thomas W. Hertel. "The Role of International Trade in Managing Food Security Risks from Climate Change." *Food Security* 7, no. 2 (2015): 275–90.

Balistreri, Edward J., Daniel T. Kaffine, and Hidemichi Yonezawa. "Optimal Environmental Border Adjustments under the General Agreement on Tariffs and Trade." *Environmental and Resource Economics* 74, no. 3 (November 2019): 1037–75.

Barrett, Scott. "Self-Enforcing International Environmental Agreements." *Oxford Economic Papers* 46 (October 1994): 878–94.

Barzel, Yoram. *Economic Analysis of Property Rights.* Cambridge: Cambridge University Press, 1997.

Baum, Rachel, Gregory W. Characklis, and Marc L. Serre. "Effects of Geographic Diversification on Risk Pooling to Mitigate Drought-Related Financial Losses for Water Utilities." *Water Resources Research* 54, no. 4 (April 2018): 2561–79.

Baum, Rachel, Jonathan D. Herman, and Gregory W. Characklis. "Designing Index Insurance Contracts to Manage Hydrologically-Driven Financial Risks Using Machine Learning." *Water Resources Research* (forthcoming).

Baylis, Patrick, and Judson Boomhower. "Moral Hazard, Wildfires, and the Economic Incidence of Natural Disasters." National Bureau of Economic Research, NBER Working Paper 26550, December 2019.

Bebchuk, Lucian A., and Roberto Tallarita. "The Illusory Promise of Stakeholder Governance." Working draft, Harvard Law School, March 2020.

Beck, Marisa, Nicholas Rivers, Randall Wigle, and Hidemichi Yonezawa. "Carbon Tax and Revenue Recycling: Impacts on Households in British Columbia." *Resource and Energy Economics* 41 (August 2015): 40–69.

Becker, Gary S. "Public Policies, Pressure Groups, and Dead Weight Costs." *Journal of Public Economics* 28, no. 3 (December 1985): 329–47.

———. "A Theory of Competition among Pressure Groups for Political Influence." *Quarterly Journal of Economics* 98, no. 3 (August 1983): 371–400.

Bennett, T. M. Bull, Patricia Cochran, Robert Gough, Kathy Lynn, Julie Maldonado, Garrit Voggesser, Susan Wotkyns, and Karen Cozzetto. "Indigenous Peoples, Lands, and Resources." In *Climate Change Impacts in the United States: The*

*Third National Climate Assessment*, 297–317. Washington, DC: US Global Change Research Program, 2014.

Berkes, Fikret, and Dyanna Jolly. "Adapting to Climate Change: Social-Ecological Resilience in a Canadian Western Arctic Community." *Conservation Ecology* 5, no. 2 (January 2002): 18.

Bernstein, Asaf, Matthew T. Gustafson, and Ryan Lewis. "Disaster on the Horizon: The Price Effect of Sea Level Rise." *Journal of Financial Economics* 134, no. 2 (November 2019): 253–72.

Berrittella, Maria, Andrea Bigano, Roberto Roson, and Richard S. J. Tol. "A General Equilibrium Analysis of Climate Change Impacts on Tourism." *Tourism Management* 27, no. 5 (October 2006): 913–24. https://doi.org/10.1016/j.tourman.2005.05.002.

Bin, Okmyung, Thomas W. Crawford, Jamie B. Kruse, and Craig E. Landry. "Viewscapes and Flood Hazard: Coastal Housing Market Response to Amenities and Risk." *Land Economics* 84, no. 3 (August 2008): 434–48.

Blue Forest Conservation. "Fighting Fire with Finance: A Roadmap for Collective Action," 2017. https://static1.squarespace.com/static/556a1885e4b0bdc6f0794659/t/59c1157f80bd5e1cd855010e/1505826201656/FRB+2017+Roadmap+Report.pdf.

Böhringer, Christoph, Edward J. Balistreri, and Thomas F. Rutherford. "The Role of Border Carbon Adjustment in Unilateral Climate Policy: Overview of an Energy Modeling Forum Study (EMF 29)." *Energy Economics* 34, no. S2 (December 2012): S97–S110.

Böhringer, Christoph, Jared C. Carbone, and Thomas F. Rutherford. "Embodied Carbon Tariffs." *Scandinavian Journal of Economics* 120, no. 1 (January 2018): 183–210.

———. "The Strategic Value of Carbon Tariffs." *American Economic Journal: Economic Policy* 8, no. 1 (February 2016): 28–51.

Bown, Chad, and Melina Kolb. "Trump's Trade War Timeline: An Up-to-Date Guide." Peterson Institute for International Economics, March 13, 2020. https://www.piie.com/blogs/trade-investment-policy-watch/trump-trade-war-china-date-guide.

Branger, Frédéric, and Philippe Quirion. "Would Border Carbon Adjustments Prevent Carbon Leakage and Heavy Industry Competitiveness Losses? Insights from a Meta-Analysis of Recent Economic Studies." *Ecological Economics* 99 (2014): 29–39.

Branger, Frédéric, Philippe Quirion, and Julien Chevallier. "Carbon Leakage and Competitiveness of Cement and Steel Industries under the EU ETS: Much Ado about Nothing." *Energy Journal* 37, no. 3 (2016).

Brinkman, Todd J., Winslow D. Hansen, F. Stuart Chapin, Gary Kofinas, Shauna BurnSilver, and T. Scott Rupp. "Arctic Communities Perceive Climate Impacts on Access as a Critical Challenge to Availability of Subsistence Resources." *Climatic Change* 139, nos. 3–4 (2016): 413–27.

British Petroleum. *BP Statistical Review of World Energy 2019*. https://www .bp.com/content/dam/bp/business-sites/en/global/corporate/pdfs/energy -economics/statistical-review/bp-stats-review-2019-full-report.pdf.

Bronen, Robin. *Climate-Induced Displacement of Alaska Native Communities*. Washington, DC: Brookings Institution, 2013. https://www.brookings.edu/research /climate-induced-displacement-of-alaska-native-communities/.

Brown, Steven E. F. "Wine from Wyoming? How Yellowstone and Yukon Will Steal Napa's Crown." *San Francisco Business Times*, April 9, 2013.

Brubaker, Michael, James Berner, Jacob Bell, John Warren, and Alicia Rolin. "Climate Change in Point Hope, Alaska: Strategies for Community Health." Alaska Native Tribal Health Consortium, 2010. https://www.cidrap.umn.edu /sites/default/files/public/php/26952/Climate%20Change%20HIA%20Report _Point%20Hope_0.pdf.

Burke, Marshall, Melanie Craxton, Charles D. Kolstad, Chikara Onda, Hunt Allcott, Erin Baker, Lint Barrage et al. "Opportunities for Advances in Climate Change Economics." *Science* 352, no. 6283 (April 2016): 292–93.

BurnSilver, Shauna, James Magdanz, Rhian Stotts, Matthew Berman, and Gary Kofinas. "Are Mixed Economies Persistent or Transitional? Evidence Using Social Networks from Arctic Alaska." *American Anthropologist* 118, no. 1 (March 2016): 121–29. https://doi.org/10.1111/aman.12447.

California Public Employees' Retirement System (CalPERS). "Addressing Climate Change Risk." https://www.calpers.ca.gov/docs/forms-publications/addressing -climate-change-risk.pdf, accessed June 4, 2020.

Carbone, Jared C., Carsten Helm, and Thomas F. Rutherford. "The Case for International Emission Trade in the Absence of Cooperative Climate Policy." *Journal of Environmental Economics and Management* 58, no. 3 (November 2009): 266–80.

Carbone, Jared C., and Nicholas Rivers. "The Impacts of Unilateral Climate Policy on Competitiveness: Evidence from Computable General Equilibrium Models." *Review of Environmental Economics and Policy* 11, no. 1 (Winter 2017): 24–42.

Carey, Erin. "Building Resilience to Climate Change in Rural Alaska: Understanding Impacts, Adaptation, and the Role of TEK." MA thesis, University of Michigan, 2009.

Casey, Brendan J., Wayne B. Gray, Joshua Linn, and Richard Morgenstern. "How Does State-Level Carbon Pricing in the United States Affect Industrial Competitiveness?" National Bureau of Economic Research, NBER Working Paper 26629, January 2020.

Cassidy, John. "Steady State: Can We Have Prosperity without Economic Growth?" *New Yorker*, February 10, 2020, 24–27.

Chapin, F. Stuart, III, and Patricia Cochran. "Community Partnership for Self Reliance and Sustainability, Final Report to Communities from the Alaska Native Science Commission and the University of Alaska Fairbanks." Working paper, 2014.

Chapin, F. Stuart, III, Carl Folke, and Gary P. Kofinas. "A Framework for Understanding Change." In *Principles of Ecosystem Stewardship: Resilience-Based Natural Resource Management in a Changing World*, edited by F. Stuart Chapin III, Gary P. Kofinas, and Carl Folke, 3–28. New York: Springer, 2009.

Chapman, Theodore A., and James M. Breeding. *U.S. Public Finance Waterworks, Sanitary Sewer, and Drainage Utility Systems: Methodology and Assumptions*. New York: S&P Global Market Intelligence, 2016.

Charles, Dan. "Gardening Map of Warming U.S. Has Plant Zones Moving North." *NPR*, January 26, 2012.

Chen, Minjie, Bruno Wichmann, Marty Luckert, Leigh Winowiecki, Wiebke Förch, and Peter Läderach. "Diversification and Intensification of Agricultural Adaptation from Global to Local Scales." *PLOS ONE* 13, no. 5 (May 2018): e0196392. https://doi.org/10.1371/journal.pone.0196392.

Clark, Annette McFadyen. *Koyokuk River Culture: National Museum of Man*. Ottawa: National Museums of Canada, 1974.

Clinton, Bill. Executive Order 13175, Consultation and Coordination with Indian Tribal Governments, November 6, 2000.

Coase, R. H. "The Problem of Social Cost." *Journal of Law and Economics* 3 (October 1960): 1–44.

Cochran, Patricia, Orville H. Huntington, Caleb Pungowiyi, Stanley Tom, F. Stuart Chapin III, Henry P. Huntington, Nancy G. Maynard, and Sarah F. Trainor. "Indigenous Frameworks for Observing and Responding to Climate Change in Alaska." *Climatic Change* 120, no. 3 (October 2013): 557–67.

Conti, Katheleen. 2018. "Homes near Ocean Risk Losing Value, Even in a Hot Market." *Boston Globe*, April 23, 2018.

Coombs, Chelsey B. "Climate Change Brings New Crops to Canadian Farms." *Climate Central*, July 16, 2015.

Cosbey, Aaron, Susanne Droege, Carolyn Fischer, and Clayton Munnings. "Developing Guidance for Implementing Border Carbon Adjustments: Lessons, Cautions, and Research Needs from the Literature." *Review of Environmental Economics and Policy* 13, no. 1 (Winter 2019): 3–22.

Cottier, Thomas, Olga Nartova, and Anirudh Shingal. "The Potential of Tariff Policy for Climate Change Mitigation: Legal and Economic Analysis." *Journal of World Trade* 48, no. 5 (2014): 1007–37.

Council of Economic Advisers. *Economic Report of the President*. Washington, DC: Government Printing Office, 2018.

Craig, Robin Kundis. "'Stationarity Is Dead'—Long Live Transformation: Five Principles for Climate Change Adaptation Law." *Harvard Environmental Law Review* 34, no. 1 (2010): 9–75.

Crocker, Thomas D. "The Structuring of Atmospheric Pollution Control Systems." *Economics of Air Pollution* 61 (1966): 81–84.

Crowley, Kate. "Up and Down with Climate Politics 2013–2016: The Repeal of Carbon Pricing in Australia." *Wiley Interdisciplinary Reviews: Climate Change* 8, no. 3 (May/June 2017): e458.

Cusick, Daniel. "Climate Change a Boon for Analytics Firms." *Climatewire*, April 23, 2019. https://www.eenews.net/climatewire/2019/04/23/stories/1060201479.

Davis, Steven J., and Ken Caldeira. "Consumption-Based Accounting of $CO_2$ Emissions." *Proceedings of the National Academy of Sciences* 107, no. 12 (March 2010): 5687–92.

De Neufville, Richard, and Stefan Scholtes. *Flexibility in Engineering Design*. Cambridge, MA: MIT Press, 2011.

Di Falco, Salvatore, Marcella Veronesi, and Mahmud Yesuf. "Does Adaptation to Climate Change Provide Food Security? A Micro-Perspective from Ethiopia." *American Journal of Agricultural Economics* 93, no. 3 (March 2011): 829–46. https://doi.org/10.1093/ajae/aar006.

Dinan, Terry, Perry Beider, and David Wylie. "The National Flood Insurance Program: Is It Financially Sound?" *Risk Management and Insurance Review* 22, no. 1 (March 2019): 15–38.

Dixit, Avinash K., Robert K. Dixit, and Robert S. Pindyck. *Investment under Uncertainty*. Princeton, NJ: Princeton University Press, 1994.

Doda, Baran, Simon Quemin, and Luca Taschini. "Linking Permit Markets Multilaterally." Working paper, 2019.

Dumond, Don E. "A Chronology of Native Alaskan Subsistence Systems." *Senri Ethnological Studies* 4 (1980): 23–47.

*Economist.* "Softening the Blow: Climate Adaptation Policies Are Needed More Than Ever." 2020 Schools Brief, May 30, 2020. https://www.economist.com/schools -brief/2020/05/30/climate-adaptation-policies-are-needed-more-than-ever.

Egger, Peter, Mario Larch, Kevin E. Staub, and Rainer Winkelmann. "The Trade Effects of Endogenous Preferential Trade Agreements." *American Economic Journal: Economic Policy* 3, no. 3 (August 2011): 113–43.

Eichholtz, Piet, Eva Steiner, and Erkan Yönder. "Where, When, and How Do Sophisticated Investors Respond to Flood Risk?" SSRN, 2019. https://dx.doi .org/10.2139/ssrn.3206257.

Environmental Protection Agency (EPA). "DC Water's Environmental Impact Bond: A First of Its Kind, U.S. EPA Water Infrastructure and Resiliency Finance Center," April 2017. https://www.epa.gov/sites/production/files/2017 -04/documents/dc_waters_environmental_impact_bond_a_first_of_its_kind _final2.pdf.

Fajgelbaum, Pablo D., Pinelopi K. Goldberg, Patrick J. Kennedy, and Amit K. Khandelwal. "The Return to Protectionism." *Quarterly Journal of Economics* 135, no. 1 (February 2020): 1–55.

Fankhauser, Sam. "Adaptation to Climate Change." *Annual Review of Resource Economics* 9, no. 1 (October 2017): 209–30. https://doi.org/10.1146/annurev -resource-100516-033554.

Fell, Harrison, and Peter Maniloff. "Leakage in Regional Environmental Policy: The Case of the Regional Greenhouse Gas Initiative." *Journal of Environmental Economics and Management* 87 (January 2018): 1–23.

Fernandez-Gimenez, Maria E., Henry P. Huntington, and Kathryn J. Frost. "Integration or Co-optation? Traditional Knowledge and Science in the Alaska Beluga Whale Committee." *Environmental Conservation* 33, no. 4 (2006): 306–15.

Figlio, David N., and Maurice E. Lucas. "What's in a Grade? School Report Cards and the Housing Market." *American Economic Review* 94, no. 3 (June 2004): 591–604.

Fink, Larry. "A Fundamental Reshaping of Finance." BlackRock. https://www .blackrock.com/corporate/investor-relations/larry-fink-ceo-letter, accessed June 4, 2020.

Finkelstein, David, Andreas Strzodka, and James I. Vickery. "Credit Risk Transfer and De Facto GSE Reform." *Economic Policy Review* 24, no. 3 (December 2018).

Fischer, Carolyn, and Alan K. Fox. "Comparing Policies to Combat Emissions Leakage: Border Carbon Adjustments versus Rebates." *Journal of Environmental Economics and Management* 64, no. 2 (September 2012): 199–216.

Fischman, Robert L., and Jillian R. Rountree. "Adaptive Management." In *The Law of Adaptation to Climate Change: U.S. and International Aspects*, eds. Michael

Gerrard and Katrina Fischer Kuh, 19–47. Chicago: American Bar Association, Section of Environment, Energy, and Resources, 2012.

Forgey, Pat. "Natives Losing Political Influence." *Juneau Empire*, March 24, 2010. http://juneauempire.com/stories/032410/sta_595649976.shtml.

Formetta, Giuseppe, and Luc Feyen. "Empirical Evidence of Declining Global Vulnerability to Climate-Related Hazards." *Global Environmental Change* 57 (July 2019). https://doi.org/10.1016/j.gloenvcha.2019.05.004.

Foster, Benjamin T., Gregory W. Characklis, and W. Thurman. "Hedging Performance of Corn Futures and Forwards Contracts during Drought on the Mississippi River." Forthcoming.

Foster, Benjamin T., Jordan D. Kern, and Gregory W. Characklis. "Mitigating Hydrologic Financial Risk in Hydropower Generation Using Index-Based Financial Instruments." *Water Resources and Economics* 10 (April 2015): 45–67. doi:10.1016/j.wre.2015.04.001.

Fowlie, Meredith, and Mar Reguant. "Challenges in the Measurement of Leakage Risk." *AEA Papers and Proceedings* 108 (May 2018): 124–29.

Friedman, Milton. "The Social Responsibility of Business Is to Increase Its Profits." *New York Times Magazine,* September 13, 1970.

Frolicher, Thomas L., and Fortunat Joos. "Reversible and Irreversible Impacts of Greenhouse Gas Emissions in Multi-Century Projections with the NCAR Global Coupled Carbon Cycle-Climate Model." *Climate Dynamics* 35, nos. 7–8 (December 2010): 1439–59.

Funk, McKenzie. *Windfall: The Booming Business of Global Warming.* New York: Penguin, 2014.

Gelles, David. "Falcons, Drones, Data: A Winery Battles Climate Change." *New York Times*, January 5, 2017.

Geneva Association. "Climate Change and the Insurance Industry, Taking Action as Risk Managers and Investors," 2018. https://www.genevaassociation .org/sites/default/files/research-topics-document-type/pdf_public//climate _change_and_the_insurance_industry_-_taking_action_as_risk_managers _and_investors.pdf.

———. "Managing Physical Climate Risk: Leveraging Innovations in Catastrophe Risk Modelling," 2018. https://www.genevaassociation.org/sites/default/files /research-topics-document-type/pdf_public/ga_risk_modelling_18112018 .pdf.

Gezie, Melese. "Farmer's Response to Climate Change and Variability in Ethiopia: A Review." *Cogent Food & Agriculture* 5, no. 1 (May 2019). https://doi.org/10 .1080/23311932.2019.1613770.

Giglio, Stefano, Matteo Maggiori, Johannes Stroebel, and Andreas Weber. "Climate Change and Long-Run Discount Rates: Evidence from Real Estate." National Bureau of Economic Research, NBER Working Paper 21767, November 2015.

Glanemann, Nicole. *The Optimal Climate Policy of Mitigation and Adaptation: A Real Options Theory Perspective.* Hamburg: WiSo-Forschungslabor, 2014.

Global Commission on Adaptation. *Adapt Now: A Global Call for Leadership on Climate Resilience,* 2019. https://gca.org/global-commission-on-adaptation/report.

Goulder, Lawrence H., and Roberton C. Williams III. "The Choice of Discount Rate for Climate Change Policy Evaluation." National Bureau of Economic Research, NBER Working Paper 18301, August 2012.

Greenstone, Michael. Statement to the US House Committee on Oversight and Reform, Hearing on Economics of Climate Change, December 19, 2019. https://epic.uchicago.edu/wp-content/uploads/2019/12/Greenstone-Testimony-12192019-FINAL.pdf.

Guettabi, Mouhcine, Joshua Greenberg, Joseph Little, and Kyle Joly. "Evaluating Differences in Household Subsistence Harvest Patterns between the Ambler Project and Non-Project Zones." Natural Resource Report NPS/GAAR/NRR—2016/1280. National Park Service, Fort Collins, Colorado, 2016.

Hamilton, Andrew L., Gregory W. Characklis, and Patrick M. Reed. "Managing Financial Risk Tradeoffs for Hydropower Generation Using Snowpack-Based Index Contracts." *Water Resources Research* (forthcoming).

Hannah, Lee, Patrick R. Roehrdanz, Makihiko Ikegami, Anderson V. Shepard, M. Rebecca Shaw, Gary Tabor, Lu Zhi, Pablo A. Marquet, and Robert J. Hijmans. "Climate Change, Wine, and Conservation." *Proceedings of the National Academy of Sciences* 110, no. 17 (April 2013): 6907–12.

Harder, Amy. "Coronavirus and Climate Change Are Obvious Risks We Ignore." *Axios,* March 9, 2020.

Hardin, Garrett. "The Tragedy of the Commons." *Science* 162, no. 3859 (December 1968): 1243–48.

Hart, Oliver. "Incomplete Contracts and Control." *American Economic Review* 107, no. 7 (July 2017): 1731–52.

Hartman, Devin. "Environmental Benefits of Electricity Policy Reform." R Street Policy Study No. 82, January 2017.

Hauer, Mathew E. "Migration Induced by Sea-Level Rise Could Reshape the US Population Landscape." *Nature Climate Change,* April 17, 2017.

Hayek, Friedrich A. "The Use of Knowledge in Society." *American Economic Review* 35, no. 4 (September 1945): 519–30.

Helm, Dieter, Cameron Hepburn, and Giovanni Ruta. "Trade, Climate Change, and the Political Game Theory of Border Carbon Adjustments." *Oxford Review of Economic Policy* 28, no. 2 (November 2012): 368–94.

Hinkel, Jochen, Daniel Lincke, Athanasios T. Vafeidis, Mahé Perrette, Robert James Nicholls, Richard S. J. Tol, Ben Marzeion, Xavier Fettweis, Cezar Ionescu, and Anders Levermann. "Coastal Flood Damage and Adaptation Costs under 21st Century Sea-Level Rise." *Proceedings of the National Academy of Sciences* 111, no. 9 (March 2014): 3292–97. https://doi.org/10.1073/pnas.1222469111.

Holen, Davin. "Fishing for Community and Culture: The Value of Fisheries in Rural Alaska." *Northern Fisheries* 50, no. 4 (2014): 403–13.

Holling, C. S., Fikret Berkes, and Carl Folke. "Science, Sustainability and Resource Management." In *Linking Social and Ecological Systems: Management Practices and Social Mechanisms for Building Resilience*, eds. Fikret Berkes, Carl Folke, and Johan Colding, 342–62. Cambridge: Cambridge University Press, 1998.

Holmes, Peter, Tom Reilly, and Jim Rollo. "Border Carbon Adjustments and the Potential for Protectionism." *Climate Policy* 11, no. 2 (2011): 883–900.

Intergovernmental Panel on Climate Change. *Climate Change 2014: Impacts, Adaptation, and Vulnerability*. Cambridge: Cambridge University Press, 2014.

Jacobs, Melanie B., and Jeffery J. Brooks. "Alaska Native Peoples and Conservation Planning: A Recipe for Meaningful Participation." *Native Studies Review* 20, no. 2 (2011): 91–135.

Jeuland, Marc. "Economic Implications of Climate Change for Infrastructure Planning in Transboundary Water Systems: An Example from the Blue Nile." *Water Resources Research* 46, no. 11 (November 2010).

Jevrejeva, S., J. C. Moore, A. Grinsted, A. P. Matthews, and G. Spada. "Trends and Acceleration in Global and Regional Sea Levels since 1807." *Global and Planetary Change* 113 (February 2014): 11–22. https://doi.org/10.1016/j.gloplacha.2013.12.004.

Jin, Ginger Z., and Phillip Leslie. "The Effect of Information on Product Quality: Evidence from Restaurant Hygiene Grade Cards." *Quarterly Journal of Economics* 118, no. 2 (May 2003): 409–51.

Jos, Philip H., and Annette Watson. "Privileging Knowledge Claims in Collaborative Regulatory Management: An Ethnography of Marginalization." *Administration & Society* 51, no. 3 (2016).

Joskow, Paul L. "Vertical Integration." In *Handbook of New Institutional Economics*, eds. C. Menard and M. Shirley, 319–48. Dordrecht, Netherlands: Springer, 2005.

Keenan, Jesse M., Thomas Hill, and Anurag Gumber. "Climate Gentrification: From Theory to Empiricism in Miami-Dade County, Florida." *Environmental Research Letters* 13, no. 5 (May 2018): 1.

Kern, Jordan D., and Gregory W. Characklis. "Evaluating the Physical and Financial Vulnerability of Power Systems to Drought under Climate Uncertainty and an Evolving Generation Mix." *Environmental Science & Technology* 51 (August 2017): 8815–23. doi:10.1021/acs.est.6b05460.

Kern, Jordan D., Gregory W. Characklis, and Benjamin T. Foster. "Natural Gas Price Uncertainty and the Cost-Effectiveness of Hedging against Low Hydropower Revenues Caused by Drought." *Water Resources Research* 51, no. 4 (April 2015): 2412–27.

Kettle, N., J. Martin, and M. Sloan. *Nome Tribal Climate Adaptation Plan.* Nome Eskimo Community and the Alaska Center for Climate Assessment and Policy, Fairbanks, Alaska, September 2017. https://www.necalaska.org/PDF/6.%20 Tribal_Resources/Nome%20Tribal%20Climate%20Adaptation%20Plan%20 (Final-LowRes).pdf.

Kimmel, Mara. "Fate Control and Human Rights: The Policies and Practices of Local Governance in America's Arctic." *Alaska Law Review* 31 (2014): 179.

Knapp, Corrine N., F. Stuart Chapin III, Gary P. Kofinas, Nancy Fresco, Courtney Carothers, and Amy Craver. "Parks, People, and Change: The Importance of Multistakeholder Engagement in Adaptation Planning for Conserved Areas." *Ecology and Society* 19, no. 4 (December 2014): 16.

Knight, Frank H. *Risk, Uncertainty, and Profit.* Boston: Riverside Press, 1921.

Kofinas, Gary P., F. Stuart Chapin III, Shauna BurnSilver, Jennifer I. Schmidt, Nancy L. Fresco, Knut Kielland, Stephanie Martin, Anna Springsteen, and T. Scott Rupp. "Resilience of Athabascan Subsistence Systems to Interior Alaska's Changing Climate." *Canadian Journal of Forest Research* 40, no. 7 (2010): 1347–59.

Kongsager, Rico. "Linking Climate Change Adaptation and Mitigation: A Review with Evidence from the Land-Use Sectors." *Land* 7, no. 4 (December 2018): 158. https://doi.org/10.3390/land7040158.

Kortum, Samuel, and David Weisbach. "The Design of Border Adjustments for Carbon Prices." *National Tax Journal* 70, no. 2 (June 2017): 421.

Kousky, Carolyn. "Financing Flood Losses: A Discussion of the National Flood Insurance Program." *Risk Management and Insurance Review* 21, no. 1 (March 2018): 11–32.

Kousky, Carolyn, and Howard Kunreuther. "Addressing Affordability in the National Flood Insurance Program." *Journal of Extreme Events* 1, no. 1 (August 2014).

Kousky, Carolyn, Erzo F. Luttmer, and Richard J. Zeckhauser. "Private Investment and Government Protection." *Journal of Risk and Uncertainty* 33, nos. 1–2 (September 2006): 73–100.

Kousky, Carolyn, Erwann O. Michel-Kerjan, and Paul A. Raschky. "Does Federal Disaster Assistance Crowd Out Flood Insurance?" *Journal of Environmental Economics and Management* 87, issue C (January 2018): 150–64.

Kron, Wolfgang. "Flood Risk = Hazard • Values • Vulnerability." *Water International* 30, no. 1 (March 2005): 58–68.

Krueger, Philipp, Zacharias Sautner, and Laura T. Starks. "The Importance of Climate Risks for Institutional Investors." *Review of Financial Studies* 33, no. 3 (March 2020): 1067–1111.

Kunreuther, Howard, and Geoffrey Heal. "Managing Catastrophic Risk." National Bureau of Economic Research, NBER Working Paper 18136, June 2012.

Kunreuther, Howard, Susan M. Wachter, Carolyn Kousky, and Michael LaCour-Little. "Flood Risk and the US Housing Market." February 2019. Available at SSRN 3426638.

Langdon, S. J. "Increments, Ranges and Thresholds: Human Population Responses to Climate Change in Northern Alaska." In *Human Ecology and Climate Change: People and Resources in the Far North*, eds. David L. Peterson and Darryll R. Johnson. Washington, DC: Taylor and Francis, 1995.

Lazo, Jeffrey K., Megan Lawson, Peter H. Larsen, and Donald M. Waldman. "U.S. Economic Sensitivity to Weather Variability." *Bulletin of the American Meteorological Society* 92, no. 6 (June 2011): 709–20.

Lim, Dawn, and Julie Steinberg. "BlackRock to Hold Companies and Itself to Higher Standards on Climate Risk." *Wall Street Journal*, January 14, 2020.

Lincke, Daniel, and Jochen Hinkel. "Economically Robust Protection against 21st Century Sea-Level Rise." *Global Environmental Change—Human and Policy Dimensions* 51 (July 2018): 67–73. https://doi.org/10.1016/j.gloenvcha .2018.05.003.

Lomborg, Bjorn. "Impact of Current Climate Proposals." *Global Policy* 7, no. 1 (February 2016): 109–18.

Loring, Philip A., Craig Gerlach, David E. Atkinson, and Maribeth S. Murray. "Ways to Help and Ways to Hinder: Governance for Effective Adaptation to an Uncertain Climate." *Arctic* 64, no. 1 (March 2011): 73–88.

Lyubich, Eva, Joseph Shapiro, and Reed Walker. "Regulating Mismeasured Pollution: Implications of Firm Heterogeneity for Environmental Policy." *AEA Papers and Proceedings* 108 (May 2018): 136–42.

Marino, Elizabeth. "The Long History of Environmental Migration: Assessing Vulnerability Construction and Obstacles to Successful Relocation in Shishmaref, Alaska." *Global Environmental Change* 22, no. 2 (2012): 374–81.

Markanday, Ambika, Ibon Galarraga, and Anil Markandya. "A Critical Review of Cost-Benefit Analysis for Climate Change Adaptation in Cities." *Climate Change Economics* 10, no. 4 (November 2019). https://doi.org/10.1142/S2010007819500143.

Markon, Carl J., Stephen T. Gray, Matthew Berman, Laura Eerkes-Medrano, Thomas Hennessy, Henry P. Huntington, Jeremy Littell, Molly McCammon, Richard Thoman, and Sarah Trainor. "Alaska." In *Impacts, Risks, and Adaptation in the United States: Fourth National Climate Assessment*, vol. 2, eds. D. R. Reidmiller, C. W. Avery, D. R. Easterling, K. E. Kunkel, K. L. M. Lewis, T. K. Maycock, and B. C. Stewart, 1185–1241. Washington, DC: U.S. Global Change Research Program, 2018.

Markusen, James R. "International Externalities and Optimal Tax Structures." *Journal of International Economics* 5, no. 1 (February 1975): 15–29.

Mathiesen, Karl. "Rating Climate Risks to Credit Worthiness." *Nature Climate Change* 8, no. 6 (June 2018): 454–56.

Mauritsen, Thorsten, and Robert Pincus. "Committed Warming Inferred from Observations." *Nature Climate Change* 7, no. 9 (September 2017): 652–55.

Mayers, David, and Clifford W. Smith. "On the Corporate Demand for Insurance." In *Foundations of Insurance Economics*, eds. Georges Dionne and Scott E. Harrington, 190–205. Dordrecht, Netherlands: Springer, 1982.

McAusland, Carol, and Nouri Najjar. "Carbon Footprint Taxes." *Environmental and Resource Economics* 61, no. 1 (2015): 37–70.

McGrayne, Sharon Bertsch. *The Theory That Would Not Die: Bayes' Rule Cracked the Enigma Code, Hunted Down Russian Submarines and Emerged Triumphant from Two Centuries of Controversy*. New Haven, CT: Yale University Press, 2011.

McNeeley, Shannon M. "Examining Barriers and Opportunities for Sustainable Adaptation to Climate Change in Interior Alaska." *Climatic Change* 111, nos. 3–4 (April 2012): 835–57.

———. "Seasons out of Balance: Climate Change Impacts, Vulnerability, and Sustainable Adaptation in Interior Alaska." PhD diss., University of Alaska, Fairbanks, 2009. http://www.cakex.org/sites/default/files/project/documents/McNeeley_Dissertation_2009.pdf.

Meek, Chanda L., Amy Lauren Lovecraft, Martin D. Robards, and Gary P. Kofinas. "Building Resilience through Interlocal Relations: Case Studies of Polar Bear and Walrus Management in the Bering Strait." *Marine Policy* 32, no. 6 (2008): 1080–89.

Mehling, Michael A., Harro van Asselt, Kasturi Das, and Susanne Droege. "Beat Protectionism and Emissions at a Stroke." *Nature*, July 16, 2018.

Mehling, Michael A., Harro van Asselt, Kasturi Das, Susanne Droege, and Cleo Verkuijl. "Designing Border Carbon Adjustments for Enhanced Climate Action." *American Journal of International Law* 113, no. 3 (July 2019): 433–81.

Meyer, Eliot S., Benjamin T. Foster, Gregory W. Characklis, Casey Brown, and Andrew J. Yates. "Integrating Physical and Financial Approaches to Manage Environmental Financial Risk on the Great Lakes." *Water Resources Research* 56, no. 5 (May 2020): e2019WR024853.

Montgomery, W. David. "Markets in Licenses and Efficient Pollution Control Programs." *Journal of Economic Theory* 5, no. 3 (December 1972): 395–418.

Moody's Investor Services. "Moody's Assigns Aa1 to Energy Northwest (WA) Columbia Generating Station Revenue Bonds; Affirms BPA and Its Supported Debt Obligations at Aa1; Outlook Revised to Negative from Stable," April 29, 2019. https://www.moodys.com/research/Moodys-assigns-Aa1-to-Energy -Northwest-WA-Columbia-Generating-Station--PR_905774475#.

———. "Moody's Downgrades BPA (OR) to Aa2 from Aa1; Assigns Aa2 Rating to Morrow (Port of) OR's Transmission Revenue Bonds; Outlook Is Stable," February 12, 2020.

Moore, Michael O. "Carbon Safeguard? Managing the Friction between Trade Rules and Climate Policy." *Journal of World Trade* 51, no. 1 (February 2017): 43–66.

Naegele, Helene, and Aleksandar Zaklan. "Does the EU ETS Cause Carbon Leakage in European Manufacturing?" *Journal of Environmental Economics and Management* 93 (2019): 125–47.

Nash, John. "Noncooperative Games." *Annals of Mathematics* 54 (September 1951): 286–95.

National Climate Assessment and Development Advisory Committee (NCADAC). *National Climate Assessment Chapter 1—Executive Summary: Draft for Public Comment.* Washington, DC: US Global Change Research Program, 2013. http://www.globalchange.gov/sites/globalchange/files/NCAJan11–2013 -publicreviewdraft-chap1-execsum.pdf.

National Oceanic and Atmospheric Administration (NOAA). Cooperative Agreement between the National Oceanic and Atmospheric Administration and the Alaska Eskimo Whaling Commission (2013). https://www.fisheries .noaa.gov/webdam/download/64417380.

———. Subsistence Taking of Northern Fur Seals, 84 Fed. Reg. 52372 (Oct. 2, 2019).

National Research Council. *Tying Flood Insurance to Flood Risk for Low-Lying Structures in the Floodplain.* Washington, DC: National Academies Press, 2015.

Nordhaus, William D. "Climate Change: The Ultimate Challenge for Economics." Nobel Lecture in Economic Sciences, Stockholm University, December 8, 2018.

———. "Climate Clubs: Overcoming Free-Riding in International Climate Policy." *American Economic Review* 105, no. 4 (April 2015): 1339–70.

Nuttall, Mark, Fikret Berkes, Bruce Forbes, Gary Kofinas, Tatiana Vlassova, and George Wenzel. "Hunting, Herding, Fishing and Gathering: Indigenous Peoples and Renewable Resource Use in the Arctic." In ACIA, *Arctic Climate Impact Assessment,* 649–90. Cambridge: Cambridge University Press, 2005.

Oda, Junichiro, Keigo Akimoto, Fuminori Sano, and Toshimasa Tomoda. "Diffusion of Energy Efficient Technologies and $CO_2$ Emission Reductions in Iron and Steel Sector." *Energy Economics* 29, no. 4 (July 2007): 868–88.

Oda, Junichiro, Keigo Akimoto, Toshimasa Tomoda, Miyuki Nagashima, Kenichi Wada, and Fuminori Sano. "International Comparisons of Energy Efficiency in Power, Steel, and Cement Industries." *Energy Policy* 44 (May 2012): 118–29.

O'Neil, Cathy. *Weapons of Math Destruction: How Big Data Increases Inequality and Threatens Democracy.* New York: Broadway Books, 2016.

Ortega, Francesc, and Süleyman Taşpınar. "Rising Sea Levels and Sinking Property Values: Hurricane Sandy and New York's Housing Market." *Journal of Urban Economics* 106 (July 2018): 81–100.

Osgood, C. *Contributions to the Ethnography of the Kutchin.* New Haven, CT: Yale University Press, 1936.

Ostrom, Elinor. *Understanding Institutional Diversity.* Princeton, NJ: Princeton University Press, 2005.

Ouazad, Amine, and Matthew E. Kahn. "Mortgage Finance in the Face of Rising Climate Risk." National Bureau of Economic Research, NBER Working Paper 26322, September 2019.

Perino, Grischa, Robert A. Ritz, and Arthur van Benthem. "Understanding Overlapping Policies: Internal Carbon Leakage and the Punctured Waterbed." National Bureau of Economic Research, NBER Working Paper 25643, March 2019.

Pindyck, Robert S. "Climate Change Policy: What Do the Models Tell Us?" *Journal of Economic Literature* 51, no. 3 (September 2013): 860–72.

Pinkerton, Evelyn. "Coastal Marine Systems: Conserving Fish and Sustaining Community Livelihoods with Co-Management." In *Principles of Ecosystem Stewardship: Resilience-Based Natural Resource Management in a Changing World,* eds. F. Stuart Chapin III, Carl Folke, and Gary P. Kofinas, 241–57. New York: Springer, 2009.

Point Lay Native Village. Bylaws for the Traditional Beluga Hunt by the Tribal Village of Point Lay, June 27, 2008.

Pratt, Kenneth L., Joan C. Stevenson, and Phillip M. Everson. "Demographic Adversities and Indigenous Resilience in Western Alaska." *Études/Inuit/Studies* 37, no. 1 (2013): 35.

Richmond, Laurie. "Incorporating Indigenous Rights and Environmental Justice into Fishery Management: Comparing Policy Challenges and Potentials from Alaska and Hawai'i." *Environmental Management* 52, no. 5 (November 2013): 1071–84.

Ristroph, E. Barrett. "Addressing Climate Change Vulnerability in Alaska Native Villages through Indigenous Community Knowledge." *Sociology Study* 9, no. 1 (January 2019): 1–19.

———. "Alaska Tribes' Melting Subsistence Rights." *Arizona Journal of Environmental Law and Policy* 1 (2010): 47–101.

———. "Fulfilling Climate Justice and Government Obligations to Alaska Native Villages: What Is the Government Role?" *William & Mary Environmental Law and Policy Review* 43, no. 2 (2019): 501–39.

———. "Integrating Community Knowledge into Environmental and Natural Resource Decision-Making: Notes from Alaska and Around the World." *Washington and Lee Journal of Energy, Climate, and the Environment* 3, no. 1 (2012): 81–132.

———. "Still Melting: How Climate Change and Subsistence Laws Constrain Alaska Native Village Adaptation." *University of Colorado Natural Resources, Energy, and Environmental Law Review* 30, no. 2 (2019): 245–86.

———. "Strategies for Strengthening Alaska Native Village Roles in Natural Resource Management." *Willamette Environmental Law Journal* 4 (Spring 2016): 57–124.

Rosales, Jon, and Jessica Chapman. "Perceptions of Obvious and Disruptive Climate Change: Community-Based Risk Assessment for Two Native Villages in Alaska." *Climate* 3, no. 4 (December 2015): 812–32.

Saltelli, Andrea, William Becker, Pawel Stano, and Philip B. Stark. "Climate Models as Economic Guides: Scientific Challenge or Quixotic Quest?" *Issues in Science and Technology* 31, no. 3 (Spring 2015): 79–84.

Sato, Misato. "Embodied Carbon in Trade: A Survey of the Empirical Literature." *Journal of Economic Surveys* 28, no. 5 (December 2014): 831–61.

Schwartz, Barry. *The Paradox of Choice: Why Less Is More.* New York: Ecco, 2004.

Seo, S. Niggol, and Robert Mendelsohn. "An Analysis of Crop Choice: Adapting to Climate Change in South American Farms." *Ecological Economics* 67, no. 1 (August 2008): 109–16. https://doi.org/10.1016/j.ecolecon.2007.12.007.

Shapiro, Joseph. "The Environmental Bias of Trade Policy." Working Paper, University of California–Berkeley, 2020.

Shultz, George P., and Gary S. Becker. "Why We Support a Revenue-Neutral Carbon Tax." *Wall Street Journal*, April 7, 2013.

Smiddy, Linda O. "Responding to Professor Janda—the U.S. Experience: The Alaska Native Claims Settlement Act (ANCSA) Regional Corporation as a Form of Social Enterprise." *Vermont Law Review* 30 (2006): 823–54.

Smith, Clifford W., and Rene M. Stulz. "The Determinants of Firms' Hedging Policies." *Journal of Financial and Quantitative Analysis* 20, no. 4 (December 1985): 391–405.

Solomon, Susan, Gian-Kasper Plattner, Reto Knutti, and Pierre Friedlingstein. "Irreversible Climate Change Due to Carbon Dioxide Emissions." *Proceedings of the National Academy of Sciences* 106, no. 6 (February 10, 2009): 1704–9.

Standard and Poor's. "Delano-Earlimart Irrigation District." Ratings Direct Analysis, January 6, 2017.

Starkey, John Sky. "Protection of Alaska Native Customary and Traditional Hunting and Fishing Rights through Title VIII of ANILCA (Alaska National Interest Lands Conservation Act)." *Alaska Law Review* 33, no. 2 (2016): 315.

Stone, Andy. "Madrid Climate Conference Failed, but Silver Lining Exists." *Forbes*, December 20, 2019.

Sunstein, Cass R. "Probability Neglect: Emotions, Worst Cases, and the Law." *Yale Law Journal* 112, no. 1 (January 2002): 61–107.

Taleb, Nassim Nicholas. *The Black Swan: The Impact of the Highly Improbable*. New York: Random House, 2010.

Task Force on Climate-Related Financial Disclosures. *Final Report: Recommendations of the Task Force on Climate-Related Financial Disclosures*, June 2017. https://www.fsb-tcfd.org/wp-content/uploads/2017/06/FINAL-2017-TCFD-Report-11052018.pdf.

Thaler, Richard H. "From Cashews to Nudges: The Evolution of Behavioral Economics." *American Economic Review* 108, no. 6 (June 2018): 1265–87.

Theriault, Sophie, Ghislain Otis, Gerard Duhaime, and Christopher Furgal. "The Legal Protection of Subsistence: A Prerequisite of Food Security for the Inuit of Alaska." *Alaska Law Review* 22 (2005): 35.

Thomas, Clive S., Laura Savatgy, and Kristina Klimovich, eds. *Alaska Politics and Public Policy: The Dynamics of Beliefs, Institutions, Personalities, and Power*. Fairbanks: University of Alaska Press, 2016.

Tiger, Mary Wyatt, Jeff Hughes, and Shadi Eskaf. *Designing Water Rate Structures for Conservation and Revenue Stability.* Chapel Hill: Environmental Finance Center at the University of North Carolina at Chapel Hill, 2014.

Tonkonogy, Bella, Federico Mazza, and Valerio Micale. "Understanding and Increasing Finance for Climate Adaptation in Developing Countries." *Climate Policy Initiative,* December 13, 2018. https://climatepolicyinitiative.org/wp -content/uploads/2018/12/Finance-for-Climate-Adaptation-in-Developing -Countries-1.pdf

Trachtman, Joel P. "WTO Law Constraints on Border Tax Adjustment and Tax Credit Mechanisms to Reduce the Competitive Effects of Carbon Taxes." *National Tax Journal* 70, no. 2 (June 2017): 469–94.

United Nations Framework Convention on Climate Change (UNFCCC). "GHG Data," 2020. http://unfccc.int.

United States Army Corps of Engineers. Event Study: 2012 Low-Water and Mississippi River Lock 27 Closures, August 2013.

Victor, David G., M. Granger Morgan, Jay Apt, John Steinbruner, and Katharine Ricke. "The Geoengineering Option: A Last Resort against Global Warming." *Foreign Affairs* 80, no. 2 (March/April 2009): 64–76.

Weitzman, Martin L. "Fat-Tailed Uncertainty in the Economics of Catastrophic Climate Change." *Review of Environmental Economics and Policy* 5, no. 2 (Summer 2011): 275–92.

———. "On Modeling and Interpreting the Economics of Catastrophic Climate Change." *Review of Economics and Statistics* 91, no. 1 (February 2009): 1–19.

Williams, Jessica. 2017. "How Environmental and Climate Risks and Opportunities Factor into Global Corporate Ratings—an Update." S&P Global, November 9, 2017. https://www.spglobal.com/en/research-insights/articles/environmental -and-climate-risks-factor-into-ratings.

Williamson, Oliver E. "Transaction-Cost Economics: The Governance of Contractual Relations." *Journal of Law and Economics* 22, no. 2 (October 1979): 233–61.

Wilson, Nicole J. "The Politics of Adaptation: Subsistence Livelihoods and Vulnerability to Climate Change in the Koyukon Athabascan Village of Ruby, Alaska." *Human Ecology* 42, no. 1 (February 2014): 87–101.

Winchester, Niven, Sergey Paltsev, and John M. Reilly. "Will Border Carbon Adjustments Work?" *BE Journal of Economic Analysis and Policy* 11, no. 1 (January 2011): 1–29.

World Economic Forum. *The Global Risks Report 2019.* http://www3.weforum.org /docs/WEF_Global_Risks_Report_2019.pdf.

Yandle, Bruce. "Bootleggers and Baptists—the Education of a Regulatory Economist." *Regulation* 7, no. 3 (May/June 1983): 12–16.

Zeff, Harrison B., and Gregory W. Characklis. "Managing Water Utility Financial Risks through Third-Party Index Insurance Contracts." *Water Resources Research* 49, no. 8 (August 2013): 4939–51.

Zeff, Harrison B., Joseph R. Kasprzyk, Jonathan D. Herman, Patrick M. Reed, and Gregory W. Characklis. "Navigating Financial and Supply Reliability Tradeoffs in Regional Drought Management Portfolios." *Water Resources Research* 50, no. 6 (June 2014): 4906–23.

# About the Contributors

**Terry L. Anderson** is the John and Jean De Nault Senior Fellow at the Hoover Institution, Stanford University; past president of the Property and Environment Research Center, Bozeman, Montana; and professor emeritus at Montana State University. Much of his career has been focused on developing the idea outlined in the title of his coauthored book *Free Market Environmentalism* (now in its third edition), outlining how markets and property rights can solve environmental problems. More recently he has focused his research and writing on how ideas defining a free society apply to Native American economies. Of his thirty-nine books, four have laid the foundation for his project on Renewing Indigenous Economies (indigenousecon.org). The most recent of these is *Unlocking the Wealth of Indian Nations* (Lexington Books, 2016). He lives in Montana with his wife, Monica, where they enjoy fishing, hunting, horseback riding, and skiing in Big Sky Country.

**Ronald Bailey** is the science correspondent for *Reason*; coauthor of *Ten Global Trends Every Smart Person Should Know: And Many Others You Will Find Interesting* (Cato Institute, 2020); and author of *The End of Doom: Environmental Renewal in the Twenty-first Century* (Thomas Dunne Books, 2015) and *Liberation Biology: The Moral and Scientific Case for the Biotech Revolution* (Prometheus, 2005). Bailey was previously a staff writer for *Forbes* magazine, covering economic, scientific, and business topics. His articles and reviews have appeared in the *New York Times*, the *Wall Street Journal*, the

*Washington Post, Commentary,* the *Public Interest, Smithsonian, National Review,* and many other publications. Bailey also has produced several weekly national public television series, including *Think Tank* and *TechnoPolitics,* as well as several documentaries for PBS and ABC News. Bailey has appeared on numerous television and radio programs, including the *NBC Nightly News, PBS NewsHour,* and programs on National Public Radio and C-SPAN.

**Gregory W. Characklis** serves as William R. Kenan, Jr. Distinguished Professor at the University of North Carolina–Chapel Hill, as well as director of the Center on Financial Risk in Environmental Systems. His research involves developing systems models that integrate engineering and economic principles to better understand, quantify, and manage financial risks arising from environmental and climate variability. He has worked with many industries, including water utilities, power utilities, agriculture, inland navigation (e.g., Great Lakes), and real estate. Characklis previously spent two years as director of resource development and management at Azurix Corp. (a subsidiary of Enron Corp.). Before entering the private sector, he spent two years in Washington, DC, as a fellow with the National Academy of Engineering. Characklis holds a PhD and an MS in environmental science and engineering from Rice University and a BS in materials science and engineering from Johns Hopkins University.

**Kenneth W. Costello** is a regulatory economist and independent consultant who has worked for the National Regulatory Research Institute, the Illinois Commerce Commission, and the Argonne National Laboratory. He has conducted extensive research and written on a wide variety of topics related to the energy industries and public utility regulation for publications including the *Cato Journal, Competition and Regulation in Network Industries,* the *Electricity Journal* (where he sits on the Editorial Advisory Board), *Energy Journal, Energy Law Journal, Energy Policy, Public*

*Utilities Fortnightly, Regulation, Resources and Energy, Utilities Policy,* and *Yale Journal on Regulation.* He has provided training and consulting services to Argentina, Bolivia, Canada, the Central and Eastern European countries, China, Costa Rica, Egypt, Ghana, India, Jamaica, Japan, the Newly Independent States, and Russia. The Financial Research Institute, University of Missouri–Columbia, awarded Costello the 2017 Crystal Award for Distinguished Contribution to Public Utility Regulatory Policy. He received BS and MA degrees from Marquette University and has done doctoral work in economics at the University of Chicago.

**Timothy Fitzgerald** is an economist appointed as an associate professor in the Rawls College of Business at Texas Tech University. His research interests include natural resource and environmental economics, with a focus on energy issues; his research has been published in outlets including the *Journal of the Association of Environmental and Resource Economists, Energy Economics, Land Economics,* and *Resource and Energy Economics.* In 2017–18 he served on the Council of Economic Advisers for the White House, as a senior economist and as chief international economist. He has been a fellow at the Property and Environment Research Center in Bozeman, Montana, and at Resources for the Future in Washington, DC.

**Benjamin T. Foster** is the COO of Lotic Labs, a firm that helps companies, investors, and public institutions identify and manage financial risk caused by variation in environmental conditions. He has developed strategies for managing environmental financial risk for nearly a decade at the Center on Financial Risk in Environmental Systems at the University of North Carolina–Chapel Hill, where he worked as a researcher and is currently completing his PhD. He is also a research fellow at the Property and Environment Research Center in Bozeman, Montana. Foster previously received a BS in civil engineering from the University of Virginia and worked as an environmental engineer, designing and implementing small-scale energy projects in East Africa and Central America. Foster also dabbles in sports analytics, and his work with Michael Binns on valuing protections on NBA draft picks was a finalist in the research paper competition at the 2019 MIT Sloan Sports Analytics Conference.

**Matthew E. Kahn** is the Bloomberg Distinguished Professor of Economics and Business at Johns Hopkins University and the director of its 21st Century Cities Initiative. He is also provost professor of economics at University of Southern California and a research associate at the National Bureau of Economic Research and at the Institute of Labor Economics (IZA). Kahn has written *Green Cities: Urban Growth and the Environment* (Brookings Institution Press, 2006) and *Climatopolis* (Basic Books, 2010); and cowritten *Heroes and Cowards: The Social Face of War* (with Dora L. Costa; Princeton University Press, 2009) and *Blue Skies over Beijing: Economic Growth and the Environment in China* (with Siqi Zheng; Princeton University Press, 2016). Forthcoming books are *Adapting to Climate Change* (Yale University Press, 2021) and *Unlocking the Potential of Post-Industrial Cities* (with Mac McComas; Johns Hopkins University Press, 2021). His research focuses on urban and environmental economics. He is a graduate of Hamilton College and the London School of Economics and holds a PhD in economics from the University of Chicago.

**Bjorn Lomborg** is visiting professor at Copenhagen Business School and president of the Copenhagen Consensus Center, a think tank that researches the smartest ways to do good. For this work, Lomborg was named by *Time* one of the world's one hundred most influential people. His numerous books include *False Alarm* (Basic Books, 2020), *The Skeptical Environmentalist* (Cambridge University Press, 2001), *Cool It* (Knopf Publishing Group, 2007), *How to Spend $75 Billion to Make the World a Better*

*Place* (Copenhagen Consensus Center, 2013), and *The Nobel Laureates' Guide to the Smartest Targets for the World: 2016–2030* (Copenhagen Consensus Center, 2015). His analysis and commentaries appear regularly in such publications as the *New York Times*, the *Wall Street Journal*, *The Economist*, the *Washington Post*, *Forbes*, the *Los Angeles Times*, and the *Boston Globe* and on networks including ABC, CNN, Fox, MSNBC, and the BBC. He holds a PhD in political science from the University of Copenhagen.

**Mark Mills** is a senior fellow at the Manhattan Institute, a faculty fellow at the McCormick School, and co-founding partner in Cottonwood Venture Partners, an energy investment fund. He writes frequently for the *Wall Street Journal* and is author of the books *Digital Cathedrals: The Information Infrastructure Era* (Encounter Books, 2019) and *Work in the Age of Robots* (Encounter Books, 2018). With Peter Huber, he coauthored *The Bottomless Well* (Basic Books, 2007), about which Bill Gates said: "This is the only book I've ever seen that really explains energy." He served as chairman and CTO of ICx Technologies, helping take it public in a 2007 IPO. Mills previously served in the White House Science Office under President Reagan and was an experimental physicist and development engineer in microprocessors and fiber optics, earning several patents, at Bell Northern Research (Canada's Bell Labs) and at the RCA David Sarnoff Research Center. He holds a BSc Honours in physics from Queen's University, Canada.

**E. Barrett Ristroph** is a lawyer, planner, mediator, and researcher based in Alaska and South Louisiana. She is the owner of Ristroph Law, Planning, and Research, which provides services at a reasonable cost to tribes, communities, and agencies related to natural resources, hazard mitigation, government, and climate change adaptation. Her PhD work considered how Alaska Native Villages are adapting to climate change and the help or hindrance of laws and planning. Originally from Cajun country, Louisiana, she has gained perspective from living and working in the Northern Mariana Islands, the Philippines, Hawaii, Arctic Alaska, and Russia. Through her work, she hopes to build bridges between communities in South Louisiana, Alaska, and the Pacific Islands that are struggling with climate change and the need for sustainable development. Ristroph has written numerous articles on climate change adaptation and natural resource management. Other research has focused on international law, environmental law in Russia and the Philippines, and indigenous knowledge and identity.

# Index